THE

HEART

DOES

BREAK

George Bowering and Jean Baird

THE

HEART

DOES

BREAK

Canadian Writers
on Grief and Mourning

RANDOM HOUSE CANADA

LIBRARY AND ARCHIVES CANADA CATALOGUING IN PUBLICATION

The heart does break : Canadian writers on grief and mourning /
[edited by] George Bowering and Jean Baird.

ISBN 978-0-307-35702-1

1. Grief. 2. Adjustment (Psychology). 3. Authors, Canadian (English)—
20th century—Biography. I. Bowering, George, 1935–. II. Baird, Jean
III. Title: Canadian writers on grief and mourning.

PS8237.G84H43 2009   C818'.5403080353   C2009-901835-7

Text design by Jennifer Lum

Printed in the United States of America

10 9 8 7 6 5 4 3 2 1

CONTENTS

For Bronwyn Jean Dixon
and all the others

                              briefly
the heart does break

the aching muscle in the chest
carries more than the weight hangs from the body
                              from the barely perceiving brain
buried under the weight of loss

of grief

          brief moment of clarity

                              stillborn

                              —**bpNichol**, from *A Book of Hours*

Bronwyn Jean Dixon

Introduction

MAY I BRING

YOU

SOME TEA?

By George Bowering

I.

Winter is come and gone,
but grief returns with the evolving year.
—*P.B. Shelley,* Adonais

Every year, as September gives way to October, my wife, Jean Baird, feels a bleakness that comes with deep loss. She wanders a little, tears in her eyes that make it impossible to handle sewing needle or keyboard. She sometimes gives way to sobbing when she needs to be alone, and she has to have someone with her as autumn makes its way.

On the morning of October 3, 2006, we were wakened by the bedroom telephone in our home in Vancouver. The dread that one often feels at such a moment multiplied as I saw the emptiness in my loved one's face. I knew what it was about. Jean was shaking, sitting up in bed, the telephone in her shaking hand. She said, "It is just not getting through to my brain," and I knew for sure. I held her, feeling necessary and useless. We humans are forced to hear the worst things possible.

Jean's daughter, Bronwyn, twenty-three years old, was dead in a car crash in southern Ontario. Her aunt Jane, Jean's best friend, had to identify her niece from a photograph the police had shown her, and then telephone Jean.

That day we were all insane. While I hurried to the travel agent to buy plane tickets, Bronwyn's brother, Sebastian, went to school and Jean spent more time on the telephone. Then, while I went to the high school to bring

Sebastian home, Jean cleaned up the kitchen and read her email. We were all crazy.

Jean was just too ordinary. I waited for her to scream or fall on the floor. Sebastian at least put his fist through a wall. "I don't know what I should do," Jean kept saying. I thought about Middle Eastern women who are photographed wailing and clutching at air when a family member gets killed. Over the next few days Jean said such calm things as how fortunate it had been that it was not a two-car accident. A few times she disagreed with the sentiment that the loss of a child is the worst possible bereavement. She had encountered people in lifetime comas following brain injuries, other people reduced to immobility. But how could she imagine that anything was worse than this? I thought that she must be in that famous denial, but I worried; I loved her so. I'd thought that crazy meant berserk. But now I know that the serene Mary in Michelangelo's famous *Pietà* is completely mad.

But over the following year Jean had to have the sanest head and strongest heart in the world to survive the idiotic things that people said to her in the way of commiseration. You have another child? Oh, good. Then it isn't so bad. You must be very happy to know that Bronwyn is with Jesus in Heaven. Time will heal your pain. You should start living your normal life again. I know exactly how you feel. When a new soul comes into the world, it has already chosen a day for leaving it; you have to accept her decision.

Some of these wise thoughts and others just as sapient came from family members.

I sometimes feel that I should describe the terrible treatment of this woman by people who should have been trying to help her. But I want to respect her privacy, and give her a refuge in a time when solace is not possible. I also remember that she was treated well by her long-time friends in Port Colborne, Ontario, and by the young people who were Bronwyn's good friends. These young folks allowed her to give to them, a true exchange, because their loving mournfulness sustained her for that first week in a world that threatened to be empty. It was Thanksgiving week, and meaningfully so as friends her own age gave her food and a place to sleep and a car for her husband to drive about the Niagara region. You may imagine how precious those things were that week.

When the strange ordinariness was over and Jean did manage to break down, her best friends just let her. Just let her. They did not cajole or demand, as the thoughtless will, that she "pull herself together." Sebastian needed time with his and his sister's old Port Colborne friends, and we did not have to know what he was doing day and night, only to hear his voice on his cellphone from time to time.

———

And sure enough, as a year passed, and then a second year, the bereft mother did not "get over it." Sometimes the horror came unexpectedly, and Jean needed some time to suffer, and maybe a hand to hold. When the earth finished an orbit, and October 3 was approaching, Jean felt the sorrow and lonesomeness and compassion for her daughter almost overcoming her. The time of year does that to you. It is not a year later; it is that day again. Grief returns with the evolving year, indeed.

2.

Well, every one can master a grief but he that has it.

—William Shakespeare, Much Ado About Nothing

Jean Baird's approach to any problem or project is to get a lot of books and read. When she perceived a problem with the literary awards system, she began reading all the short-listed books for every year's Booker Prize. When someone close to her admitted to an eating disorder, Jean researched the subject thoroughly, even reading all the information to be found in hospital libraries. So she hoped that her way out of the craziness after her daughter's sudden death was to be found, if it existed at all, in books.

Jean has been around books all her life, and not only as a consumer. She was co-editor of a magazine about brain injuries, and later publisher of a magazine for young writers and artists. She worked for the Writers' Trust of Canada, and managed Canada Book Week. She began and organized the project to mandate Canadian texts in British Columbia high-school English curricula. She invented the Al Purdy A-frame Trust to save the late author's house from the bulldozers.

Jean earned her Ph.D. with a literary bibliography. She knows research. So, for a year after that devastating morning, she read dozens of books about bereavement. For a while she attended meetings of a helpful group called Compassionate Friends. There, a circle of parents who had lost their children a year ago or a decade ago told one another their stories. In their meeting room at a church in North Vancouver they had a big box filled with books you could borrow. Jean borrowed some of these and donated others to the box.

Some of the books were self-published poems. Most of them were like the ones that Jean had found in bookstores and libraries and on the Internet. There were volumes written by psychiatrists, psychologists, journalists, gurus, preachers, television stars, medical doctors and trendy therapists. Many of these authors felt that they should have letters after their names on the covers of their books. Grief "resources" are all over the Internet. They include PowerPoint treatments!

Jean read a lot of these offerings and parts of a lot more. She found one that prescribed the same twelve steps that are supposed to cure people of kleptomania or stuttering. Some of the people in the "helping professions" think that readers can "get over" their grief, or normalize their lives, or find a purpose in a world that seems beyond comprehension.

It did not take a year for Jean to discover that the really helpful books were those written by real writers rather than self-help mentors. Dora FitzGerald, a therapist and friend who lives on Galiano Island, listened to Jean's questions and gave her a copy of Joan Didion's *The Year of Magical Thinking*, arguably the most famous grief narrative in recent times. In 2003, a few weeks after Didion's daughter lapsed into a coma, her husband, the novelist John Gregory Dunne, died at their dinner table. The book both narrates the dreadful details of suffering its author faced and describes the operating principles of grief and mourning. Didion has always been celebrated as a stylist. Here, she never romanticizes a life of relentless shocks, offering a reality no twelve-step program could ever approach.

Another marvellous writer is Isabel Allende, who wrote a similar story. Allende's daughter, while living in Spain, was attacked by porphyria, a dreadful blood disease, and fell into a coma from which she would never awaken. Allende and her son-in-law brought the comatose woman to Allende's home in California, where the mother began to tell the story of her life in South America and Lebanon to her sleeping daughter. The result was the supernal memoir *Paula*.

Another therapist and friend, Karen Tallman, who had lost her own son in a dreadful accident, and who had grown up with parents who were experts in both the literary world and the therapy world, took Jean to a specialized bookstore and showed her which writers about mourning were the best. One was Thomas Lynch, a successful poet and essayist who lives in Milford, Michigan. He is also the third-generation director of Lynch & Sons funeral home, and the author of two books about life as an undertaker, *The Undertaking* and *Bodies in Motion and at Rest*. He was the subject of a 2007 PBS television special and the inspiration for the serio-comic HBO series *Six Feet Under*.

A village undertaker is a different thing than a cosmic-energy maven. The human beings who come through his place of work are people he knew in life, and he will see their families in town. He is not going to be on late-night TV, telling you to get out your credit card. As a writer, he takes the care you expect from your hometown friend. So he says, at the end of "Local Heroes," his poem about the aftermath of Hurricane Katrina's destruction of New Orleans:

> But here the brave men and women pick the pieces up.
> They serve the living tending to the dead.
> They bring them home, the missing and adrift,
> They give them back to let them go again.
> Like politics, all funerals are local.

It may seem strange that a woman seeking some sense in a world from which her daughter has been taken would turn to stories about the handling of dead people. But the words written by a writer rather than someone looking for a "client" saved my wife's spirit.

Jean has spent a good part of her life reading and promoting Canadian writing. During her first year of grieving her own daughter, she found no Canadian narrative on the subject, none that can reach one's soul—or is it spirit? Jean will always be grateful to Karen Tallman for introducing her to Katherine Ashenburg's *The Mourner's Dance*. After her daughter Hannah lost her fiancé to a car crash, Ashenburg began to research varieties of human mourning and to think about a book to be subtitled, simply, *What We Do When People Die*. Thus, for Jean Baird the reader, Ashenburg's book was a godsend. Finding out the ways in which human beings have learned to live with mortality and inevitable horror meant that Jean knew there were better ways than some of those that had been visited upon her. And the reason for this solace was the quality of Ashenburg's writing.

In 2008, after the work on our anthology had begun, Abigail Carter's *The Alchemy of Loss* told the first-person story of a wife and mother whose husband had telephoned her from the stricken World Trade Center, and never come home. It is a memoir of five years during which the expatriate Canadian lived through both her family's grief and the public U.S. tragedy. The writing is done by a first-time author, but the words are plainly felt and honestly depict the promised "alchemy" that transformed Carter's "loneliness and isolation" into a highly readable narrative. It is the kind of book that both Jean Baird and Abigail Carter wished had been there for them while the world was crazy.

3.

I will teach you my townspeople
how to perform a funeral
for you have it over a troop
of artists—
unless one should scour the world—
you have the ground sense necessary.
—*William Carlos Williams, "Tract"*

Jean always has a number of projects under way, so I was not surprised when she decided to look for some Canadian writing about grief and mourning. We are a country of poets, so it was not hard to find good poems about loss, such as Dennis Lee's *The Death of Harold Ladoo*, or good novels, such as Matt Cohen's *Last Seen*. There are also scads of tributes to the departed, memoirs in verse and prose, fictive and less so. We did find a few excellent non-fiction pieces, and recommend reading, for example, Patrick Lane's two pieces about losing his mother—see his book of mixed verse and prose, *Go Leaving Strange*.

But the editors and publisher of *The Heart Does Break* decided on new material, commissioned stories rather than reprinted ones. There were writers that we coveted shamelessly who said that they could not, for various reasons, approach the subject. There were others who said that they were too busy writing or publicizing a novel. There were some who almost wrote a story for us, and others who almost didn't.

The variety of stories that did arrive on our desks told us again something we had learned over the past couple of years—there is no limit to the number of ways in which grief occurs or in which human beings mourn. Katherine Ashenburg's book describes some of the many ways in which differing cultures perform a funeral. Our stories tell us that individuals, too, are various in their mourning.

A lot of people are ill at ease around someone who is in extreme grief. They don't know what to say or they fall back on clichés. They want to say something that will help the person "get over" it. But a grieving person does not want to get over it. Mourning is love for the one so sadly gone. "While grief is fresh," said Dr. Johnson, "every attempt to divert only irritates." If you want to say something to a widower or mother or brother, say it simply: "I am sorry for your loss. May I bring you some tea?"

4.

As long as skies are blue, and fields are green,
evening must usher night, night urge the morrow,
month follow month with woe,
and year wake year to sorrow.
—*P.B. Shelley,* Adonais

The word "grief" has an old family. Its Sanskrit ancestor was *gurús,* and it showed up in medieval Latin as *gravis* and Gothic as *kaurus.* From the beginning it has meant heavy. Curiously, medieval Latin has the form *gravidus,* signifying heavy with child. What a grave attitude the Europeans had of our mortality back then!

But in the heaviness that joins the grave to the womb, there is a reason to write an elegy—that poem that begins by relentlessly immersing us in sorrow, but then, after a long wait, tells us about birth, or rebirth. In Shelley's poem, the departed John Keats takes his place among the stars, "the abode where the Eternal are." Next time you go to a wake, see the way the adults act around the newest baby or most pregnant mother in the family. They gravitate, perhaps. Check Linda McNutt's story here.

Grief is the weight we feel, the gravity that orders us when loved ones die, even as we know that they must, even as we still hold an unspoken hope that the next one never will have to accede to the general rule. Grief is what finds us, mortals that we be. Mourning is what we learn to do. William Carlos Williams told us that we are called on to perform a funeral, and so we do; mourning is not something given to us, as grief is, but a challenge. It is the true subject of all the stories in our anthology.

The word "mourning" derives from the Old English *murnan*, which is from the Sanskrit term for both memory and anxiety, an interesting doubleness. Perhaps that says something about the sense we have of our own mortality while we are engaged in commemorating someone's life, or in solemnly attending a memorial. Maybe that is why we now talk about "celebrating" the subject's life rather than memorializing it. A century or so ago, Europeans and North Americans experienced a lot more family deaths during their lifetimes than they do now. Now, the ubiquity of death is filtered through television screens, statistics and abstractions between us and Middle Eastern wars and African famines.

To be anxious. To grieve. To perform our love and respect. That is mourning. Sometimes, as you will see, writing itself can be an act of mourning. Despite the given procedures, mourning is not easy. The heart does break. At my father's graveside ceremony, I was shocked to observe myself rushing from my Protestant family formation to kiss his coffin. So we find ourselves re-enacting stories told by our forebears. When my first wife, Angela, died before the eyes of her daughter and me, I tried to close her eyes, which had gone empty, and they would not, as they always will do in movies and novels, close. But one does at times of our most focused insanity desire to perform the olden story, properly to mourn.

5.

The day breaks not, it is my heart.
—John Donne, "Daybreak"

Another way to mourn is to tell the personal tale, not to eulogize the departed mortal, but to narrate the survivor's story.

Sometimes it can be a depiction of solitude. All the while that the Newfoundland novelist Bernice Morgan was in the hospital attending her dying husband, the rest of the world was experiencing the destruction of New York's twin towers and the chaotic television screens of the days afterwards.

At the Woody Point, Newfoundland, writers' and musicians' festival, we went to hear Bernice Morgan read (and if you get a chance to do that, don't let it slip by) and, naturally, asked her to contribute to our book. Eventually we received a beautiful handwritten letter from her, telling us that she had come to the conclusion that she could not write about the grief she has felt since her husband, George, died. Then, with the help of her daughter, she had come to realize that much of what she felt had found its way into her novel *Cloud of Bone.*

It is a peculiar and delicate act, asking a writer to narrate his or her days or years of loss. A man who has garnered a lot of awards for his work told us that he is "without words" to deal with the death of a family member. A novelist whose grandson had been killed by an unrepentant driver put the question to her family and told us that they could not bear to see their story in print.

As we would hear many times, there are many ways to mourn, and some of them will not allow for written words at all. Some of our writers found the words slow and elusive, and had to rewrite and revise, in a way to piece through their re-enactment of the process. A few managed to be theoretical. Some viewed their own responses and behaviour with humour, various sorts of humour. Others followed their memories right down into the frightening hole behind the broken heart. Bill Whitehead's story of life after Timothy Findley continues to amaze me with its depiction of both despair and laughter—a reminder that in the theatre, tragedy and comedy need one another to continue, and that we live and die in a theatre.

So yes, some people, even some highly successful writers, cannot write their grief, while others can tell about their being in the world that a loved one has left.

Just about everyone in our society wants to write a goodbye poem to their dead—just look at the obituary notices in the classifieds. But why would one want to write about being left behind? I think that your father's death, your daughter's, your best friend's death means that you are another person now. You need to be redefined. For one kind of person that might mean quitting your job and heading to Africa. For a writer it probably means writing.

For Jean Baird and me it meant editing a first anthology of that writing. Some of its readers will be people who are mourning a person who had defined their lives. Some might even find a kind of therapy. In all likelihood, most will be readers who look for good stories from Canadian writers. The human touch, the art of such a thing, is our reason for collecting and offering these stories.

> **They are there like breath, instantly when something, anything, touches us.**
> *—Rudy Wiebe*

Leonard Francis Brett

TASTING

MY

FATHER

By Brian Brett

My wife, Sharon, and I packed the jeep with the clutter of
a classic camping trip—propane lamps, popcorn and marsh-
mallows, the gummed-up camp stove and the tent with
missing pegs. My mother watched in awe as Sharon artfully
wedged the whole mess into the jeep.

We were hungry to make this a real camping trip, so
we instinctively began committing all the sins these journeys
demand. Sharon wanted coffee and doughnuts within the
first hour. By noon we were halfway up Vancouver Island,

ordering ice cream cones. I turned to my mother to ask what kind of cone to buy for Father. It was an instinctive reaction, but I was quick enough to shut my mouth in mid-question. Father's ashes were in the back of the car and we were going to Rebecca Spit to take him home.

The son of cockney peddlers, he was always a big, tough man. He'd piled a stolen car into a telephone pole at the age of seventeen. The other guy walked off into the night with a broken back. Father spent a year in hospital, got gangrene and lost his leg. In an odd way, the accident helped him change his life for the better. After he was released from the hospital, he worked on a green chain in a relative's small sawmill—it was a brutal job even for a man with all his limbs. But he'd hop the long boards off the saw and stack them while someone hand-carved a new leg for him—in those days it took months to make a wooden leg. The accident might have changed his moral direction, but not his energy. A few years later he eloped with my mother—a child of refugees from the deep poverty of southern Italy—and they set up their first home, climbing out of the working-class ghettos of Vancouver immigrants to a comfortable middle-class existence.

My father was always a wanderer, and my mother loved to follow. In those days she was a quiet young woman, secretly inclined to adventure, and that was just another word for my father. He worked all winter as a potato peddler, junk dealer, deliveryman, riveter in a shipyard, coal packer, whatever work he could find, so he could take his summers and travel the West Coast landscape. They moved endlessly into the sunshine before they found Rebecca Spit on Quadra Island, which became their spiritual home. The salmon constantly lured them back until Mother and Father were too frail to return.

It was called a park on the maps then, but the bureaucrats hadn't got to it yet, so the wildlife remained. We lived on a beach full of oysters and clams, the shallows littered with the sandy detritus of giant moon snails. One year, the morning after we arrived with a cluster of relatives, an aunt discovered a ling cod trapped in a tidal pool. The ocean was rich with surprises in those days. All of us gorged ourselves, laughing, on the cod gift. So much life flourished in these waters that it hadn't even occurred to the government to invent saltwater fishing licences. Those only came when it began to seriously manage the destruction of this rich country. They legislated the fish and shellfish into near extinction within little more than thirty years. These were serious bureaucrats, and they were very good at their job. If you talk to them today, you'll find that many are proud of their "management" of the environment they wiped out. And we were just as clueless, tasting everything, until we reeled away from the mighty clam pot, overfed and blissed out.

There were four-foot-deep oyster beds so razor sharp we couldn't beach the wooden boat. My father often refused to fish for cod because they were too common. They were beneath his dignity. He was a salmon king. But I liked cod, especially in batter with chips, and I'd whine at the bow of the boat until he steered us to a cod hole, and warned me .

not to tell his friends that he'd jigged for bottom fish. Now try and find a cod.

This summer, perhaps because of the latest salmon fiasco—their rush towards extinction—the tourists were few. We camped near our original spot, alone within its newly defined boundaries. Where we once inhabited the whole beach, there were twenty-foot-wide camping spots. How strange, I thought, to come from our farm, where we can't see a neighbour's house, to a wilderness experience where the tents can be as close as 10 feet apart. What was free before cost us seventeen dollars a night. We didn't even think about it as we paid our fees. This was the thing called progress, which Father would often smirk at.

In my teen years we camped at the spit for weeks off and on during the summer months. After helping Father clean his catch, I'd tie a salmon head onto my hookless line and hurl it onto the beach. The bald eagles would swing down and grab the head, my line singing as if I had the biggest salmon, and for a brief period I would "fish" the flying eagle in the air, as it fought for its prize until it snapped the line. This would be considered cruelty today, and I wouldn't have the heart to play them like that anymore, but I loved it then.

Father infected everyone in our family with his desire for wilderness. He was a hungry man and he wanted to eat the world. My parents were on the road from their earliest days together, hunting and fishing, or playing cards under a hissing Coleman lantern in a snow-shrouded cabin while a blizzard howled outside. Then, the raincoast sang with life. A few of the tidal narrows, such as the Burnaby Narrows at Haida Gwaii, and some tidal reefs in the unique archipelago known as the Gulf Islands, once held more species per square metre than anywhere in the world. The forests and meadows were equally rich. What we didn't eat, my generation polluted.

When we came upon the spit in the early sixties—that bridge between the land and the sea where nobody made demands—we just drove up and camped, and felt welcomed, both by the local community at Heriot Bay, and by the landscape. When we explored the north island and Cortez by boat, we found eerie rocky inlets and haunty forests where immense cedars and fir, draped with old man's beard and tattooed with bracket fungi, soared into the green canopy far above us.

One year the northern coho were so thick that their finning awoke me—there was an enormous rustling whisper and I snuck out of my tent to watch the dawn reflect on their black-shadowed fins surrounding the spit like an army of spirit fish. At first, the fishing was so easy we never bothered with Tom Macks or other lures. We used a white rag on a hook. The killer whales used to surface suddenly and spy-hop our dory, scaring us before they rolled over and disappeared, and the seals would snap our salmon right off the hook. Once, a humpback whale came up under my father's boat, shaking him around, before diving again and leaving a huge hole in the water off the stern.

For several camping trips to Quadra Island, Mother decided to travel in style and made Father move their bedroom suite into the back of the big peddling truck. You just had to lift the canvas flap and there was a double bed and dresser. The flap served to protect a full, improvised kitchen on a picnic table. She soon had Father gathering firewood—for breakfast, lunch and dinner, served as punctually as clockwork.

———

This camping trip flooded me and the rest of my family with those memories. Only now, my father wasn't here to tell the tallest tale, or duel with the pegs on a crib board, cursing and gloating over fate and the failure of justice in a card game. He'd been one of those men who took over whatever he inhabited. He ate the world. Everyone wanted to follow him. Now, we were following him for the last time.

Death is not about the dead. It's about the living. Our grief, and our inability to speak it. The tragedy of death only exists when you are still alive. He knew he was dying before they told him. He grew uncommonly nervous, fixing the house, the roof, the windows, repairing the locks, as if he was trying to make Mother's future safe. When he was told the cancer had him, it was as if he was relieved of a great duty.

He began sitting for hours, silent, alone in the living room, staring at the TV set. It wasn't on. Who knows what he was seeing written on that blank screen. There are no comforting words for the news of mortality, and I never had the courage to talk to him about it. Other times he could be ironic. When I was sitting with him shortly after he received the news that the cancer was terminal, he said, "Good. At least now I can eat everything again." He'd grown mighty sick of his "heart smart" and low-cholesterol diet. And there was an ironic twinkle in his eyes. He'd have his last shot of crackling from the pork roast.

Sharon is a critical care nurse who's also worked at palliative care. She's seen the extreme moments of too many lives. She tells me that everyone reacts differently. The dying follow whichever death infects them, whether it's an angry spirit or a gifting spirit. Some are dragged into the dark kingdom; others fade away, glowing with the life before death, the warm light only they can see.

Their families, friends and care workers react with equal creativity. How do people sit with the dying and the dead? Some will pester and mistreat the nurses, even mistreat their loved ones as they die. They will scream at the dying and shake their frail bodies, demanding that they come home—as if they believe that they own the dead and the death. Most are sad, and sometimes relieved if there's an excess of pain. Some quietly cry for the dead, as much as for themselves. And how they will keep the house?

———

The day he died I was working in Dawson City, and I thought he had longer. But Father had held back the pain too long. He was a big tough man, 220 pounds (and that with a missing leg) of muscle in his prime, but unused to medication; he never recovered consciousness after his first shot of morphine.

I think I'd like to die like that. He fought until death knocked on the door, and then he just folded up and took the hand of his dark companion. I'd spent the day standing on the banks of the Yukon River, watching the ice break, grinding its way towards the oblivion of the Bering Sea, a thousand miles downstream—thinking about him, yet not knowing how close to the gate he was. We received the phone call near midnight, telling us he was sinking fast, and I didn't sleep much. We were gone before six in the morning, timing our departure so that we'd reach the Carmacks gas station when it opened and then complete the dash to Whitehorse. I remembered my brother telling me a week earlier that I'd have trouble living with myself if I arrived too late. Here I was, coming home too late. In truth, I always had trouble living with myself, and this misadventure was only one among many.

Father would have loved the wild run Sharon and I made. Four big moose on the road. He'd laugh and call for his gun when he saw game, even in a zoo, or wink at them and say, "Catch you next time." He was like a cat in a window, teeth chattering at the sparrows. A wolverine dashed across the road in a kind of mystic circle—in the scary way a wolverine can run—a low-flying magic rug inhabited by demons. Oh, he would have loved to have seen that wolverine!

I was bawling the entire way, through the fire-burnt hills, past the skinny bears coming out of hibernation, and the mountains. When we reached our hotel room in Whitehorse, I phoned home. He'd died five minutes earlier, and I'm sure everyone in the hotel heard me howl. The plane to Vancouver was leaving in little more than an hour, and there was only room for me, so Sharon had to catch another flight. I waited at the airport, sobbing into glasses of whisky in the lounge while young adventuring students, on their big Yukon rite of passage moved away from me, but not before someone stole my credit card.

I was in Vancouver within three hours of his death. What a strange new world we live in. A good friend drove me to the hospital. They usually remove the body quickly, but the kind staff had closed the room until I arrived, and I sat with him for the last time. It was a barren, lifeless room, the usual sterile hospital quarters. He didn't get to die in his bed at home. But there were two lively crows dancing on the railing outside his room, like sentries guarding his journey into what none of us will know until we reach it— the oblivion both he and I always assumed. He would have liked the crows. His body was so shrivelled and small, a shadow of what he once was. All that hugeness had disappeared.

Sharon tells me that when she encounters a death at the hospital there is always a presence in the room, usually around the body, and she opens a window to let it go free. The glass door to the balcony was open in this room. I leaned down and kissed the body of my father on the lips— the first time I had ever kissed him on the lips in my life. He wouldn't have liked that, but his death was no longer about him. He'd gone out the window.

Afterwards, I joined our family at the house. Everyone was quiet and strangely distant, as if a taboo had entered the room. We drank a few glasses of wine and ate, and talked quietly, but I wanted to shout and I wanted a party I wasn't capable of participating in. I wanted to cry, but I knew it would ruin everyone. It was a weird conflict. When I die, I hope my friends and family wreck the place, but I know they won't, and that makes me sad.

————

At the campsite beyond the twisted shore fir, our nearest neighbour, an old man, dragged his boat up from the beach, proud and happy. He'd caught an 18-pound chinook—his first catch after two weeks of hard trolling. We all shook our heads when we realized how poor the fishing was, glad that Father wasn't here to learn this, but he would have liked the fish. It was fat and beautiful.

My mother, as fiercely strong as ever, had divided his ashes into four little plastic bags recycled from the local supermarket. Neither of them believed in waste. Father would have been outraged if she'd spent a penny more than necessary for his death. Do it right, and do it without ostentation. The ashes in the bags were small for so enormous a man. We helped her down to the spit; the logs and the rocks that she used to scamper over were barriers now that her knees were ruined with age. We stood before the incoming tide, my brothers and I and my mother, scattering his ashes on his old fishing ground, now almost barren.

My mother said, "Does anyone want to say anything?" I was so thick with emotion I couldn't hear the words my younger brother spoke beyond her. I remember my own voice, distant and wretched: "Nothing we could say would be enough."

I had to return to the Yukon for my work, and there was nowhere to live except a cheap motel suite that gave monthly rates. Every night Father returned and my dreams made me shout and troll my ugly rooms like a predator. Then I'd hear another voice and walk out on the snowy deck, and there was my dead father singing "O Sole Mio" to me from the scrubby, half-shovelled parking lot below. He was out of tune. He was always out of tune, and he had the words scrambled as usual, but it was enthralling to listen, because he put his heart into every note. Meaning, as usual, meant nothing compared to desire.

It was the song of the dead, and hard to miss. It demanded to be heard. Father was gone, but the song drifted through the arctic night, a reminder that the problem was me, not him. He was gone, but he still had that terrible, impish look in his eyes, the one that said "Follow me," the one that would always lure me into covering his back when we went down to hell, and returned a little singed but happy. It said: "Here's where we get into trouble." And he was right. I was in trouble, standing naked in the snow on the deck of a cheap motel, gazing down at an empty parking lot.

————

Sharon has seen so much death during almost forty years of emergency rooms and hospice care, yet she's never been hardened by it. I've seen her weep over kittens and puppies and lambs. She can't weep at a hospital or a death room in a home; it's not professional, but wet-eyed is permissible, perhaps even encouraged by the authorities who no longer understand how to deal with death beyond the mechanics of it. She brought me a package for caregivers, detailing care programs, insurance money, inheritance—yet the spirit of life, the spirit of the dying, was barely mentioned. Our institutions fear death as much as we do, perhaps because we are now a truly multicultural nation and every family brings a different agenda to death, but they are trying to sort out the different cultures and their different deaths. That said, our local hospital district has two little fold-over pamphlets that are almost thrilling in their depth and compassion, explaining how to deal with death as a caregiver or as a relative, and discussing how children react. Salt Spring Island is in its own universe, and it has an educated palliative care program, a lovely dying room and professionals capable of dealing with the knotty cultural and spiritual questions that face the dying and their community, but this is rare in our society.

While our world is changing, we still live in a society that wants to encounter death only in theatres and on television, or in books. It remains the thing we do not speak, as it was the day my father died. Even our doctors dodge the subject of death. Yet the nurses of our hospitals generally know how to introduce the dying and their families to death, and apart from a few callous or dumb nurses, most act as the bridge between life and death. They know the physical needs while recognizing the emotional paths of the living and the dying.

We are such complex creatures. We reject, we withdraw, we dream, we go dizzy, we crap ourselves, and we weep, we weep endlessly, we go numb, we calculate insurance money and inheritances, we regress into childhood, we are sleepless, we skip down the street, we seize the cars of the dead, blame god, and then we blame god for not existing.

Years ago I knew this attractive, decent woman who worked in the same building. She suddenly disappeared. When I came in for an early shift a few days later, I saw her crying at her desk. Her face was so tragic, I knew there was a terrible anguish behind her sorrow. I sat with her and she told me her story.

Her ancient mother had suffered a stroke and the doctors had pronounced her brain-dead, but a few days later she suddenly sat up in her bed, and said, "Where the hell am I?" As healthy and sharp as she had been the week before. My friend rushed to her mother's apartment to fetch her housecoat and slippers, only to discover that the apartment was gutted. Empty. Her sister had taken everything in a pre-emptive strike because she feared "the inheritance wouldn't be fair." That unfortunate sister went into shock when my friend told her their mother was fine and coming home and everything had better be back by the time she returned.

The unhappy secretary had fixed everything in one day, yet she hadn't fixed it, of course, and her sorrow was at her new awareness of the ways of the world—the horror of it all, and her powerlessness when the wheels of death came around the corner.

This was how I felt in Whitehorse. My father was singing to me about the sun in his face, the sun he would never see. That's how I feel now. His death ten years ago came back like a roller-coaster ride to hell as soon as I began writing these words, the pain as immediate now as it was then. Forgetting is the only cure for grief, and it ain't much of a cure because it's so easy to remember what we forget. Closure is merely the current mythology we feed ourselves so we will believe there is an end to grief. Grief is complex, and complexity can be dealt with only by learning it, understanding it, living in it, and then gradually playing "The Forgetting Waltz" less and less as time passes.

———

When I returned home, I found the plastic bag in my pocket, and it was white with his dust, so I wet my finger and dipped it into the bag and then stuck it in my mouth. I tasted my father, and it made me remember the ways he had lured me into tasting the treasures of our world. He was always in me before, but now it's for real. I tied the empty bag to a Balinese sculpture of a hero riding a demon. Ten years later, it's still there. On a shelf four feet from my desk. I cannot avoid looking at it. And this is perhaps the third time in all those years that I can speak my grief.

Today, when I recall the sea of treasures he introduced to me when I was a trouble child, I often wonder what it was like for the First Nations before the European invasion, this damp paradise of endless riches they inhabited in their winter villages and the cricket-crackling summers of the inland meadows—the boundaries, like the Rebecca Spit of my childhood, where the worlds of water and earth met.

That was the last of my father, the day I tasted his ashes. Now he is only memory. I miss him. I miss being unable to rip at my hair and claw my skin and cover myself with ashes and wail until all the crows flee the trees. I miss my youth, I miss the feasts, the grief and the wild glory of it, everything that has been taken from this coast that I was born into and taught to celebrate—the taste of tasting itself—the crazy song of all that my father taught me to sing.

Raymond Sydney Bush

THE

EMBRACE

By Catherine Bush

If it's possible, in the wake of a parent's death, for that parent to retreat to the point where he or she is barely thought of, I don't know it. My father, dead nearly twenty years ago, remains an absent presence, or a present absence, not because I long for something from him, not in the way a child is taken over by a longing that will inevitably remain unfulfilled, but because, given the gaps and silences and concealments in his life, or his life as I know it, I am continually trying to reconstruct a version of him that will make sense to me, to track a path through what I know and don't know, to incorporate both him and his death. Which is not grief but what grows out of it. Not one story but stories.

In the months and weeks leading up to his death, stories were what I wanted from him. In my journals of the time, I voiced this repeated cry. I wanted him to tell us about himself. Of course he didn't deliver. He died, just turned fifty-nine, of lung cancer, not a smoker's cancer, as he assured us, he the smoker of a pipe not cigarettes, and we figured that he should know, being a cancer specialist, a radiation oncologist, and, until two years before his death, the director of the Princess Margaret Hospital, Ontario's leading cancer-care centre and the Toronto hospital in which he died. He'd worked there, in the old Princess Margaret near Sherbourne and Wellesley, now demolished, virtually all his professional life—the whole of his medical life. On his way to his own cancer treatment, he would first walk and later was wheeled past his portrait hanging in the hospital vestibule, not a bad likeness, if one that in no way captured his vitality. He weakened, lost his hair, aged in the accelerated way that terminal illness forces. The portrait did not. Some of the younger staff, the radiation technicians who were treating him, say, had no idea who he was, were oblivious to the significance of his history in this place, and this, too, must have been painful—although it was my mother who described these things, his pain accessible only through hers.

I had returned to Toronto from the United States less than a year and a half before his diagnosis, less than two years before his death. In retrospect, my timing looked felicitous, as if some internal sensor, piloting me towards this last period of proximity, had brought me home, although at the time my reasons looked nothing like that. (I was finding it difficult to write fiction in New York, I had reached an immigration impasse, I was curious about a Toronto different from the city in which I had grown up). I had just turned twenty-seven and was twenty-eight at the time my father died.

If his death itself did not come as a shock, his diagnosis did. Days before Christmas, 1989, I accompanied my mother to a performance of the *Messiah*, filling in for my father, my mother and I already distracted by a death. My brother-in-law's best friend had died days before of lung cancer, three months after diagnosis; he was thirty-one. I did not know this man and had only glimpsed him once through the gauze curtains of a house in Waterloo, but he was someone near to those I love, and so his death, shocking because of his youth and its speed, pressed close. As my mother drove me home, west along King Street towards Parkdale, I asked after my father, who'd been suffering from something like the flu and an ache in his leg and had gone in for some tests. She wouldn't speak. I suppose I could have forced her, but in those moments I was too taken aback to do so. Instead, once home, I spoke to my middle sister, with whom I shared a house, she living in the first-floor apartment with her boyfriend and I on the top floor, a tenant between us, and my sister was the one (not that night, but the next) who called our parents and begged them to tell us what was up. They'd hoped to wait to break the news until after Christmas. I'm not sure how they thought they would pull this off. Word, when it came, came by phone, only I was on the phone talking to my boyfriend in New York as my father tried to reach me, until my sister came sobbing up the stairs between apartments, screaming that I had to get off, so wild that I was convinced something catastrophic had happened—someone had broken in and stabbed her boyfriend. (It was Parkdale.) When I heard my father's voice, I must already have known something—but he was good at this, very calm, a professional delivering a prognosis that nothing could have prepared him for. And then it was the four of us—my remarkably normal-seeming father, my white-faced and sleepless mother, my middle sister and me, gripped by nightmares of earthquakes and tumbling ceilings, my youngest sister being far away in Africa—who spent Christmas concealing the news of his terminal cancer from my grandparents, his parents, visiting from my aunt's farm outside of Ottawa.

———

In the wake of his death, the first forms of grief were both obvious and unexpected. There was, beyond loss, solace in the knowledge that we had, as a family, managed to come together and give him a version of a good death. My youngest sister had returned twice from her temporary home in Kenya and had, especially during her second visit, when my father was between hospital stays and close to the end of his life, been able to help my mother with his care, at a time when his atypical reactions to pain medications were giving him a form of dementia. He was supposed to be attached to a tube of oxygen but would often wake and wander the house at night. In this stretch of time, between his first near-death and his actual death, a period of a few weeks, he was out of the hospital long enough for my middle sister to get married. He himself was the one who said, if you want me to be there, better do it now, and so a wedding, held in my parents' garden, was organized in a week. During his last days, back in the hospital, we were able, finally, to reunite his two worlds, the world of the hospital and his domestic life, which he had so long kept separate. As children, we'd visited the hospital for Christmas parties, or to watch my father inject mice in those long-ago rudimentary labs, not like those of today, sealed away behind air-locked doors—not only inject the mice, but, with a neat crack of their necks kill them before tossing their bodies in a garbage can. We played with the real human skeleton in his office and scribbled on his chalkboard. In subsequent years, we'd had almost no access to this side of his life, to the man with the remarkable bedside manner, so we were told, to the place where he was at home in his authority. Colleagues paid awkward, terrified visits to his bedside, while we kept a vigil around his bed, eating Sri Lankan takeout, watching World Cup soccer and the Liberal leadership convention, massaging his feet, swabbing out his mouth when he could no longer drink, listening to the gurgling shallowness of his breath. For the first time in my life, I heard my father say I love you, not to me, but over the phone to my sister in Kenya, the rest of us in the room, perhaps the only way that he could speak directly to us. I love all my daughters and my lovely wife. The words he spoke to me, once when we were alone together in those last days, were simply, you've been so good to me—meaning not me, but all of us, his acknowledgement of what we'd given him at the end, and these words made me cry.

He was adamant that nothing be done to prolong his life. I have no sense that he wanted to die, but he did not in the end fight death or rage against it, and though my middle sister did his raging for him (why weren't they feeding him, figuring out ways to keep him alive?), it seemed to me that what he was asking from us was a similar accept-ance. He was given a six-month prognosis and died six months later, almost to the day, my sister and I almost missing the moment of his death because our car wouldn't start, my mother ragged with fear because she couldn't get hold of us, this in the days before cellphones. Then we were at his bedside, along with a nurse who'd worked beside him for years, as his heart, slowed by morphine, stopped.

And then we were holding his hands, and touching him, as the temperature of our bodies slowly reversed, his cooling as ours warmed, while one of the nurses made a pot of tea.

Perhaps the most potent early form of loss was itself a displacement, an assaultive sense of my own mortality. Grief has its self-absorptions. Anything, it seemed, could lead to death. Stepping into a car or off a sidewalk. It was impos-sible to know what lurked inside the body, waiting to uncoil itself. I'd swallow a pill to tend a headache and feel as if the tiny lozenge were stuck in my throat, unbudgeable, although it wasn't. So much of this was about a loss of control, the loss of any illusion of control being the eternal loss—a vertigo, in the wake of my father's death, so intense as to feel unfathomable. The passing of time seemed overwhelming, the velocity of it, my father an astronaut who'd gone tumbling through space, his aging zooming ahead of ours, although even my own temporal trajectory felt terrifying. Others might rage against death, but it was fear that gripped me, a fear that reached its apotheosis one night, a year later, in a tent by the shores of Lake Turkana in northern Kenya. My mother and I had gone to visit my younger sister and her husband, timing our journey to be away from Toronto on the anniversary of my father's death. We headed out on an overnight camping trip, into the desolate scrub desert, not far from a few remote Turkana villages and, close to the lake, the dimness of a hotel, perhaps from the seventies, already falling into ruin, although what seemed most overwhelming was the ancientness of the place, this the land that hominids first sprang from, and how far I was from anything I knew or depended on to orient myself. I was somewhere from which I could not escape on my own, and this in itself was terrifying, as I lay rigid in the dark, under a sky in which the southern stars themselves were unfamiliar. This fear, too, had to be passed through.

And through all this, I wrote. In the midst of my first novel, I kept writing. When friends asked me how I could do this, I said I didn't see how I could not. I kept going, I think, because the interior displacement of fiction became a necessary form of order to set against the chaos all around me. I dreamed of him. In the week after his death, I dreamed of him, lifelike, tending a barbecue, although in the dream I knew him to be dead; the encounter with him in the dream was a confirmation of his death, as if, perversely, seeing him alive was a way of registering his absence. In subsequent months, I would dream of him dying, as if my growing acceptance of his death allowed me to move away from that point of finality, back towards a landscape in which he might once more be anything.

And though I feared travel—every journey being full of possible death and leading inevitably to death—I made the decision to take a job, the September after my father died, at the Fine Arts Work Center in Provincetown, Massachusetts, where I'd been a resident writing fellow two years before. In part I took the job because I was desperate for money, but I was also desperate, in the short term, to get out of Toronto, away from the enclosure of family, to seek some other form of consolation, and in what better place to do so than by the sea off-season, at the tip of Cape Cod.

The first time I'd come to Provincetown, I'd also been fleeing death, if in an entirely different way, leaving behind a downtown New York in which death from AIDS, or the fear of it, seemed omnipresent—one man I knew well enough to visit in hospital, others I knew of, or the lovers of those I knew, this being my first exposure to death, that of peers and near-peers, not the elderly, since all of my grandparents would remain alive for years. Not that Provincetown was a place where I was freed from death, death only being transformed by it.

During that first stay, I would learn of the suicide of a high-school boyfriend, who jumped through a window when the schizophrenia that was already engulfing him began to return. Early that winter, something—toxic algae, a form of red tide—was killing the humpback whales that populate the waters of Cape Cod Bay, their bodies washing up onshore. I went one sullen, windy afternoon to look at one of the bodies, on a beach near Truro. Other people were there. The stench of decomposition was stupendous, but the body was still largely intact, apart from a core sample that had been drilled for an autopsy through the layers of flesh, and there was a scouring sadness at the sight, at the wreckage of it, a whale stilled and huge as a house, and yet there was something momentous about being able to touch its body, lay my hands against its skin, against the delicate fibres of its mouth through which it sifted tiny fish—to have the whale, in death, offered up as something so acutely corporeal.

The year after my father's death, I lived in a house that backed onto the town beach, where my fisherman neighbour mended lobster traps and hung deer carcasses on his back porch to swing and cure beyond my kitchen window. Within the house, where once more I lived up on the third floor, I would feel, for the first time in my life, the full circular force of a gale, the way the wind will turn as it passes, from north to east to south, the water, whipped up by wind and high tide and full moon, flinging seaweed against the third-floor windows and ripping planks from the deck below as if they were no more than twigs, while down the street, beyond the protection of the breakwater, the entire backs of houses and a restaurant were torn away. Puny humans, we were nothing in the storm's path, and there was consolation in this, in the implacability of such violence and such cycles.

Death came swooping close in other ways, with the advent of the first Gulf War, news arriving via television and radio, through the voice of the president, who shared my name, through the appearance of yellow ribbons tied around trees and fears for the family of my Israeli brother-in-law, hunkered down in their southern Israeli town to escape possible attacks from SCUD missiles (as my own parents' childhoods had once been indelibly shaped by war). On the radio, a voice intoned about the calculus of possible death. I was not trying to kid myself that there was any escape from it.

My father—did I miss him? It had come to me early that loss was always tied up with longing, that all longing is informed by the possibility of loss, that to desire something is to understand that it can be snatched away. What I wanted, then, as much as anything, was to make some sense of him, this man who concealed himself without cunning, of my relationship to him, and of the manner of his dying.

His cancer had no obvious cause—most cancers don't, as he himself had taught us. He would have called his death random, bad luck as much as anything, and he did say this, yet it was impossible not to look, not to want to look for connections. There was the intense stress of his job. For years, as hospital director, he'd been engaged in the Sisyphean task of trying to extract funding from the provincial government in order to build a new and bigger hospital, presciently aware of the coming demographic bulge that would make the need for more cancer resources inevitable. He was the youngest hospital director and the last to fill the position, the job no longer the possible domain of one man. From the outside, it looked at times as though administration was eating him alive. If the fight for the new hospital consumed him, it was a struggle that he wholly believed in. And he succeeded in it. In the dark of his hospital room, swimming in and out of consciousness, he would ask us what year it was and whether the new hospital had been built, this preoccupation a ferocious part of him right until the end. Stress might have made him vulnerable to other predations, stress and the strange release that succeeds it when the body becomes most exposed, and he perhaps vulnerable in other ways, cut loose from a job that had so wholly defined him, struggling to adapt, as he himself once put it, to some new role.

Then there was the tricky question of radiation, as in, had he been exposed to too much of it? His parents thought so. They went to their own deaths convinced that radiation exposure had led to his. He said no. Of course, there was no smoking gun. His words did only so much to reassure us, to reassure me. (Did he truly believe his denial, or was he saying what had to be said because there was no proof, or was he lying to protect us?) He was involved in the very early days of setting up Cobalt radiation units. At the time of his death, one of his colleagues was dying of another cancer down the hall. The possibility lingers, of connection if not cause, and there's some reassurance in it, as possibility, even now, even as there seems no point in trying to pursue it, for knowing more would not alter his choices, or that fact that he died committed to saving others, in the grip of a pro-fession that he loved.

———

Even in the immediate aftermath of his death, I was able to feel relief, glad—glad?—that if my father was going to die early, that he hadn't died when either he or I was any younger. At twenty-eight, I was still something of a mess in his eyes, rootless, jobless, in the midst of a first novel, having done nothing outwardly worthwhile with my fancy Ivy League degree. Which he had paid for. His concern could take the form of anger—I was refusing to think about my future; I was a snob for balking at taking a full-time job. He'd read an early draft of my novel and admitted that he had no idea what to make of it. I knew that I was like him in some ways—I'd always felt this—but in my twenties, I was also beginning to understand, through my mother, through my questions to her during long car trips south through the Adirondacks, that much of my father's more imposing demeanour hid insecurity and real shyness. I remember being initially startled by the thought, though the knowledge made him more comprehensible and more like me, once again—and like my mother, too, herself a shy woman.

During the years of my adolescence, my father had not been an easy man to live with. He was terrified of teenage boys getting their hands on his teenage girls, and I, the eldest, was the first to run that gauntlet, not the best rebel because, even as I resisted his authority, I internalized both his judg-

ment and his fear—this, too, being territory it's impossible
not to return to, part of my lifelong renegotiation with him.
He wanted to spare me, at sixteen, from potentially dangerous situations—his words—situations that were, as I
wrote at the time, equally inexplicable to him. Naturally he
would not tell me directly what such situations were. My
male classmates were terrified of him (so his technique
worked, sort of). He was made nervous, perhaps rightly, by
my intimacy with my last high-school boyfriend, a troubled
intimacy, given my own habits of withdrawal and my
boyfriend's capacity for anger and judgment and fear in the
face of my fear. My father's attempts to part us, late at night,
days before my boyfriend left for university, ended in threats
of violence. The doctor, I called him on the page, while also
noting how he ran his knuckles down my back as I sat
hunched and daunted over pages of university applications,
noting, also, the comfort in the gesture.

When I left for university, I was desperate to get out
not only of the city but out of the country (a passage not
unlike that my parents had taken before me), desperate to
prove the ways in which I was not like him, like either of
my parents (this being the common passage of all children),
to find a voice (so much was about finding a voice), though
in the years since I have sometimes wondered, if he had
died when I was still caught up in the heat of that struggle, desiring escape above all, if I would have remained
trapped in some far more unresolved legacy, endlessly
resisting him, though even at the time I wanted, as much
as anything, to understand him.

A year and a half after his death, I would sell my novel and, for the first time, move in with someone. And the four of us present at his deathbed—my mother, my sister, my brother-in-law and I—would reconvene in another hospital room for the birth of my sister's first child, a daughter.

———

What I want is to construct a journey for him, a trajectory, out of a family life that has been full of journeys, people endlessly trying to connect one place with somewhere else. On the surface, my father's looks like a typical immigrant success story, that of a man who escaped a class-bound past and made good. He grew up in England, a scholarship boy who played national junior-level soccer, who boxed. Until his death, he kept his accent. In the hours after his death, as we stayed with his body, a Greek-Canadian cleaner who worked in the hospital came to pay his final respects, saluting my father's body, heralding him as a new Canadian, a man who as director had held doors open for him, a mere cleaner, the two of them sharing this path as new Canadians, which was true, except for the fact that my father had been born in Toronto.

His parents had come out at what turned out to be the depth of the Depression. Before leaving, my grandfather, in a fit of optimism, spent good money on a bowler hat in order to look smart in Toronto, only to discover on arrival that no one wore bowler hats in Toronto, and so, in another fit of optimism, as he walked one day along the top of the Scarborough Bluffs, he tossed his new hat off the

cliffs and into the waters of Lake Ontario. (It was my grandfather who told me this story that last Christmas we all spent
together.) Unfortunately, my grandfather, a mechanical
draughtsman and designer of radios, couldn't find work. For
a while, he and my grandmother ran a fish-and-chip shop
out on the Danforth in the city's east end. He worked for
the gas company, digging lines. After two years, they gave
up and took my infant father back to England.

My father returned to Canada as a young man, eager
to begin a new life, and it was in Toronto that he met my
mother, no typical immigrant either. Born in England, she'd
grown up in Toronto as a war guest; at five, she was one of
the youngest sent over in a government-sponsored program
that sent English children to safety overseas during the
Second World War. She returned to her natural family in
England at eleven—not an easy return, her own father a
troubled and difficult man. It was in the Leaside house of
her Canadian foster parents, who would become my
Canadian grandparents (card-playing, gin-drinking, so different from my bookish grandparents back in England), that
she met my father, by then a young medical student, at a
party. He was just back from Burma, where he'd spent some
months setting up portable radiation units to help pay his
way through medical school, still tanned, driving a baby
blue Triumph convertible. She was in the midst of a post-
university trip across the country but had stopped in Toronto
to work, having sworn to her parents that she would return
to England. My father, the new Canadian, offered her a pro-
posal. Keep travelling or marry me. She married him.

———

It is through stories that we make sense of the absent ones, attempt to pull them close—or that's how I do it. I can't vouch for the veracity of all the details I'm offering, for I'm a fiction writer who practises her own habits of indirection. I can vouch for the baby blue convertible because I have seen photographs of it, and we spent evenings as children watching the films of my father's Burmese days played from an old projector onto the living-room wall of our Don Mills townhouse—monks racing barefoot across stones rimmed with fire—a trip that would inspire my youngest sister, a year out of high school, to set off on her own trek across Africa. We all fled the country as soon as we left high school, a gesture that looks meaningful, even as it was something that as a family we made jokes about.

I was eighteen when I learned from my mother that my father had been married before. The two of us were on the subway, heading home, when I asked what seemed a simple enough question: How had my father met the family friends we'd been visiting, whom I knew had preceded her arrival in his life? And so she told me. Perhaps the most peculiar thing was that we had grown up surrounded by traces of his first wife, even though we had never known this crucial fact about her. Her parents had always been a part of our lives, another set of Canadian grandparents; we knew her sister. We'd seen the black-and-white photograph of her in her nurse's uniform hanging on the wall of her parents' house, knew her name

and that she'd died, just not that she'd died of toxemia in pregnancy and that she'd been married to our father. Before
meeting my mother, he'd had another Canadian life. He'd
lived in Ottawa and worked for Atomic Energy of Canada.
It was because of his first wife, and her death, that he went
into medicine, or so he told a reporter writing a profile of
him for the *Toronto Sun*, which is how I know of it.

His first wife's father was a pharmacist, her mother of
United Empire Loyalist stock. When my father was court-
ing her, they were living and working in a pharmacy in
west-end Toronto, at the corner of College and Dufferin,
not far from where I live now, and so, strangely, this is the
part of my father's geography that remains closest to me.
Passing that corner, as I often do, I find it hard not to think
of him, though I know that he believed it was possible to
outstrip the past, not possible but necessary, that my parents
shared a generational belief in putting the difficult parts of
the past behind you. If he did not speak of his first wife and
her death, it was because he wanted us to believe in the
intactness of our own family, yet his grief must have been
present to him in some form. In those early years, he must
have felt raw loss and been engaged in his own acts of nego-
tiation and willed transformation even as, once more, he
embraced a new life. And he must have suffered fear, too,
of all that can be snatched away.

On the day of my birth, my father, then an intern at East
York General Hospital, took my mother to what was then the
Salvation Army Grace Hospital at the corner of Bloor and
Church, not far from the apartment where they were living,

close to Bloor and Sherbourne. Upon leaving the hospital after my birth, he stepped off a curb and felt one leg go numb, slipping a disc, as they used to say, or herniating it, the pressure on the nerve severe enough that he required surgery, though they were quicker to operate on backs in those days, and besides, he was an intern, and wanted on the wards at work. He ended up flat on his back, in his own hospital, the only time he'd be in a hospital as a patient until his death, and it was my mother, leaving me in the care of another medical student and his wife, who went to visit *him*. He would be the first to acknowledge the humour in this story—the trauma of my birth felling him—as well as the first to declare the injury simply another instance of bad luck.

Although I'm leery of straightforward emotional explanations for the physical, I find it hard not to see something revealing in the physical slippage of my father's body at my birth, the body saying something in its language of displacement, and I found myself returning to this moment recently, after a disc injury laid me up and left me lying, evenings at a stretch, on the living-room couch, watching dusk filigree the trees outside. My own injury flared at the end of a long and difficult relationship, and so I lay there, pondering this emotional congruence and wondering at the moment when, in the aftermath of my birth, my father stepped off a curb and fell as his back seized up. As I watched the trees dissolve, I searched for something—his fear, his loss, his longing, what he must, no, might have felt, the joy and peril of new beginnings. I don't know how he'd tell this story; all I have is what gets passed on and what I wonder at, the fear, the longing, the elusive language of the body, what you think you know and something else, for there is always something else.

Part of the journey away from the externality of death, from the moment when someone is physically taken from you, is towards incorporation, the lost one finding a home in the body of those who are left—this, the embrace—because this is the only place to put him. After a loved one's death, the only way to reach the unreachable is through indirection: everything becomes metaphor, one thing standing in for something else. Stories are one way to replace what can never be replaced, and the telling of stories is my work, not his.

In a folder at the back of the bottom drawer of my filing cabinet, I keep a tiny collection of the last things that I have from my father, two items that speak volumes if you're adept at reading through indirection and seeing what isn't there. There's the last prescription he ever wrote for me, for Tylenol 3s, *for the treatment of severe pain*. And a blank pad of paper—not a note but the impression of a note, the indentations of his pen upon a plain white page. What remains is something almost corporeal, not ink marks but the pressure of his hand through the pen, as close as I can get to a physical trace. These many years later, the traces may be fading. I don't know. I don't take out the pad very often. It was an ordinary note. He was asking my mother to do something. What I can make out now, when I tilt the blank paper towards sunlight so that a shadow is cast across it, is this: *Margaret*—and at the end: *Thanks, Ray.*

Steven Carty

Gladys Irene Clarke Luke

(with her daughter-in-law, Shirley Luke)

THERE IS

NO GOOD

IN A

BLACK NIGHT

(Thoughts on my personal grieving)

By Austin Clarke

I was drifting in and out of sleep, after my arrival in America, in New Jersey, in the suburb of Willingboro. I was here and I was there back in Barbados, at the same time in the same time, in fact and in fantasy, one church melting into the other, and both soaked in the song that filled the church, just like water rising in a flood sweeps over table and bed.

I am in a flood. The water is brown. And cool. Even though it is in the Tropics there, and in the middle of summer here, torturous as the humidity is. And I am sinking. I never learned to swim. I am drowning. But before I am aware that I am drowning, I can feel the beginning of death. The water is coming into my mouth. Just as the words of a song the congregation is singing are coming out of their mouths. It is a beautiful song. A song that was sung also on the Island in the little ashen-grey church painted in that colour by the unforgiving sun; back there; that was sung in the Cathedral-church.

The family has come from the four corners of the Island, and South Carolina, and Montreal, and Manhattan, and Miami, and Canada—meaning Toronto—to Brooklyn. And there is a wake; and there is pudding-and-souse, and macaroni pie, and baked potatoes, and oxtail stew, and roast pork, and drinks of all denominations and proofs, and two large rooms in this first house (of six that she owned), in an all-Jewish neighbourhood of Avenue A, in Brooklyn, that my mother had bought in 1969; and we go upstairs and come back downstairs like tributaries in a river that has no strong current to keep the flow in one direction; only a languishing of movement; and we laugh and drink and go back over the years, and we hear that "she died a natural death." At age ninety-two—the first time any of us knew for certain when she was born on the Island; and plans are made for who, who amongst us, her children and her cousins and her friends, shall be allowed to say a few words "for Gladys" in her memory; in her honour; and we hear where the funeral service shall be held; and what time; but we are concerned with the amount of food and alcohol that are already consumed; and what we need that will be consumed later. For no one, children, grandchildren, great-grandchildren, one "great-great-gran," says too much about her. Yes! She died from natural causes! People think she died from unnatural causes? No-no! She died a natural death. Although, it is true, she fell down in the shower her last morning on earth, when she was taking a shower . . .

I have seen her laugh. Her head would be held back, and the gold filling her teeth in specks would glisten. And if her laughter could have a colour to identify it, a colour put to it, to distinguish it, her laughter would be golden. I have seen her cry; weep; in tears: from the ferocity of thunder and lightning and the torrential rain in the Island; stormy weather; and I have seen her tears as they gouge out two lines in the powder running down her face; and could taste them almost, for they were often shed on my behalf, and I had seen the cause that caused them, like the origin of a river flowing from some origin of unkindness; or of disappointment.

"She want to be dressed in her best dress, with a hat, with the veil attach', and her jewelleries. Her rings. And her gold wristwatch. She want her wedding ring on her finger. And she want everybody to have a good time. The second thing, the second wake, is to be held in her house up in New Jersey. And she want to be buried next to Daddy. Next to her husband . . ." And I go over all the details in our lives, hers and mine, that began in the small Island, when she sat at the front window "studying her head," calculating the meaning to her health and to her budget, of killing the pullet, "the last pullet big-enough to eat, at the door," and boiling-it-down in a pot with watery white rice, something I would come to know in Canada as "sticky rice," made famous by the Chinese, another cautious, saving race, but which in the Island we knew to be the result of bad cooking . . . "too much water in the pot for the number of rice grains"; but this was done deliberately, to stretch the rice; and rice in the Island, during the years of the Second World War, was as scarce and precious as pearls; and the beginning of a storm, or a hurricane, or a heavy downpour of rain—all of which we gave the same name of terror to; in these times, she would be the first to hear the rumbling and then the clap of unforgiving noise in the distance, in the thickness of the clouds, high over the Caribbean Sea, which she told me, from the time I was five years old, was "join-on to that Ocean, the Atlantic . . . a terrible body of dirty water . . . puke mixed with blood of our forefathers"; and she followed the peal of the thunder, like the collapsing sound of the tongues of bells hitting steel, hearing them with her ears, keen as a jaguar's or some other wild animal's, seeking prey . . . which, in our neighbourhood, these would be wild dogs . . . she heard the thunder in the distance first, like the roll of bass drums at a parade of the Island's Volunteer Force on the Garrison Savannah Parade Square, where royalty in the local white eyes and faces, and the poor black men, privates and lance corporals, their highest rank in the Volunteer Force, met in a colonial equality, drilling and marching in formation, to "Onward Christian Soldiers," and moved their rifles timed in measured notes to the bagpipes' sad wail, rifles left over from the Boer War, in "Royyul Sah-lute, Pree-zent Armsss!" in the voice of a local white, tinged with an English accent, making us, the privates and the lance corporals, disobey the officer's command; and we mocked the drill sergeant and felt better about the warning in the clouds and the sound from the clouds of the bass-rolling of drumsticks, "Bramm! . . . Blax! . . . Brah-laaxxx!" and it was the lightning like a cruel cutlass just sharpened for cutting, ready for the soft skin and peel of the sugar canes in the fields surrounding us, just like, in a few quick seconds, we were surrounded in the darkness under the bed, as if it was night and blackness over the Island, by the sheets and the blanket and the darkness under the bed . . . me and my mother. I wondering if people anywhere in the "outside-world" lived their entire lives in tents; and what they did for light and fire. And my mother, who remembered to bring her Holy Bible with her under the bed, darkened by her fear of the natural darkness under the bed, and holding the Bible in a grip of purposefulness, unopened, tight-tight-tight . . . making me think of the nursery rhyme

> *Hiddy-Biddy*
> *Shut-up yuh lap*
> *Tight-tight-tight . . .*

But my mother had no time for children's rhymes. The damage of lightning (a man was killed standing under a mango tree), sheltering from the rain, and frightened by the thunder rolling over the Atlantic Ocean, waves high as the sails in the masts of schooners, some of whom had brought African citizens to Barbados, now anchored in the Careenage

in the Wharf, in Town . . . and my mother cut into my
thoughts, reciting something from the unopened Bible:

> *By Sin-Peter, and by Sin-Paul . . .*
> *By Sin-Peter, and by Sin-Paul . . .*

She had to have forgotten the rest of the prayer, taken from
the Book of Common Prayer . . . but then, it returned to
her memory . . .

> *Don't let this storm,*
> *And this thunder*
> *Crucify we, Lord,*
> *For you is a good God, Lord . . .*

And the thunder clapped. Like the palms of giants. Like the
host and tribe of Polyphemus. Announcing victory. And the
bass drums rolled and I remembered the garrison Savannah
Drill Square, with the regality of spit and polish, and the flash
of lightning and the sound of thunder came together; and
they struck my mother dumb. The soft purr of water drib-
bling from one corner of the house to another, outside; and
the bleat of one of the three sheep we kept, for meat and
for Easter and for Christmas, and the swaying clammy-cherry
trees, and the pawpaw trees, their fruits and the seeds inside
them that looked like caviar, good for moving the bowels;
near the outdoor closet; and the helpless crowing of a cock
up on the highest bar in the roost of the fowl shed that
Daddy made one Sunday after Matins, came under the bed

with us, and then, as always happened, a cool wind found us under the white sheet hanging down from the mattress made with guinea grass to the floor which let in no light upon our incarceration; but we could see the late-afternoon sun, in rays like rivers of fire, greeting us when it was over. Or the flash of a "forty-leg," my mother's name for a centipede, well fed and dark brown, and so large that I always heard the noise of its forty legs when it walked. But it was only a flash. Fast as the travelling lightning in the sky. And that was the signal to search, and kill. Every piece of furniture, every cup and saucer, every glass, every plate, in every drawer, every layer of bedclothes upon every bed in the house, every shoe, every pair of socks, every shirt, every skirt, trousers, pants and panties, brassieres, housedresses, dresses to wear to the Church of the Nazarene and to the Anglican church, St. Matthias, and Daddy's three-piece dark brown, jet black and grey pin-striped suits: inside the linings, inside the innumerable pockets, including the fobs, under the inside lining of hats, inside the hatband, and in all my school books. My mother felt that "forty-legs" liked school books, especially.

And when this was over, like the waves in the sea become calm and even and buoyant as a freshly made bed, and you lie upon it, you feel a newer vibration of peace. And my mother finished the pot of yellow split-pea soup, with thick juicy pieces of pig tail in it, fresh eddoes for soup, fresh sweet potatoes, fresh pieces of beef bought in Town, on account from Goddard's & Sons, Limited; and dumplings, whose flour is kneaded to make them heavy and tight, and when you bite into one, you hear the click; and if there is no click to greet your teeth, then the dumplings are not well done . . . and you move into the rest of the sun-setting late afternoon, and the cleanness and the clearness and the sweetness of food and memory that "we were near death in this damn storm, boy!" (I pardoned her the exaggeration); "and that," she said like a philosopher, "is why we have to be grateful for this food, and to God, for sparing life."

I was the schoolboy "champeen" athlete in the whole of Barbados. For many years, counting 1946, 1947, 1948, 1949, 1950 and 1951, and not once did I see her appear on the track, at the Combermere School for Boys' Pasture. Or, at Harrison College—also in those days, a school for boys—to watch me run. Or long jump into a pit of sand brought from the beach. And neither my father nor my stepfather. Perhaps, the three of them, in unison, felt that their presence might take away from my concentration; perhaps they thought their watching me run the 100 yards might be bad luck, that I would fall, and the spikes built into my home-made running shoes by the Village tailor, a man who himself liked running, the running shoes of the boy chasing me, might punch holes into my feet. And how would I, with a little accident like that, be able to continue being schoolboy "champeen" for six years, crowned Victor Ludorum, cham-pion of the games? Perhaps, it was for some of these reasons.

Her life was spared for ninety-two years. All of us, children and close-family, were amazed she had reached that pinnacle of years. We knew that, many years ago, she subtracted five years from her legal count, in order to work five years more than legal before legal retirement. And she didn't have to tell two lies, only one, that she was five years younger. She always looked ten years younger than her true age; and she didn't have to open her mouth and state the lie. People who knew her, and strangers, all thought and said, "Jesus Christ, Gladys, how you always looking more younger than your age?"

"Hard work," she told them. And laughed and showed her teeth with the gold fillings . . .

She impressed all of us with her wisdom. And she impressed poets, too. Strangers painted an image of her, from hearsay, from the tales, some tall, some short, of her imagination. She liked scary stories, and terrified me, night after night, in her darkened narratives about men with three heads, and one eye in the middle of each head, and four feet who roamed the gutters and lanes and back alleys of our small Village, in Barbados; and turned themselves into donkeys and other animals, made out of steel; and dwelled in the sugarcane fields. The skin, the flesh, the softness of humanity was transformed into the fierceness of the "steel donkey" . . .

"This is my big-son," my mother used to introduce me when I visited her in America. "Lives up in Canada. A big professor. At Yale. In the Ivy Leagues, boy!"

One poet of Canada said this of my mother, when she died:

The stars hang particularly low,
particularly bright, on this crisp
early December evening, sparkling
up the thin frosted bare armed

shadowy ash trees, everyone
scurrying home to electric lamps
and gas fires, heading into the
long night, when you have restored
to us the meaning of the season,
bells ringing along the lit busy
streets of Brooklyn, to celebrate
the passing of a grand old queen,
immaculate mother of Africa,
Barbados, Canada, New York,
and her formidable children, dread
locked, jazz bejeweled, honorary
gowned, that was a gorgeous
lived life, of heroic engagements
and delicious digressions, Gladys
Irene, and these are tears of
happiness from the flower bearing
grateful multitudes, bon voyage,
good job, mom, long live the queen.

And we, family and friends, and strangers who did not know her, a granddaughter who had never seen her in the flesh, living; and in the cold winds of New Jersey, standing over the open grave, like celebrating guests at a birthday party, looking down into the cruel, dark, cold, thick Willingboro clumps of mould, slippery in the December frost, when the grave-digging two men in coveralls, the one I saw dragging the green snake of a hose, the other with the shovel, now reappearing as two uncaring "grave attendants," found words spoken to us in their cold irony, "We are not allowed to bury the coffin in these conditions. We have to leave the coffin on top of the grave, because someone might slip, in these weather conditions, and fall in . . ."

But all of us wanted to accompany her in this portion of the journey back home, to ashes from which the Bible said she had come; that all of us came from; and in my bravery, casual as a bad habit, I nodded assent to the two grave-attendants; and we hurried back to her mansion out of the cold, to drink the strong rum from Barbados, and the single malt that my brother, brewed and schooled at Columbia University, near Harlem, learned to drink; and the turkey breasts and legs which she loved above all cuts of other meats; and to play dominoes, and cook other meals into the long non-grieving ungodly night, when the tales of her personality of kindness were exchanged, and circulated; and they all said, "You know something that I just realize? You are the spitting image of Gladys! Jesus Christ, you look just like your mother, boy! I can see her features in your face! That is a blessing, boy. When a son look like his mother! The same smile. The same eyes. The same way you turn your face when you happy, the same way you turn your face when you angry, the same way with her . . . you are just like her . . . you really take after her . . ."

————

I had stood over her coffin, and looked into her eyes, and I swear I saw her eyes close, and open again. She winked at me. Acknowledging that I, the resembling firstborn, was just like my mother; and did not waste a tear, did not feel the tug of loss, did not feel the loss. I said goodbye to her. Mother. Role model, using that manufactured term, foreign to us in Barbados, as I had said goodbye, not farewell, when she left on Sundays, at the same time, fifteen minutes before eleven o'clock, to go the rocking, tambourine-ridden, hot Sunday mornings, to sit in a pew that shook as the Sisters and Brothers and the Pastor recited, "Jerusalem, my Happy Home . . ."

She is gone now, and I am like a tourist returning from a vacation. Coming back to Canada.

———

And from the first day, after I returned, I started to hear things; and see things. And being cushioned in the certainty and force of witchcraft, "obeah": a dependency upon spirits, the ghosts of deads, I feel her presence, in the floor beneath my bedroom; and I wait for her to declare herself, declare her presence; make me know her intention; and I feel it, although I cannot see it, only in my imagination. But my imagination this time, in these two following years, after I had left her coffin at the side of the open grave, like a mouth wide open, in the middle of a yawn . . .

It began, her welcomed ghostly presence, with the ringing of the doorbell. No one had touched the button. But the doorbell still announced the arrival and impatience of a visitor. The visitor is my mother. Come back from the open grave, to tell me the truth: that I have enemies; that all my enemies are friends; that "only yuh friends know yuh business!" She and Bob Marley; that I am being watched, being protected; just as she had protected me under the bed in the total darkness, when the darkness was not gentle; when the lightning flashed like the Sword of Damocles, when the thunder, like the bass drums in the Volunteers' parade, rolled, demanding attention and order; and military precision.

The house in which I live, now with the spirits of my mother's haunting visits, at all hours of the day and night, was lived in by one of "the Negroes" who came by railroad, underground from the slave plantations of America; and its romantic history was uncovered in the days of acknowledgement and apology and confession, and the pouring out of guilt, in the terms initiated by Archbishop Desmond Mpilo Tutu: truth and reconciliation. The Archbishop was made more glorious and universal through the trumpet of Miles Davis, who named one of his masterpieces "Tutu." I was, by this music, already surrounded by ghosts, the spirits of slaves and "African Negroes"; and I glorified in my safety. There is no better guardian than the ghost of your forefathers. Than the ghost of your mother. Warmth, and confidence and assurance and strength and the company of voice and silent advice and the selection of the role I am to play. Just as the voice of the doorbell ringing the arrival of guest and friend, lover and postman, by the beginning chiming notes of the tune, similar to "Big Ben," chaining me to an earlier colonialism, and earlier slavery, the breath of my mother whispering warnings and advice; caution with friend; wariness with lover; a backward glance at the person walking at the rear of my friendships, so too did the breath of her presence wrap itself around me, like a suit made out of rubber, like the costume of men who swim like dolphins in a pool much smaller than the Atlantic Ocean.

No show of emotion. She had told me this, from the time I could understand words, not only hers, but the world's words. No crying. For help or for surrender. No tears. It is not a funeral, she also said. It is a departure. A natural going away, implying that there will be a sure arrival, "on the other side," and a certain return: if not in this world, then in the other world of spirits that she now is a citizen of. Heaven. Dust. The ending up of skin and hair and bones, veins and blood; air and breath, now stultified, in the cold Willingboro air, putrid as fruits left rotting in the ground.

. . . And we had left her, in her box, in her mansion of deep brown, rich mahogany casket, beside the mouth of the grave, her grave, just as she had been left standing in the late, frightening, cold nights, after her double shift as a nurse providing care to old men round the clock, in those money-making days when she had subtracted five years from the years the official stamp on her birth certificate testified to . . .

. . . And she was left, lying beside her own grave, just as she had been left standing beside the road when the fifth taxi in a row refused to stop to take her out of the bone-chilling-cold, money-making exclusive Brooklyn district where her terminal patients lay. It had happened in Manhattan. It happened in Brooklyn. It happened in Willingboro. It happened at her own funeral; at her burial. But it was a clear afternoon, no later than five o'clock.

———

In that December sunset, when there was no sun, when
there was no cloud. When there is no sky. Just the emptiness of the day, taking on the tint and colour of lead.

I did not cry then. I did not enter into the skin of rage.
I did not just walk away. I did not even notice that it was
not a good night. I just followed the mourners, into the twi-
light, in the long, slow drive along the grey road, along the
trees that were silent, that were dead, that were blackened
by the wind blowing on their bodies, in this normal, cus-
tomary six black months of the year; and on the plane coming
back to Canada and then in the car from the airport, and
then into the bell-ringing house that was empty. I fell to the
floor. And all the things I should have felt, should have
suffered, should have spoken, at her viewing, at her trolleyed
drive over roads that had no bumps in them, and detours, at
her drive, slow as a funeral, to her last spot, where years
before, when Daddy was in his coma, refusing to be a man
and throw the blanket of silence from off his shoulders, and
his loins, here in this same spot where she chose the "spot"
into which, in time, when he stopped breathing, she would
throw his body into the dark mould, and cover it up; in this
same spot where she offered me a rectangular-shaped hole in
the ground, in Willingboro, in New Jersey, for my body, "just
in case you dead before you think you're going to dead . . . ,"
leaving it there, unfinished, the thought unburied . . .

For there is no good, no good at all, in a night that is
always black.

William Clarke

THE

BAGGAGE

HANDLER

By George Elliott Clarke

I.

When I was nine, my mother baked a Halloween cake (orange and brown frosting on chocolate) for me to take to school to share, in small slices, with my classmates. As I handed out each piece of cake, I began to laugh, then, suddenly, to cry. No, sob. My tears actually ran into and disintegrated a section of the dessert. My teacher, who I adored in a subconsciously sexual fashion, took me to one side, and, after rescuing the dry part of the cake, hugged me and asked me to explain why I was feeling so sad. Already vaguely embarrassed by my crying jag, though delighted by her maternal and perfumed comforting, I answered, with honesty (but also distressing consciousness of my manipulation of the classroom and of her), that I had read in the Bible that we all had to die, and this knowledge upset me. Now, my beautiful blonde teacher pressed me wonderfully against her and then sent me home. There, having been telephone-alerted about my precocious Weltschmerz, my mother now also offered me solace, and I obliged the drama I had prompted by managing to dutifully summon fresh tears.

The moment was memorable for me because my disturbance was simultaneously genuine and manufactured. My tragicomic terror did answer to a deep sense of unfairness: Why should I be subjected to mortality, especially as a child? But, as I bruit above, my crisis was also fake: I knew damn well, even as a nine-year-old, that my—our—doom was sealed, all because of Adam and Eve.

Yet, despite that early recognition that every life carries an expiration date (and further proof was provided by the demise of my maternal grandfather, an event that also transpired in my tenth year, and which was the probable provocation of my otherwise inexplicable Halloween tears), I must admit that I was absolutely unprepared for the death of my father, William Lloyd Clarke, on August 31, 2005, at age seventy. It didn't matter a bit that I had already had practice mourning the deaths of my mother's parents in 1969 and 1979; my father's mother in 1979; my cousin Debbie, age thirty-three, in 1995; my cousin Mona, age forty (by suicidal gunshot wound), in 1999; my cousin

Blair, age forty, in 2001 (I literally trembled in reading the
eulogy over his body: I knew it could have been me laid
out so coldly there); and even my mother, age sixty-one,
on August 6, 2000, whose passing on was actually a mer-
ciful termination of a terminal illness. Despite all these
breathtakingly painful precursors to my father's death, his
end hurt me most, wounded me most deeply, and was the
most psychologically crushing, perhaps because we had not
been as close as I would have liked, even though I now
know his influence—for good and for ill—has been indeli-
ble upon my life.

It is a truism that children can list, with forensic cool-
ness, the imbecilic, immoral or just bad-luck failings of
parents—or a parent—and I did possess a catalogue of my
father's faults (which, nevertheless, I have reproduced
"admirably" in my own life). Indeed, only five years before
his death, I had resolved to never speak to him again. Why?
He had brought to my mother's funeral his second wife, and
had told my two brothers and me, "Now we can be a family
again," thereby suggesting it had been our mother's fault
that our family had broken up, when the greatest blame fell
on him, due to his affair with our blonde, Québécoise maid.
His statement struck me as characteristically insensitive, if
not outrageously stupid, and it was unforgivable coming
as it did on the day my always stylish, beautiful and self-
sacrificing mother—so vastly superior to my father's mistress
and also to his second wife—had been laid to rest.

Thus, my attitude towards my father in his last five
years of life was essentially distant. Sometimes, when I took

my daughter home to Nova Scotia, I would take her to see her Africadian grandfather last; sometimes we would not visit him at all. When his second wife passed away, only a year after my own mother's death, I avoided her funeral studiously, while dispatching a tremendous floral display. Yet, thanks to that woman's vanishing (a death I never mourned nor assisted my father in mourning), I was able to retire my vicious vow not to speak to him, and a kind of uneasy—but maybe typical son–father—relationship began to falteringly evolve.

Part of me still felt the need, though, to punish him for not loving me enough as a child. I was the result of a pregnancy unplanned, with a woman who was not his heart's desire, but who he chivalrously wooed and married once he had assured himself I was indeed his child. As uncharitably as I viewed his decision in the past, I do now recognize that he was accepting a responsibility that his own father, Morris—or Norris—Clarke (of Barbados), had not, abandoning my father and his siblings shortly after marriage to their mother and their births.

I think I also wanted to chastise my father for having quit on my mother, for exposing her to adultery and poverty, and releasing her to enter into serially lousy relationships with utterly exploitive and conscienceless men. True, she had made her own bed, as the saying goes, but he made it harder by robbing her of a just share of the house she had established with him, being parsimonious with child support and being vindictive—inflicting a myriad of woes upon a woman, a person, who was so soft, and likely too soft to survive such blows. (I suspect my father's ill treatment of my mother, plus the exploitive handling she received from other men, hastened her premature death.)

It is also probable that I wanted to deny my father my full love or sympathy because he had treated my brothers and me so harshly when we were children. He was a man who frowned upon us, who exorcised his demons as a black working-class intellectual in a white-ruled, essentially segregated city by frequently assaulting us—verbally and physically—and our mother too. I classify my childhood as "happy," for there was much that was good about it, but it is also true that we came close to seeing our father killed when we called the police to our home during one of our parents' violent arguments. I look back on that moment now and I understand that, had my mother not calmed the situation by putting on a show of refreshed family harmony, my father could have ended up as yet another black male victim of white force.

Make no mistake: he was a hard man. Born in the midst of the Depression to an abandoned and socially shamed mother, he was raised in a barn, in straw-and-newspaper-floor poverty, and had quit school in Grade 10 so as to help his mother and siblings. Marginalized within the already marginalized black Halifax community, he learned, in childhood, to keep a closed heart, to exercise stunning discipline, to count pennies and to be the tyrant in his castle. His apprenticeship in parenting enabled him to literally throw one teenage son (my brother) onto the street and to tell me, "You're eighteen: time to leave." (For the record, I left home the very next day, much to his surprise.)

But I must also acknowledge that, after the birth of my half-sister, the daughter of our maid, in 1974, my father began to mellow. He was never as harsh with her as he had been with us sons—perhaps because of the gender difference, or perhaps simply because he had chosen this child, her biological mother, and then her stepmother, as opposed to his situation with my mother, whom, in a sense, chance had chosen for him. Nevertheless, he had no contact with his second-born son between 1978 and 1990 or so, and the same was true for me, the eldest, between 1983 and 1990. In those years, mellowing or not, he tried to erase his first family from his life.

Although this familial psychodrama lay behind my bitterness, love and ambivalence for my father, I still did want to see him, in his later, latter years. My motives were mixed: when I did well in school, my father would reward me with great praise and even a quarter to spend on candy, chips and pop. In my adulthood, when I won wider praise for my writing or my scholarship, my father would also applaud my success, and, frankly, I would relish these salutes. I knew he was an artist manqué, and I wanted him to recognize my "superior" achievements, to ask for forgiveness, or at least a truce, a real, warm peace. Too, my happier memories of him, from my childhood, are of a man whistling while doing carpentry or painting actually good landscapes and seascapes while listening to classical music. He was the first artist I ever knew, and the first intellectual, and we continued to hold erudite and expansive conversations throughout our adulthood, sometimes over a beer at his home, or over coffee and doughnuts at Tim's. So, even as I kept a distance, I sought him out—to be edified, to be uplifted, to share with him, for our mutual delight, talk of politics and history and books and film. He was the richest interlocutor on these subjects, though he remained reticent in emotion.

Yet, although my father had a troubling bout with prostate cancer in 1995, one serious enough that he had had to have surgery, I still refused to admit his mortality. I just didn't think he could die, at least not before we had—no, I mean, I had—concluded satisfactorily my contest with him.

In the summer of 2005, after not having seen each other for a year, we finally met, in late June, over two Sprites, in Halifax, and had a sprightly conversation, documenting the evils of George W. Bush and the rich ability of banks to profit from regular folks' misery. He asked me if I would attend the White Family Reunion (we are descended from this largely African-American family thanks to my father's mother's father) the next month, in July, and I answered, honestly, that I wasn't sure.

In late July, I flew to Dallas, Texas, toured Dealey Plaza, where President John F. Kennedy died, then flew on to Corpus Christi, Texas, to do research for a book. When I returned home to Toronto on July 30, 2005, I was beyond feeling tired: I was exhausted, I was worn out. The next day, July 31, was, though, the date of the White Family Reunion, being held, this time, in Ottawa. All that day I was convinced I would not attend the gathering. Then, at

5 p.m., I pulled together a suitcase, drove to the airport and flew to Ottawa. When I walked into the Family Supper at the National Arts Centre at 7 p.m., I was surprised utterly—and thrilled: there was my dad! He'd taken the train up from Halifax—a poignant trip, because he had worked most of his life for the railway: a baggage handler when I was born, a sales agent when he retired. We spent the evening talking and eating and drinking, even as I found myself still alternating in mood towards him: angry, enthralled. He was my father; he was my foe. It turned out to be the last time I would see him alive. We hugged in the lobby of the Lord Elgin Hotel. Our last conversation was partly about my visit to Dealey Plaza: we were both J.F.K. fans—and assassination buffs.

In mid-August 2005, I flew to Finland for a conference, then went to Scotland for the Edinburgh Book Festival, then on to England to meet the local publisher of my first novel, *George & Rue.* I was in Britain, a nation my father loved but never saw, when he checked himself into a Halifax emergency room with what was soon diagnosed as inoperable leukemia. Everyone tried desperately to reach me, but I had left no contact information, and my wife was travelling with me. As I later learned, the day after we left Canada my father had gone into the hospital. When my wife and I returned home to Toronto on the night of August 30, I encountered a slew of faxes, e-mails and answering machine messages, all advising me that my father was gravely ill in the hospital, was comfortable if delirious under his morphine feed and was asking for me.

I made plans to fly to Halifax on August 31. I wanted to make it to his hospital bedside. But my (half-)sister called me to say, "He's dead." It was 1:30 p.m. E.S.T., August 31, 2005.

My heart did break, is still broken. I think about both of my parents every day, and I remain astonished that the one I felt furthest from is the one I most greatly mourn.

2.

Although I was not the executor of my father's estate, the duty devolved upon me to sift through his personal papers and library and determine what should be trashed, what should be archived, and what his children should keep. I did throw out boxes of mouldy newspapers, because I realized that these would duplicate already well-established holdings. However, one box of clippings turned out to be particularly important because it was a one-man file of every scrap of news produced about the crash of Swissair 111 off the coast of Peggy's Cove, Nova Scotia, in early September 1998. Another box of clippings surprised me and left me sobbing: my father had also collected, over the years, every piece of news about me and all my locally published writing. I had had no idea that he had been so assiduous in following my "progress."

Just as surprising was my discovery of dozens—no, hundreds—of old photographs of his motorcycle days in the mid- to- late 1950s, his lady loves (including, poignantly, my mother) and his first family (my brothers and me, as boys, and our mother). Finding these photos was a shock, for, after his second wedding in January 1975, his new wife telephoned me and told me to come and pick up whatever photographs I wanted because the rest were going into the garbage. So, I had gone, at age fifteen, over to his house (I was living with my mother at the time), selected just a few dozen photos, and then biked away, believing, for the next thirty years, that all other photographic evidence of his first marriage and family had been lost. Instead, as I could now see, he had hidden these photographs in a box marked RAILWAY, and so had continued, unbeknownst to all of us, to hold some nostalgic sentiments for the family he had lost to divorce and remarriage. I wept at this recognition, and it still summons tears now. I wonder if my mother would have passed away more happily if she had known that her once-and-only husband had not totally renounced any affection for her.

The most personally affecting aspect of my father's estate was the only item he willed expressly to me: his 1959 diary. With it, he included a handwritten message: "For George, So He Will Understand." A whole year passed before I could read it. However, as soon as I mentioned my possession of it to my agent, Denise Bukowski, she said, instantly, "He wants you to write about him," and I knew, just as instantly, that she was right, and that I would.

I began to read and transcribe the diary in August 2006, in Vichy, France, and I finished it in September that same year, in Radford, Virginia. I could read it only through a veil of tears, because it revealed to me a man I had never known, one with great self-doubt, a broken heart and, at one point, a budding and lucrative career as an artist. The diary also bore witness that the narrative I had always believed, that he had rejected me at birth, was untrue. Instead, and my mother's siblings confirm it now, she had kept her pregnancy and my birth a secret from my father. It was only when I went into the hospital with a life-threatening illness some two months after my birth that my father was informed of my existence, and then came to see me and woo and wed my mother. This fact does not change the truth that he was a harsh and difficult parent, but it does underline the notion that he felt a responsibility to be a father and husband, and then moved rapidly—with some sacrifice of his other dreams—to fulfill those roles. Indeed, as an artist myself, I have fresh respect—mixed with sorrow—for his decision to abandon his just-beginning career as a painter, to return to the security (if also drudgery) of the railway. Similarly, he sold his motorcycle to buy a pickup truck, to do odd jobs to earn more income for all of us. The most personally angst-ridden choice for him was his surrender of any hope of marrying the student nurse he truly loved. Instead, he wed the student teacher, who was, really, a "friend" he saw, on and off, over an eight-week period in April–June 1959, and whom he managed to impregnate sometime in May. (I wonder if my father felt any regret for the nurse, who, as it turned out, did not marry anyone.)

These revelations gave me new insight into the emotionally complex man who sired me and then parented me—at least for the first fourteen years of my life. I was also filled with sorrow for not having heard some of these stories earlier, but was also forced to reflect on the troubling truth that, in so many ways, I am my father's son, right down to repeating, more than once, some of his errors and experiences.

When I weep for him, and I still do, my wife tells me sagely that it's really my own mortality I am grieving. (I do think of Gerard Manley Hopkins's poem on the subject too.) But, no, there is more to it than my own hesitations around the fact that I must die that might still cause me to weep into a piece of cake. What bothers me about all these relinquishings and deliquescences is their apparent, pernicious finality. I don't want to say goodbye to my parents, just as I don't want to have to leave my daughter in this hard world, without my protective embrace. And I don't want to give up coitus; and I don't want to surrender family and friends to the grave. Damn it all, I don't. It's not death I grieve, but *subtraction*—destruction of a certain community of memory and feeling and communication.

There are only two antidotes to this grief: 1) faith that one will see one's loved ones again; 2) the writing of their (our) stories. In some small way, my current project to novelize my father's 1959 diary allows me to revive him, to parley with him and to understand him—and, crucially, myself—better. This essay returns me to the novel manuscript, *The Motorcyclist*.

Gail Victoria Tulloch

ON THE

MATERIAL,

or,

GAIL'S BOOKS

By Stephen Collis

I.

Just after our parents' fiftieth wedding anniversary—an August day, garden sun, her flower print dress—my sister Gail learns she has cancer and I recall that dress her smile and the sun. On December 19, 2002, she dies. Enduring her final lucid moments trying to talk and something in her tongue seems gone and as a kind of resignation the only word that comes out again and again is "okay" "okay."

One thing we shared was a love of books and learning. Hers: poetry, psychology and spirituality. Mine: poetry, philosophy, history. Poetry was the hinge, the place our worlds swung one into another's.

On January 19, 2003, one month to the day she died, her house burnt in an accidental fire. Her study and books were destroyed, the firemen having cast the burning volumes through broken windows into a yard of rain and darkness. Many landed in a small fishpond where I found them blackened soaked and crumbling the next morning. Only one book was recoverable. The fire had taken everything else—anything she had written, her books, personal effects, clothes—any material reminder.

There are other books that were hers, which I took in the month between her death and the fire. Books I took because they were hers and the hinge between us was always a book's spreading binding, gutter and spine. Kathleen Raine's *Selected Poems,* published in 1988 by Lindisfarne Press, has four purple flags protruding sideways from passages and poems she marked to return to, quote or recall. Rilke's *Book of Hours*, translated by Anita Barrows and Joanna Macy and published by Riverhead Books in 1996, was a favourite of hers: she bought me a copy too and now I have both hers and mine. Novalis's *Philosophical Writings*, translated by Margaret Mahony Stoljar and published in 1997 by the State University of New York Press, she appears to have bought at the University of British Columbia Bookstore. And finally Peter Ackroyd's Blake biography, published by Minerva in 1996, with the poet's "Good and Evil Angels" on its cover: tilting its glossy surface in the right light I can make out the impression of a telephone number pressed into the soft cover—a North Vancouver number she no doubt took down using the book as a writing surface— her hand has engraved it exactly between the two figures, on the evil angel's outstretched arm and down across the flames sea sky and earth.

I hold what she held, touching hinges. There is nowhere else she is. The door creaks open to oblivion— hence voices. I try to look where her eyes looked, reading reunion. The flag flutters the eye open and closed. August print dresses. May she is born. December she dies and begins again. This is her belief and I can only hold it in my hands and watch the words play across in near perfect print.

2.

This slip marks the moment of your absence
Books you have left shuttered gifts
Glyph or glimpse of reading rent
Margins I want marked meander
Feeling evening roses sound fear holds chaos against cold
It is questions I would pour into deserts
Swamping silence

3.

Days she was home and we waited for her to die—comatose and her breathing laboured. Took turns sitting with her or in small groups hushed voices or read to her—or Rita played her harp in the cedar room a skylight above the bed and all the forests of North Vancouver at her door. I read Rilke's "Duino Elegies," a poem we had both loved.

> *Yes—the springtimes needed you. Often a star*
> *was waiting for you to notice it. A wave rolled toward you*
> *out of the distant past, or as you walked*
> *under an open window, a violin*
> *yielded itself to your hearing. All this was mission.*

I kept waiting for words, for her to make me understand for some sort of task or commission to be given but my sister died in silence. No words came okay that would have to be okay. Perhaps I expected too much of her perhaps it was she who needed words to build a lexical raft to carry her across strange waters or Shield of Achilles poetry made to protect her in this battle we both knew the outcome of.

Once she had died someone was to be with her at all times for the three days after so we continued in our shifts sitting beside her now complete silence reading or watching her impeccable stillness her poise her incommensurate with-drawal—flowers wilting in her white hands her bed her raft to afterward. This time I read Whitman in the 1855 edition of what would eventually be inaccurately titled *Song of Myself* but which in 1855 was simply *Leaves of Grass* like every other poem in that book. Read the whole poem through into the room my voice growing hoarse the words seeming to exist for their own sake for the space they take up between people—all their own autonomous region—now where can between be when everything becomes between?

I celebrate myself,
And what I assume you shall assume,
For every atom belonging to me as good belongs to you.

After three days her husband Les and I must place her body in a simple pine coffin. Dry ice has kept her body stiff and light like some wood we must take out to the fire. The coffin is in the living room and from the bedroom to the living room is a narrow hall and it will not be an easy passage with her. There is no dignity in death, but no, there is dignity for there are things and the love and significance we bestow upon them and sometimes receive from them or discover between them and ourselves. I hold Gail's body and it is Gail's body like Gail's books or her brooch or her painting—only it isn't it is more some one-and-only place she was—the impression she left in wax that must now melt away. I look into her expressionless face or face I read all significant expressions into like the colour white all colours have run into to give it its snow as we jostle and lift and maneuver her and settle her into the box her red hair stiff and short and holding its place. Being tall she only just fits and we are careful only I can't help thinking this is wood simply a thing I am holding and placing in a box for safe-keeping—a memento to stow away—only there are no simple things.

Distance is how we deal with difficult matters but there was no distance here from matter and its most intimate difficulties. Only there was distance as it was my body carrying my sister's body and I watched as from outside quiet and unthinking amidst the strange everydayness of material objects and their movements in time and space.

If in this I found my sister reduced to a "thing" by death what is most strange is the complete erasure of all the things she was in the events that followed. Her body was cremated and the ashes in a small cardboard box brought home and placed in her room where she had died. Then the fire came candles falling on the bed she had died in the fire consuming her room every material object her dresses clothes jewellery photographs toiletries every last "thing" she was—the fire falling through the floor to her study below burning her library her papers her writing her sewing her fabrics her craft supplies her contemplative figurines handmade candles icons and postcards every single "thing" consumed and gone. No thing to carry memory no object to console us. Even her ashes burnt again and mixed with the ashes of her things. The erasure was complete. Except for the books I had taken and the book that survived the fire.

4.

These are your
Selected poems now I
Cannot choose otherwise
You are on the edge of
Rain the shimmer of
Fire forms a screen
Oracles wind Medea

Not return murmur
To sorrow go to nest
I shiver the moment self
Incarnates the Pythoness
Moves towards origin

5.

By coincidence of space and time, six months after my sister's death my family and I moved—our new home close by a simple cemetery as far south in Greater Vancouver as her home had been north. Eagles made their nests in tall firs and we watched crows taking turns harassing the nests the size of small cars. Carrion littered the yard: a Canada goose's head and neck cleanly severed, one morning a complete mallard's wing from shoulder to farthest tip, its blue and green array spread beneath the trees.

I began to take daily walks amongst the small stones of our cemetery, the flat stones settled in the grass at the newer lower end of the rectangular lot and the standing stones rising up at the older high end overlooking the farms and bay below the bluff. "In what way," W.G. Sebald asks, "do objects immersed in time differ from those left untouched by it?" I have known no "untouched" objects or rather I know them only in memory and imagination where some things remain seemingly untouched—a dream in which four tornadoes appeared near my parents' house, the look of light reflecting off water onto the side of a fibre-glass canoe and the pong of a paddle against its hull, my sister's face in animated conversation in her kitchen, her shrug and quip. These "things" remain as long as I do. Beyond that there is no marker no object to mark Gail's passing to which anyone can go or which can be seen to alter via its "immersion in time."

Sebald also writes of the "autonomous existence of things" which "outlast us" and which "know more about us than we know about them." I have a hunger for such things but cannot find them except in books and then is it the fact of the book's material presence that lends this or is it still what the books "contain," their precise memories and imaginations? With the few of Gail's books that I have it is probably more the former than the latter—it is physical contact with the pages she held—it is the fact that etymologically at least a "thing" once meant an "assembly," or public meeting, which meaning hovers still I guess when we speak of "conversation pieces." I want things where we meet and speak. I want to take to the "hustings" which meant assembly place—*house things*—and speak the reality that we are only ever together and then we are not and this is politics pure and simple: let's gather together while we can.

Inseparable from Gail's death is the sale of my parents' home at Shawnigan Lake—though they had only lived there twenty years it had been my grandfather's cabin and it meant summers all our lives. And though its loss was separated from my sister's death by several years they go together because everything in our family has become mutable and tenuous and uncertain since her death—familiar places unvisited, brothers drifting off, my father's stroke. Summers at the lake were where I could always look forward to time with my sister to books to conversation to ideas to the challenge of meeting her spirituality. We were different but we pried into the hidden life of things from opposite directions like two teams building a tunnel we hoped to meet in the middle of some mountain and embrace. The blackberries at the lake were numerous and we spoke together the being of our numerousness picking berries or eating a pie at the table outside or sat late with our children watching the numerous stars and their summer fall from the sky. Went mornings to the lakeside each with our books and settled into chairs to read and swim and talk, books spread on the grass between us—a wrinkled page where a lake-wet finger pressed bookmark or marginal note or notebook writing down something the other said or read.

Peter Ackroyd's *Blake* opens by telling us that "In the visionary imagination of William Blake there is no birth and no death, no beginning and no end, only the perpetual pilgrimage within time towards eternity." So I think my sister believed too. But when I take down my sister's *Novalis* I read in the first entry of the poet's "Miscellaneous Observations" that "We *seek* the absolute everywhere and only ever *find* things." So I suppose I believe but sometimes when it comes to my sister I seek things and cannot find them, turning up instead strange absolutes disappearances vacancies places we once were and are no longer, blanks in the record memories become iconic overdetermined emotionally overwrought absolute and yet entirely ephemeral.

———

6.

Because a tear is an
Intellectual thing
This rainfall will
Cloud vision towards
Deeper thinking where
You keep sleep
In a box and your
Voice amongst reeds
Will be the presence of
Pomegranate seeds
Sparkling red multitude
Silent and awaiting the
Decay of December and
Rebirth of May

7.

In the middle of our cemetery between the lower and higher grounds is a lovely and old dogwood tree. At night a lamp lights it up so it is the only bright thing in the whole dark place. Where the trunk splits into spreading branches some four or five feet from the ground there is a curious thing. A blackberry cane has taken root here and grows each spring out of the crotch of the old tree, its canes curving to the earth to touch the face of lichen-covered stones below. Some years it is allowed to grow as it will and it becomes heavy with berries, which I will eat pondering the

cane fed by the tree fed by the earth with its other passen-
gers buried below. Other years come late July or early
August gardeners come and cut the cane back almost completely eradicating it but then next spring it shoots out soft
and green again. This plant has become a talisman or totem
for me—something that holds forth profoundest truths and
which I cannot separate in my mind from my sister's death,
—its discovery coming close on the heels of her vanishing.
One thing always depends on at least one other thing. But
that dependence may be to the detriment of the other thing.
I am not sure whether the blackberry will eventually kill
the dogwood but it seems possible, rot having set into at
least one big bough rising from the bramble's seat. Or maybe
the gardeners will manage to kill the blackberry to save the
tree. It's not certain. But in the meantime these things are
tangled together and everything seems circular and inter-
dependent and fruit comes unbidden—a gift of sustenance
amidst the death that surrounds. This is when I smile at
those "untouched" things of my sister's, those memories
where she is the beacon I wrote every poem towards.

8.

Go back again
To the time of recollecting
Who speaks hears
Fragile forests holds
Metallic dreaming
If we are any

Antinomies affirmations
Not holding is an orbit
Round the emptiness where
You read aloud to me
Writing to ward off
With words going
Into governance to unlock
Laws shout out of disasters
We are here we are here
This failing inscribes
On sheer volatility
Volumes I cannot read
No matter it was you leaving them
Ephemeral rain falling out of rain

9.

My sister was the source of (in poet Robert Duncan's words) "first permission." She was the first to allow poetry to be for me a significant act and activity—gave it weight, made it "matter." Paradoxically, because she was a dualist believing in hidden significances we see only the visible signs of. Though perhaps poetry's paradox is similar in that it makes the inarticulate articulate, as in making the absent present via recollection it remains painfully absent, so in poetry the articulate inarticulate remains stubbornly inarticulate. Sounds its impossible speech or is a face always turned away from us to listen to a music we cannot ever hear or gaze upon objects we cannot ever see; though we see the poem's listening and looking we witness only the backs of words the props behind the scenes of language. This is what it means to speak of language as "material"— it is building stuff beautiful things for fashioning assemblies; we can take shelter there. Perhaps after Gail's death there is no other shelter left but also since her death words have been revealed as well to be things that is assemblies that is talking points and places, their every use a political act of marking where one and others may meet—our divergences yes but more important the hope and possibility of our convergences too. So I also go to words to meet my sister for there to be objects untouched by time though they are touched and it is this ability of words to touch and be touched that I value so much—I would carry each one of them in my arms to its resting place on the page carefully laying them out for ever.

It has only been poems I have been able to write to my sister's absence but then it was only ever poems I wrote to her when she was alive and this was the way we could converse about the things that mattered—or more accurately it was poems I wrote in the felt presence of her the heart and mind she was and I still feel her presence when words surpass their divergences and become the folding together that is poetry once again.

As I hold Gail's books in my hands her Blake or her Rilke or the book rescued from the fire—*Art and Human Consciousness* by Gottfried Richter, —its page ends seared and swollen from water the smell of smoke everywhere about it still—as I hold these things I think of that blackberry bramble that does not itself grow out of the ground but relies instead on another's grounding there and I wonder which of us sister or brother is the bramble and which the supporting tree that may eventually die of the burden of bearing the other. So it is to be human and conscious and making art so it is so it is—we go on being there for one another or our absences or our needs.

Frank Davey and bpNichol

THIS

GENTLEMAN,

bpNichol

By Frank Davey

Barrie ("bp") Nichol would frequently tell his friends the story of how we had first met—how I phoned him shortly after moving to Toronto in 1970 and arranged for us to meet for lunch. He'd been surprised and in some odd way flattered. That meeting had rather quickly led to our collaborating on numerous literary projects, my wife, Linda, becoming his literary agent (and eventually his lawyer), and Barrie becoming a close friend to us and our young family. He was the only Toronto writer that summer I wished actively to contact—and in the summer of 1970 there were a lot of young writers in Toronto. The fact that Barrie had been so moved by my having sought to get to know him, and kept recalling that moment, endeared him to me more than I ever thought to tell him. Not that he needed to know. I last saw him in June of 1988, while passing on to him the files of my literary journal *Open Letter*, which he was going to manage during my 1988–89 sabbatical in France. As we parted, Barrie said that he would miss me and I said I was only going for a year and he replied sensibly, "You never know what will happen in a year." "Our" grief was beginning—his missing of me and mine of him. One of us was departing—inevitably—and I thought it was me. Part of grief is recollecting the missed opportunities: the call that could have been made, the things that could have been said more clearly, the farewells that may not have been farewells.

So I was never part of the collective remembering and public mourning of Barrie, in various parts of Canada, that followed his unexpected death during surgery that September. I wrote to him several times from Paris during the summer, and received one long cheerful telephone call in return. I think it may have been difficult by this time for him to sit and write. That spring he had rarely sat down during his late-night visits, but had drunk his tea and talked about his new work while pacing back and forth, his left hand often behind him, massaging the most troubling area. That back pain had become worse, he told me during the phone call, but there was new hope that surgery could deal with it. The pain had caused him to cancel plans to travel with the rest of the Four Horsemen, sound poets, to Tarascon to perform at the Rencontre Internationale de Poésie. He would not be visiting me in Paris.

In late September, Linda and I were on the patio of our small Université Canadienne en France villa, on the Grande Corniche above the Col de Villefranche. The university's dean—"Dean Doug" Parker of the Laurentian University English department—came by with a telegram from my home department at York University: "Regret to inform that bpNichol has died." I thought it might be important, Doug said. Linda and I had no knowledge of Barrie's planned surgery. Had he fallen from a canoe and drowned? Had he been run over by a laundry van? Had he tumbled from an apple tree? What time was it in Canada? Who could we phone who would know?

But when I recall that moment I also find myself involuntarily recalling W.C. Williams's response to the publication of Eliot's *The Waste Land*: that "it wiped out [my] world as if an atomic bomb had been dropped on it." Any death of someone close to us is in a sense the end of a world, but in Barrie's case that world for me had been enormous—personal, literary, cultural, political. He had been the only writer in Toronto whose work I had ever envied and learned from. He was by far the most active contributing editor to *Open Letter*, viewing the carte blanche editorial role I had offered him back in 1970 as an ongoing, almost daily opportunity and responsibility. He had been, with me, one of the two most active editors of Coach House Press; during some periods, we had together edited more than 50 percent of the press's publications. Moreover, unlike the other editors, we usually conferred with one another about the titles we were separately editing, and read them eagerly once they were printed. After editorial meetings, Barrie, Linda and I would usually have a second, more reflective, meeting over a pot of Earl Grey at my house. During 1986–88 the press had been undergoing an acrimonious transformation from an unofficial co-operative into a corporation. Barrie had been in my view the only trustworthy literary voice on the new board of directors; when I returned to Toronto in the summer of 1989, I would find that his death had permitted two of the directors to repopulate the board with non-literary strangers. For me, Barrie's death bitterly symbolized the end of the activist literary community that had been dying as Coach House was occupied and transformed by neoliberal writers and businesspeople—the death of trust among its editors, and of the once-welcome voluntarism of our contributions to it. My feeling as I held that telegram, and looked out over the olive groves at the Baie des Anges towards Antibes, was that there would be little in Toronto for me ever to return "home" to. Numerous possibilities within my self had died. It was a feeling I would have again in a much more personal sense a decade later, when Linda died.

"Home," of course, is not a place; it is a context constituted by ties and expectations and shared obligations and projects. A single person does not make a home. All those things that constitute a home also contribute to our inner understandings of who we are. Our identities shift and evolve around the things we do with others. When a close friend and collaborator dies, the things that only you and that person could do together, and could not have done separately, also die, and along with them die as well the effects and influence those activities would have on others. The bell that was tolling for Barrie was tolling for many, including me. There would be no more "No-tay-shun" issues of *Open Letter*, no more proposals for special issues on R. Murray Schafer or Canadian 'pataphysics. There would be no John Beckwith issue, no issue on the theories of teaching creative writing, no issue on the use of computers in artistic production (issues Barrie had planned to assemble during my absence)—and no more visual-poetry books from Coach House Press, no more jointly written essays on prosody, no more late-evening visits by an excited Barrie eager to read to us that day's addition to *The Martyrology,* or to chuckle over his astonished misreading earlier in the day of a highway road sign.

What do you do when a huge part of who you were and what you thought you would be doing vanishes? To dwell inside the loss would be incapacitating—the very kind of self-destructive self-indulgence against which Barrie as a lay psychotherapist had battled in his clients, and which he had also written about, personally and allegorically, in the first two books of his long poem *The Martyrology*. In a sense Barrie had already set a high standard for the way in which he should be grieved—just thinking about him evoked questions such as what he would want me to do, questions that critic Catherine Bates would later describe as ones of how "to mourn responsibly." Thinking about him was, unfortunately, what I fell asleep to each night that fall and woke to each morning. "*C'est normal,*" my daughter Sara reassured me. Together we had been taking note of the rhythms of everyday French. "*Ce n'est pas grave.*" But a grave nevertheless, Barrie would have undoubtedly in some way punned. Dear grave Barrie.

That temptation to dwell inside one's grief and masochistically "enjoy" one's sense of loss, amputation and indignation can be huge. To be bereaved means literally to be deprived, robbed, stripped, dispossessed. Why bother trying to continue? Or, as the cliché response goes, what is there now to live for? Let others pity me. Let them see the depths of my bereavement. Let historians explain why x, "shattered by grief," fell into silence, inactivity, bitterness, reclusiveness. For there is both pride and anger within grief— pride that one can suffer so greatly, anger that this robbery has occurred to oneself, anger at the unfairness to oneself, anger that can narcissistically wish to punish the unfair world through one's own melodramatic withdrawing from it. All of which Barrie knew, and had known that I knew.

Linda very quickly returned to her law practice and began researching the events in Barrie's extensive medical record that had delayed an accurate diagnosis of his back pain and allowed a tumour to grow around his spine, unde-tected, to such a lethal size. I was also fortunate to have responsibilities, things to do—two teenagers to cook for and make a home for, a university course to teach in exchange for the villa we were enjoying, and the book I had planned as the basis for that course. The course schedule was to be my writing schedule, and with the "Barrie" within me watching, it continued to be. The book came to be titled *Post-National Arguments*—a book that became more and more one of allegorical grief for the fading of a communal, internationally contextualized Canada and Canadian literature, which Barrie had tirelessly worked to create, and towards which his 1970s efforts at Coach House and *Open Letter* had been only two of numerous parts.

When my father had died three years before, I had abruptly felt alone and vulnerable—not because I had been close to him (ours had been a mutually wary friendship), but because suddenly there was no family male of an earlier generation between me and death. I was now on the front line. Barrie's death had a similar effect on me—I felt alone, without allies, in the Canadian arts world. This was not strictly true, yet it was also effectively true inasmuch as the personal chemistry between Barrie and me that enabled us to work collaboratively, and at similar energy and long-term commitment levels, was not replicated in my relations with other allies such as Barbara Godard, George Bowering, Lola Tostevin, Steve McCaffery, Fred Wah or Victor Coleman; their cultural work seemed to intersect with mine only intermittently. My sense now is that, among my friends, only Barrie experienced all the various aspects of his life not as rivals for his attention but as related parts of one huge interactive project. Everything eventually connected; nothing distracted. Even the "bp:if" cards of *The Martyrology Book(s)* 7& on which he wrote—and left to be "interleaved"—his own death. Like the flies at the end of Alden Nowlan's

"And He Wept Aloud," I was now going to have to rebuild my world, replacing Barrie's daily contributions to it with a collage of occasional ones. And I would be doing this in part because he would have expected no less.

That is, my grief had to be constructive. That had been one of his messages to the artists' workshops he had helped conduct as a lay psychotherapist. I wonder sometimes if we truly grieve the deaths of those who leave us little to construct—those whose relationships with us have been worked out, their limitations accepted, our narratives together completed. I did not mourn for long the uncle whom I had admired, my dad's brother Orrie, a jazz musician who could play passages from Tchaikovsky on a ukelele, and who died at ninety-one, a year after giving me the banjo he had played during the 1930s in Vancouver in Barney Potts's orchestra. I do not expect to deeply grieve my mother, who has now reached a hundred in a nursing home in Abbotsford. I think I have grieved her as she has aged. But the deaths of my father, Barrie, Greg Curnoe in 1992, and then Linda in 2000 all seemed to leave me with extensive work to do. All of them died before my hopes and expectations of my interactions with them had ended. All of them ended a world and demanded a rebuilding and reworking.

Of course, what we then work out is one-sided, no matter how indeterminate or ambiguous our speculations. The dead are dead because they have at best problematical access to discourse—our discourse. I had already been carrying on a one-sided dialogue with Barrie that summer as he awaited his final surgery. I had been writing a lengthy poem about French funerary customs and celebrity—a poem that had begun as a reflection on Père-Lachaise Cemetery in Paris and evolved into one on the celebrated French film of that summer, *Camille Claudel*. I had sent him a draft of the poem and a letter about some of the issues the cemetery and the film seemed to raise. I was trying to approximate some of our late-night living-room discussions. But the pain in Barrie's back was already rendering his access to written discourse problematical. With his death, the "matter" of that poem was transformed, or perhaps not so much transformed as revealed to have been other than what I had believed it to be. I had been having an imaginary dialogue about death with one of the dying. The deaths of people I could only know as names or stories had been joined by that of someone whose story was also my story.

Until writing the present essay, I had not thought to consider Barrie's death other than obliquely or allegorically—as in *Post-National Arguments*, or my essay "The Beginnings of an End to Coach House Press," or this poem "Dead in France," in which the deaths of Oscar Wilde, Gertrude Stein, Jim Morrison, Camille Claudel and Héloïse and Abelard all "stand in" for that of Barrie. I understand this obliqueness as in part a response to the sentimental humanism through which so many others experienced his loss. An "H in the heart" indeed, I have grumbled. Barrie was so much more than a writer who could evoke sublime moments of longing, loss or suffering in the early books of *The Martyrology*. He was one who had learned to transcend such moments with making, often ironic makings, in books themselves oblique, such as *Zygal, Art Facts, Two Novels, Selected Organs*. Among the impossible responsibilities of the griever is not to sentimentalize, not to reduce the specific work of the dead to myths of bonhomie and goodwill, what Darren Wershler-Henry has called the "anecdotal 'I knew bp when' mode"—not to use them for one's own maudlin pleasures or aggrandizement. These are risks I do not escape here. "Dear Barrie," I began my Paris letters.

In the fall of 1989, when I returned to Toronto, it was as I had anticipated: without Barrie, a much different city. Coach House was now only a print shop. The publishing corporation also known as Coach House was now next door, with a separate entrance. It was evaluating manuscripts in terms of potential profitability, expanding its debt load and calling this "capitalization," and getting most of its books printed elsewhere in cheap ink on cheap paper. There were no more monthly meetings of editors, and no more editorial discussions of the press's goals. One morning, when I came down to the print shop to work on a new issue of *Open Letter,* there were around fifty boxes of 1960s and '70s Coach House Press books stacked in the laneway, awaiting garbage pickup. The corporation's new manager had thrown them out to make warehouse space for new titles. Many of the titles in the boxes had been edited by Barrie, some written by him. The laneway had been renamed bpNichol Lane, but the literary values he had championed were being dispatched to an unmarked grave.

I still have a pang when I recall rescuing a hardback first edition of his elaborately printed *Two Novels* from those boxes, much as I do whenever I drive past Choate Road on Highway 401 near Cobourg and recall his excitement at being sparked to write the first lines of "Inchoate Road" by noting that road sign and a car stalled beside it. He had been commuting back and forth to Cobourg to work on the production of his musical *Tracks*, which he had co-written with actor Marye Barton. He read the first draft of the poem to Linda and me a few days later during a characteristic late-night visit. "Inchoate Road" became a long meditation on the opaque liquidity of events, a car stalled where the driver did not expect it to be stalled— i.e., "you never know what will happen in a year." Some of the cartons in the alley had contained copies of the late Gerald Lampert's *Chestnut, Flower, Eye of Venus,* a novel edited by Barrie. Lampert had unexpectedly died just before the book was released, and a hostile reviewer had boorishly but presciently titled his commentary "Bury the book too." Barrie had been appalled.

Grief means gathering up what one can and moving on. I would never have left Toronto as long as Barrie were living there, and his death seemed almost to require me to leave. A bpNichol Lane littered with discarded bpNichol books was at best a bad-faith gesture and at worst a desecration, a violation. A few months after receiving that terse telegram, I had flown from Nice to Victoria to consider an offer to teach at the university, but the overall context did not seem especially promising. A year and a half later, I would accept a research chair at the University of Western Ontario and move 200 kilometres west to London. Being away from the spaces in which Barrie and I had worked together—Huron Street, Admiral Road, Spadina Crescent, Lyndhurst Avenue, York University, bpNichol Lane—meant that they could no longer taunt me with the apparent deterritorialization his absence had helped bring to them. With the addition of Barbara Godard, Lola Tostevin and Terry Goldie to its editorial board, *Open Letter* moved on also—away from Barrie's multimedia and writing-as-research interests and towards issues of gender and race. My own writing moved in several new directions and resulted in six books in the first half of the 1990s. I thought of Barrie as an imaginary reader while writing each of them.

But the pain over his surprising death continued through Linda's research. Grief is so often the gnawing desire to know why. Barrie's surgeon had reported finding a tumour the size of a roast of beef wrapped around his vertebrae and spinal cord; he had successfully detached it and various entangled matter—once he had started, there was no going back—but had done such damage to Barrie in the process that massive bleeding had exhausted Toronto's blood supply. Barrie's last hour was enabled by a machine that cleaned and recycled the blood he was bleeding. The surgeon wrote that a tumour of such large dimensions should have been routinely detected much earlier by the doctors Barrie had been consulting over the preceding five years. "This gentleman" should not have had to die. There were other documents whose messages were equally painful to read. Linda's own grief at these overwhelmed the confidentiality in which they should have been kept from me. We sat together with a pot of Earl Grey and brooded over the hidden story they implied. Barrie, of course, in those fatal hours had suffered no pain. But his surgeon had, and those who came to read about them. Like most who encounter seemingly avoidable death, we grieved the "if" and the "what-if" as if the unfairness had been unwittingly directed at ourselves— as indeed it had.

Margit Farkas

WAITING

TO GRIEVE

By Endre Farkas

Death is the most certain thing in the world; at some point everyone must face it. When confronted by death, only an insensitive and unsympathetic person would not become concerned and would neglect to observe the mourning of loved ones.

—from a tract on Jewish burial traditions

Lately, I have been attending more funerals than births. As I come closer to shuffling off this mortal coil, I get farther from baby showers and *brisses* and nearer to wakes and unveilings. I assume it comes with aging. And although I am not yet at the stage where I first turn to the obit pages in my morning paper, I do glance at them on a regular basis, not only for familiar names, but for the birth year, comparing it to mine. As well, I do expect the worst from early-morning and late-night phone calls.

In the last two years, I have lost two close friends. Actually, that's not true. I did not lose them; they were not lost. They might have been lost while alive, but not now. Now they are dead.

Dead: Middle English *deed*, from Old English *dēad*; akin to Old Norse *dauthr, deyja,* to die; Old High German, *tōt*, dead. Said of things that have been alive.

My friends are still alive in the way recent losses are, in ways that lost limbs feel present. They are still alive because not enough time has passed for death to have done its job. Ruth comes to me when I drive a certain stretch of the Highway 20 West and see the shock of sumacs, especially in fall, when they become the colour of Spanish onions. She made me see them. She makes me see them.

I have inherited Artie's bookshelves of wooden boxes and his poetry books: Spicer, O'Hara and others he took the time to know. Whenever I pick one up to read, I hear Artie's admonition not to crack spines or allow cat hair near it. Every time I flip through one of his notebooks and see one of his small and mean comments, I hear his childlike, gleeful cackle.

They are not yet dead.

Dead. Our times seem to be afraid of this word. Maybe it is because there is a solid, earthy finality to the sound of it. And as the tract on Jewish burial traditions states, "Death is the most certain thing in the world . . . ." There is no escaping the reality of it. Not that we don't try. We spend billions on ways—from cosmetics to religion. We seem to recoil from it. I can certainly see why. From where I sit and from what I have seen, it's not a pleasant experience. But, since there is no getting away from it, we might as well call death death and the dead dead.

The dead are our memento mori. They remind us that there was a time before us, that there is our time, and that there will be a time after us. They are also our *carpe diem*. Their deaths are a note to us about the now.

I have been looking at various funeral home brochures, which are being delivered to my mailbox with more frequency than diaper coupons. Funeral home: a euphemism if there ever was one. The closest any pamphlet comes to using the word "dead" is in the phrase "Death Notice." Even "deceased" is a rarity. We don't want to think of our loved ones as dead; we prefer to think of them as having *gone on* or *passed on, gone to heaven* or *gone to spirit*.

The Montreal *Gazette* recently ran an article entitled "Motif and Mortality," which featured Montreal mortician Elisabeth Lehoux, who has created a designer urn line called Dressed for Eternity. According to Lehoux, "It's about making rituals that surround our just reward more beautiful, and therefore more significant by marrying an artistic sensibility with practical reality of dealing with human remains." That same article described a funeral home that has won an architectural award for its design. It includes a café and a library, and a sunny terrace during the summer months. It also hosts art openings once a month and celebrates Mexico's Day of the Dead. I don't know whether to applaud the liberation of death from faux grief to haute chic, or to lament it.

Every society gives itself ways and means of dealing with death and the dead. Rituals are our collective way of grieving. Many of these are as old as the hills and were relevant when we did, in fact, "live in them hills," when everyone knew everyone else. Losses back then were deeply felt because everyone was a part of everyone else.

As part of the Jewish tradition, there is a ritual time, before Rosh Hashanah and Yom Kippur, to visit the dead. I've been doing this since my bar mitzvah. Before the New Year, my parents and I and my maiden aunt would go to the cemetery to visit the dead—as an act of soul cleansing. We would park the car outside the cemetery and stroll to my uncle's grave. Every year since his death in 1968 and until my aunt's in 1997, we would repeat the same ritual.

"It's always colder inside," my aunt would say as we entered the cemetery.

"It seems farther away," she would say as we walked along the path.

"Are you sure we turn here?" she would ask each time.

Every year we would stop along the way to visit the graves of the same family friends.

"Did you bring enough pebbles?" she would ask.

And I, guide and pebble source, would every year nod and reply, "Yes, yes, yes, yes."

And when we finally got to my uncle's gravesite, the first thing she would do was look to see if the flower arrangement was right. Since it was paid for by her sister-in-law, with whom she didn't get along, it was never to her liking. This seemed to give her immense satisfaction and an excuse to continue the ongoing feud with her sister-in-law for the coming year. Now carefully avoiding stepping on the grave itself, she could walk to the tombstone, lean on it the way Jews for countless thousands of years leaned against the Wailing Wall, and exhale a sigh that could be heard for miles. Or so I imagined.

Then came the catalogue of hardships she suffered during the year: the long hours in the restaurant, the fatigue, the ungrateful whore-of-a-waitress, the rotten-louse customers, the general dishonesty of her suppliers. All of which would get her sobbing. Body shaking, she would end with her lament of how lonely she was and how much she missed him.

The first few years, I was embarrassed by her performance. At a time in my life when everything was about me, the visits with the dead seemed to be an intrusion. I lowered my head and snuck glances at the other graves to see if those mourners were watching us, certain that they were, and were talking amongst themselves about how gauche, how "greener" (new Old-World immigrant) my aunt's behaviour was. But they weren't. In fact, most of them were engaged in similar acts of soul cleansing.

Then, as abruptly as she began, she would cease her lamentations, step back and let my father step up to the stone. He would place a hand on the tombstone and rock back and forth, reciting Kaddish, which he knew by heart. He, too, with his free hand across closed eyes, would cry, but quietly. When done, he would place his pebble on the tombstone, kiss the tips of his fingers and touch them to the stone.

My mother was next, stepping up quietly, placing her pebble, leaving her hands there and staring off into the distance. She never cried; rather, she stroked the stone the way a mother unconsciously soothes a baby.

Last, I performed the same ritual, but I always felt it was more of an act on my part, something I was expected to do. I was not grieving.

I wondered what I was supposed to feel. I was sixteen when he died. I had known him for eight years. He was the first family member and the first person I knew who had died. I stared into the distance, feeling nothing. At least nothing that I could call grief. I was always trying to figure out how long I had to stand there before I could step back and leave.

Leaving the cemetery, my aunt, holding on to me, would emit a sigh of relief and launch into her latest bawdy joke.

I don't know when I evolved from embarrassment to detached anthropology. It must have been during my undergraduate years at university when I began to classify my aunt's behaviour as an "old world" ritual, an interesting cultural artefact, the act of a vanishing species. I became intrigued by our annual visit to the cemetery, which I viewed as a "removed" outsider all too aware of the elements of the ritual of mourning. I now felt too sophisticated to indulge in the wailings and mumblings in a language I could read but not understand. I still stood at the tombstone, but spent my time wondering how this ritual had begun. As well, by this time I had a sense of how long I should stand there.

A time came when my aunt became too ill to make

the pilgrimage. I was already watching over my parents; my mother had just had major surgery and my father was nursing her. Now I was my aunt's caregiver, too, watching her mind disintegrate. I watched her, in her confusion, beg for death. One day when I was teaching, a colleague interrupted my class to tell me to go immediately to the hospital. In the car, it occurred to me that I was on my way to see my aunt, a human being, die. Perhaps now, driving to the hospital, would be a good time to grieve. But I didn't. It was as though I had to wait until I was there with her, seeing her final moments, hearing her final breath.

By the time I got to the hospital, she was dead—eyes closed, mouth open. Dead. Her mouth without her teeth looked like the blackest abyss. The first thing that came to mind was Irving Layton's poem "Keine Lazorovitch," in which he describes his dead mother's mouth as a "black rent in the universe." I had been teaching it to a class of bored and disinterested teenagers. They, of course, were never going to die.

This would be a good time to grieve, I thought. But I didn't. I remember looking at the doctor and nurses who were eyeing me, ready to come to my aid should I collapse. They looked worried and seemed too young to know what to do, too uncomfortable with the idea of a potential "situation." So I didn't. I just leaned over her paling face and kissed her goodbye. It seemed enough for the moment.

In the Jewish tradition, burial must occur within three days. This ritual is a holdover from the time when Jews were a nomadic desert people whose corpses had to be buried quickly for obvious practical and sanitary reasons. So it became God's decree.

From the time of death until burial, a corpse must not be left unattended. Candles are usually lit nearby. The dead are never put on display; they are washed before burial and then dressed in plain white linen shrouds that cover them, including a hood over the head and gloves over the hands and feet. Males are wrapped in a tallit (prayer shawl), females in a plain sheet.

Here and now, my aunt became the body and the body became the remains that disappeared into the basement of the hospital and then magically reappeared at the funeral home. It's amazing how quickly it happens—the depersonalization, the deconstruction of a person who, hours before, was a living being.

Here and now, she was removed from the hospital to the funeral home. Whatever happens there happens offstage, with no family member attending, witnessing and wailing. And most of us do not want to attend, witness or wail. Most of us do not want to wash and dress a corpse. Not that I had thought of doing any of that then, but now, I wonder. Would it have made grieving more real? In a different time, in a different place, probably. Time alone with the body of a family member or a friend, time to touch it, time to say what we never have the time or words for or even dare to say; time to let tears be the pebbles on the tombstone of the flesh. Time for one last joke.

It's amazing how much paperwork the dead require. There were power-of-attorney forms. There was money to take care of: all her pennies saved by buying day-old bread and bruised bananas, dollars saved working from before light, on her feet all day, cooking and sweating in a closet-sized kitchen until after dark, until retirement, when every day she'd shuffle off to the bank to check her account and sit with her safety deposit box. She knew that a watched pot never boils over. She was convinced that everyone was stealing her blind.

It's amazing how many phone calls the dead require. The disconnecting. Companies needed to be informed that my aunt no longer needed their services. I signed papers. Bureaucracies needed proof that she was no longer here. I signed papers. Her body needed to be released. I signed papers. The undertaker needed permission for this and that. I signed papers. I signed papers. And then she was gone.

It's amazing how much preparation the dead require. There was a coffin to buy; a myriad of choices. There was the guilt about how much to spend. There was an obituary to write, the pecking order of relatives and the phrasing to figure out. The experts are right: there is nothing like work— having to do things, having others to look after—to keep you from thinking about the dead and about death as real. I felt removed, outside of myself. Observing but not feeling.

The rabbi, who hardly knew her, offered up some generalities about how good she had been and how everybody had loved her. The eulogy is the first step towards canonization.

I wrote my own eulogy for her. I crafted sentiments, choosing words for their meaning, their sounds, their rhythms. It was a satisfying act. I aimed for a striking opening image, good transitions, a moment of levity and a tearjerker ending. Because art makes it real.

My aunt had been a very fine cook. She owned a restaurant specializing in old-world Hungarian chicken soup, goulash, palacsinta (crepes) and stuffed cabbage. The Hungarians of Montreal used to flock to her little hole-in-the-wall restaurant on Prince Arthur Street (before the neighbourhood became trendy). She fed them all, she fed them hearty. I inherited her well-cooked pots and pans. I am now slowly learning the secrets of the pots, those peasant-soft-blue pots.

Sitting shiva is the ritual time of mourning. It follows the burial and lasts a week. During this time, the family sits on low stools or on the floor to signify being brought low by the death. During this time, the family does no work, is not even allowed "marital relations." For seven days, visitors bring food and remember. I remember sitting on a footstool, with my tie cut as a symbol of loss. It used to be the rending of jacket lapels, but that's become too expensive a gesture nowadays. I recall thinking how surprised she would have been at the number of people who had shown up. I think she would have known that all this wasn't for her but for the living, and she wouldn't have liked it. And I was still waiting to grieve.

The unveiling was a year after her death. Unveiling is the gathering of family and friends at the cemetery to dedicate the tombstone. A white apron covering the tombstone is removed and Kaddish said. In some ways, it is closure; in some ways, it is the beginning. It is the beginning of a new relationship.

It is always cold here. The visible breath is a tap on the shoulder, it is a memento mori. The old hold on to the young, who feel a shiver from what is not the wind. Along the path we know by heart, we walk towards the grave. Every year, our steps get slower. Every year seems to come more quickly. Every year, each has a private moment to murmur a prayer, to say nothing, to wail at the heavens, to ask what is to become of us. We promise nicer flowers and a footboard next year.

We place pebbles on the headstone—as a note to the dead, to the living—to show that we are never finished building monuments to the dead. To say we were here, to say we will be back. Afterwards, feeling unburdened, we turn to leave.

Memories of the dead wash us of the year's gathered pain. This is the way the dead cleanse the living. This is the way the dead keep on living. It reminds me of a joke . . .

Duncan Hartley Fawcett

MY

FATHER'S

BLUE

SKIES

By Brian Fawcett

My father, Duncan Hartley Fawcett, died a couple of months short of his 101st birthday in January 2008 after a remarkably happy life. He was a man who set his goals early on, achieved them all by the age of sixty, and then spent the next forty years enjoying himself, doing exactly and only what he damned well pleased. He was in relatively good health until two weeks before he died, and he knew where all the cards in his deck were until the last forty-eight hours. Through most of the last several decades of his life, he was appreciatively conscious of just how good he had it. He believed he possessed everything a sensible man could ask for, and when I looked at the world through his eyes, I could see why he thought so.

When so happy a life ends after a century, it really isn't relevant, it seems to me, to regret its end, and any grief experienced by others is likely to be somewhat stained with selfishness. Whatever the polite and relevant gestures are, I'm really not sure. But I've experienced little regret or grief since he died, even though I miss him and the cheerful wisdom he dispensed in the last few years of his run, and I sometimes grow tearful when I think about him.

But for all that, I'm aware that my emotions about my father aren't what count, despite our culture's insistence on my having them long, loud and in public. What matters more—or ought to—is tracking down the sources and resources of his exemplary happiness, and then coming to terms with them. It seems to me that not examining what made him a happy man would be deeply foolish and dishonourable, particularly since he himself vastly preferred life lessons to maudlin ponderings. What was this guy about, anyway?

There's an "X" factor here. My father's last seven years were his happiest: he married for a second time, had innumerable other affectionate and occasionally erotic relationships with an amazing assortment of people, and became progressively sweeter and more attentive of others as the final years accelerated. Moreover, he'd become both conscious of and curious about what made him so sanguine a man, and he'd kick my ass if I didn't at least try to figure out what transformed him and what it all means. So here goes.

While I don't feel much grief about my father's death, I do see him every day when I look at the nine 5x7 photographs of him I've hung on the walls of my coach house/ writing studio/library/guest house in Toronto, where I've lived since 1991. In one of my two favourite photographs of him, he's in his mid-thirties, sitting on some boxes in a rail yard. He's wearing a dark three-piece suit, tie and a snap-brim hat on his head that just covers his eyes. He's good-looking in a square-jawed, square-shouldered way, and until you see how large his hands are—farmer's hands—you might think he's a dandy or even a gangster. In his left hand, which rests on his knee, is a piece of paper. It's probably an order form, and the boxes he's sitting on are probably the order. He was a salesman for a meat-packing company at the time (the photograph was likely taken during the Second World War). The other favourite, taken in the late 1920s, has him on a motorcycle, and in this one he's glowering at the photographer, almost certainly in play, but looking tough anyway. Next to him is another motorcyclist, not quite as convincing, and their two motorcycles are leaning in towards one another slightly, allowing the third person in the photograph, an attractive young woman, a perch to stand on. In both photographs, and in nearly all the others I have of him as a young man, one can see a kind of coiled vitality that has made at least two visitors to my office, one female and one homosexual male, ask who the good-looking guy is.

He was better-looking than I ever was, actually, even though we're built similarly, erect, broad-shouldered, tall enough. In his prime he stayed handsome in a heavy-set way (he carried about 200 pounds until he was in his late seventies) and he was as strong as an ox. He also had a very, very long prime. Into his nineties he was consistently taken for a man twenty years younger. He doesn't look either happy or sad in those favourite photographs on my wall, but he's mostly happy in the others, and when my older brother, a month after his death, sent me a CD containing several hundred colour slides of the family from the 1950s scanned into JPEG formatting, the overwhelming impression was of a comfortable and engaged man in a world he understood and felt on top of.

The most obvious source of my father's happiness, not surprisingly, was extreme good fortune: he had good looks, good health, he made enough money, and nothing bad happened to him. He lived his entire life in western North America, the most stable region on the planet during his century. He was born in Edmonton, Alberta, and grew up on a quarter-section family farm about 60 kilometres north of that city, near a farming town called Morinville. He married my mother in Edmonton in 1936, lived in several locations around Alberta while he worked as a salesman, and then moved to northern British Columbia in 1943. He made his fortune there, running a soft drink bottling plant and an ice cream manufacturing operation, then retired to the B.C. Okanagan in the mid-1960s, where he lived to the end of his life.

There were no man-made disasters in his part of the world, and the worst natural disaster he witnessed personally was a 1952 river flood in Prince George, B.C. Even there, the house he'd built for our family was on a plateau well above the reach of the floodwaters. He'd planned it that way: it's okay to be a bystander, he'd have said, but only morons do their bystanding from the middle of a highway or on the banks of a deep, wild river. He believed that you needed to be a fool to become a victim. That's how he saw his life, and everyone else's too. Given the sorts of things that happened to people during the twentieth century, those were the words of someone deeply, and maybe obliviously, fortunate.

Location was only part of his good fortune. His placement in history was just as lucky. He came of age in the mid-1920s, and thus missed the First World War, where combat was probably the most psychologically destructive and physically lethal mass event human beings have ever consented to take part in. He then avoided military service in the Second World War without trying: he was in his thirties in 1939, married with children, had a job that was deemed necessary to the "war effort" and, characteristically, didn't put himself in harm's way by volunteering.

If he might have been shirking personal danger, he didn't ever avoid hard work. He'd been able to get and keep a job throughout the Depression, managing to save enough to put a down payment on a house when he married my mother. His post-war industriousness made him a moderately wealthy man, despite a lack of formal education. As luck would have it, all of his children survived childhood and adolescence, and generally inherited his good health while experiencing reasonable degrees of prosperity. Another part of his luck was that he didn't outlive any of us.

He was lucky in still other ways. At the beginning of his life, he was the adored youngest son of a doting mother who breastfed him intermittently until he was almost seven years old. He then enjoyed lifelong good health, wasn't accident-prone, and was never, as they say, in the wrong place at the wrong time. The worst injuries he suffered in his several auto accidents were minor cuts and bruises. This is a bigger deal than it sounds, since through his twenties he was a motorcyclist, and for fifteen years after that he was a commercial traveller for a meat-packing company in an area with primitive roads and in an era of poorly built cars. His mishaps remained minor as he grew old, and because he continued to do everything his own way, they often carried powerful elements of slapstick. He fell off roofs and walked away barely shaken up, he tumbled down steep embankments and crawled back up, ruffled but undamaged. This continued until, on his ninety-ninth birthday, he fell, landing on a hefty roll of twenty-dollar bills he'd taken to keeping in his hip pocket instead of a wallet. Its bulk broke his hip. Even while he was near death in the weeks that followed the fall, he understood the irony of the accident and played it for the rich practical joke on him that it was. Armed thus, by laughter and his still-intact will, he turned what should have been a life-ender into a good time within a few months by marshalling his considerable charm and making himself the favoured patient/resident at the extended care facility he went into.

So he was a man who got some breaks in life, yes. Yet on a thousand occasions his wilfulness and practical intelligence gave those breaks that little shove that transformed here-now-gone-tomorrow luck into progressive and accumulative good fortune. He was hard-working, frugal and very shrewd, both in his business decisions and in his judgment of people and situations, and so he did well financially if not always socially. He may have been a man in the right place at the right time, but he always made that place more than its slippery surfaces naturally allowed.

Until he was well into his nineties, I didn't, any more than he did, think about whether he was happy, or about what sorts of materials that happiness was constructed from. I was the rebellious youngest son of a rebellious youngest son, and so my father and I wasted nearly all of our time together with nose-to-nose stare-downs and contests of will, neither of us able to see or appreciate one another beyond the uneven conflict of two alpha males. The things that appeared to give him the most pleasure were making money and telling everyone around him what to do and what was right and wrong, and I curled my lip at both. Since I was the weaker alpha, I tried to keep a distance between us, but when I couldn't sidestep him I fought back blindly against both his authority and his influence. The fights were loud and ferocious, and when I was younger, sometimes physical.

But by the time he was approaching his last decade, the battles between us had become less intense and more rare, maybe because the war was no longer compelling. He was growing tired of fighting, and while I'd learned how to

win battles, I'd decided I was never going to win the war—
which is to say, he wasn't going to change his mind. As his
nineties began, there was a wary truce between us, if not
quite an armistice. Finally, the war simply ended, because,
well, he changed. And I let go, too, a little. It was impossible not to admire his courage and resourcefulness, and his
growing sweetness made it possible to forget what an over-
bearing shithead he'd been for so many years.

My mother died when he was ninety-three, and that's
when he truly went into overdrive. In the year that followed, he taught himself to cook and keep a house clean.
Despite being virtually blind, he regained his driver's licence
with his own unique combination of charm, pleading and
bully-ragging, and then managed to drive for six more years
without killing anyone or demolishing anything except a
few garage doors. He forced himself to go into unfamiliar
circumstances to gain companionship, and he never once
whined about how hard any of it was. When he was ninety-
four, he courted a seventy-year-old woman, asked her to
marry him, and only after she'd accepted mentioned how
old he was. Thus, he married for the second time at the age
of ninety-five, the two newlyweds danced until after midnight on their wedding night, and I'm not even going to
speculate on what happened when they got home.

It was around that time that I found myself enjoying his
company for the first time in my adult life, wishing I'd found
ways to get along with him when he was younger and decid-
ing I'd better find out who he really was before he wasn't
around to talk to. But he wasn't the man I'd grown up with.

He began to ask questions of family members we'd never dreamed he'd ask: What did we think about things? What did we feel? As far as he was capable—he was seriously deaf by this time, although some of us suspected he'd merely perfected "selective hearing"—he listened carefully to the answers. He and I began to talk, tentatively at first, but gradually with increased—and to me, gratifying—openness. After he went into the extended care facility, that openness took another leap, and the last half-dozen long conversations we had there were wide-ranging and affectionate.

He survived twenty-one months after he broke his hip. During that time he lost his second wife, who'd suffered a crippling stroke less than a year after they were married, and for almost three years he'd visited her daily in the same institution he would land up in. As his second institutionalized summer wound down, he lost a girlfriend he'd liked enough that the two of them, six weeks after his hundredth birthday, were busted climbing into bed together without a stitch of clothing on. After the girlfriend died, he seemed to lose interest in companionship, and he started to talk, between the increasingly gentle philosophical soliloquies he delivered to anyone who visited, about being tired. "How the hell do I get out of this life?" he asked me the last time I visited him.

I answered that I didn't know, and left the question hanging without offering him any idiotic opinions about it being okay to let go. I preferred it the way he'd put it several months before that, when I asked him how he was doing and he recognized that I wanted the truth.

"Not so good," he'd said. "I can't hear, I can't see much, and I have to wear diapers most of the time. I'm not really having much fun at all." Then he paused, as he'd taken to doing recently, giving himself time to calculate the greater truth of whatever he was pondering. "But you know," he concluded, "this is still a hell of a lot more fun than being six feet under the ground."

When he first entered the facility, he keyed a lot of our conversations with what I thought was a rhetorical question: "How in hell did I get this old?" I learned, after a while, that it was a real question to him, and that he didn't know the answer. His best resort, when no pat answer appeared, was to use it as a springboard for stories about his past, many of which I'd never heard before, and which he told as if he were himself hearing them for the first time. He seemed to be testing their truth at times, too, searching them for insights he'd have never entertained a decade before if they'd clubbed him over the head and called him "Charlie."

When I visited him close to Thanksgiving, after his first summer in the facility, I was startled to find him sporting a George Hamilton IV–level suntan. He'd taken to sitting outside most of the day, even when the days began to grow cool in September. "I like to feel the sunlight on my skin," he said, when I asked him what it was about.

There was that now-familiar pause as he thought over the implications of his most recent thought. "You know," he said after a moment or two, "I built five houses in my life, and not a goddamned one of them had a place where you could sit in the sun." Another pause, as he thought this over. He smiled, not quite ruefully, as he settled in around the interesting new thing he'd uncovered about himself. "I guess my mind was on other things."

It wasn't a self-accusation, but the recognition was satisfactory to both of us, and there were many more like it to come. He kept himself busy thinking through his life, sorting memories and weighing their value and verity right into the last month of it. There was no self-pity, no self-stroking and startlingly few regrets. He was exploring a part of himself and his experience that he'd ignored for almost a century, and I think he was honestly curious about. As Remembrance Day approached, he began thinking over the John McCrae poem "In Flanders Fields," which he'd always liked but now decided he ought to memorize as a way of, as he put it, keeping his mind from getting stale. I think he was circling the last verse of the poem and its fuzzy ideas about passing the torch from the dead to the living, but when I talked to him on the phone a few days after November 11, I was startled to hear that he'd gotten interested in the first two verses—the good ones—and he talked for several minutes about "those poor boys" and how stupid the government was to be again sending young men not much different to "get their asses shot off in some godforsaken shithole."

He was up to other things, too, one of them momentous: he was changing his will to leave his estate, most of which he'd long since dispersed to us via tax loopholes, to his grandchildren. I think he'd realized that his children weren't exactly suffering financially, and that he could do a good turn to everyone by leaving what remained to his ten grandchildren. Here, as generally seemed the case over the last several years, it wasn't ego that moved him. This was the fruit of his improved powers of domestic observation, and it carried a predictably strong element of practicality. I believe he'd been rethinking the power of parental wealth to control and corrupt children—something he'd employed, or tried to, with his own. But now he decided to take some of that corrupting power away from us, while (not incidentally) saving us from having to pay taxes on the money we did transfer to our children. A week after he signed the new will, pneumonia, the old man's friend, set in, and he began to spiral downward.

I got the call to come five days before the end, and I was there for the last thirty-six hours of his life. One of my sisters had arrived a day earlier to relieve my older brother, who'd stayed with him until his collapse simply became too painful to witness. When I arrived, my sister told me he'd lost consciousness a few hours before my plane touched down, and the doctor didn't think he'd come out of it again. I'm not sure he knew that two of his children were with him, but he did grip my hand firmly enough to let me know he was aware that he wasn't alone. This was his show, and companionship was what he really wanted: being alone had been the one thing in life he'd truly disliked.

He had a hard death even though he'd been at peace with the idea of dying. He—or maybe it was life itself—hung on for more than twenty-four hours after there was no reason to expect he could, or that he wanted to. I held his still-huge but lifeless hands for hours on end during that painful day, watching his lined face collapse and become, in the last twelve hours, the fretful face of an infant entangled in troubled dreams—remembering his century-ago passage into the world perhaps, or hesitating before the one he was about to enter now. Death, as I'd learned from my mother's last agonies, doesn't necessarily offer Hollywood comforts to the dying: no theme music in the background, no slo-mo Defining Moments, no backlit tableaus. There did seem, with both my parents, a point at which the conscious will dissolved and the darkness poured into their minds and bodies, unhurriedly and almost casually, without permitting either of them a shred of dignity as they departed. "Peaceful" wasn't what came to mind for what I saw either time. Death is about itself, not about those who witness it, and maybe not even those who experience it. It is painful, raw and humiliating, and the only illumination from above comes from the fluorescent tubes in the ceiling—if there is any light at all.

Witnessing my father die as he did brought back my mother's more difficult death, in December 2000. Hers was a death that hadn't exactly been infused with conventional grief, either. She'd been "only" ninety when she suffered a massive stroke, and like my father, she'd been prepared to die, albeit in a different way. She'd known for several years that it was going to be a stroke that killed her, and she'd had time to orchestrate as much of her exit as she could. She made the preparations primarily, I think, to keep us and the medical system from heroically, as they say, prolonging her life. Beyond that, she wanted to keep her family from scrapping over the sizable estate she left behind. She achieved the latter

goal by writing a precisely detailed will that actually speci-
fied "no fighting"—and by tagging names on or under virtually everything in the house. It worked as well as she could
have hoped. There wasn't a single disagreement over the
estate, and after the funeral reception was over, the twenty or
so females in the extended family retreated to her bedroom
and, amidst much laughter, told stories about her while they
took turns picking their favourite things of hers. She would
have enjoyed every moment of it, and particularly the fact
that there was very little left after they were done.

The graceful and painless exit she'd planned for herself
hadn't gone nearly so smoothly. I think she and her physician had a side deal that would have seen her gone in two
or three days. It wouldn't have been outright euthanasia,
which is against the laws of British Columbia, but it would
have amounted to the same thing. But a chance remark by
one of my siblings—"Can't we do something?"—queered
it, and the doctor retreated to let the living will my mother
signed play out its "natural" course.

That course required almost two brutal weeks, during
which I stood around and watched the woman who'd spent
her life making mine easier die of starvation and dehydra-
tion. About the only good thing I can say about it is that
all of her children were present when she died, and that not
once during her agonized descent was she alone. But when
it was over, I felt nothing that resembled conventional grief.
I was filled, instead, with rage that she had been made to
die so barbarically, and beneath that ran a feeling of shame
that I'd been able to do nothing to avert it. Neither the

anger nor the shame has since gone away, although the anger has diminished.

My older siblings, in their different ways, experienced similar emotions. My brother, the most sensitive and emotionally reserved of us, put up a brave front despite his unresolved issues with our mother, who he felt hadn't ever adequately connected with him because, in his view, she'd preferred me or my sisters. I knew that she'd always practised a scrupulous emotional democracy amongst us, and that what he saw as her lack of interest was the dynamic of having had three children within seventeen months of one another, of whom the elder two were identical twins and he the by nature less-demanding third. But it was true that the two of them had never quite worked it out, and so at the moment of her death I was more moved by his pain at losing her with all that unresolved than by any sense of my own private loss. My mother and I had always talked, and there was nothing unresolved between us. I'd even had a long telephone conversation with her a few days before the stroke irrevocably truncated cognition and left her unable to speak, and we'd tied up the few remaining loose ends that remained. I think she'd felt a blood vessel inside her brain begin to give way, and so decided to assure herself that I at least was okay with her going, understood what she wanted done and how she wanted her children to respond.

My twin sisters handled their anger by taking most of it out on my father, who'd reacted to the end of his sixty-four-year not-always-happy marriage like a man being released from jail: by rapidly, openly and almost giddily attempting to get on with the rest of his life. At the top of his agenda—this was a man who hated to be alone, remember—was companionship. He was trying to pick up women at the funeral reception, and my sisters took an extremely dim view of it. I didn't understand what he was up to either, and found myself wondering whether he'd lost his mind.

A complete break between my father and me was, at that moment, a possibility for the first time in my life. My mother, you see, had imposed a non-negotiable rule at the centre of our family life: we could fight as much as we wanted, any and all of us, but we still had to come home. It had been her way of preserving the family in the face of my father's often clumsy and aggressive attempts to control us, and I suppose it was also her way to get past the stubbornness and stupidity of young adults. She made it clear that there was nothing any of us could have done with our lives horrible enough to nullify the rule. There was probably a line across which we couldn't go, but she made a fair show of trusting our good natures not to. None of us ever challenged the rule or came within a country mile of serious approbation.

Now that she was dead, I coldly considered breaking contact with my father, making him the scapegoat for my helpless rage, punishing him for what I hadn't been able to do to protect my mother. Before I left town after the funeral, I shouted at him, rattled my sabre at him. But it didn't go anywhere, because he began, quietly, to argue his case—or rather, to plead it. I'd never seen him sincerely plead for anything, and I was so astonished that I listened. He told me that he was a man with no idea how long he had left, and so he just didn't have time for a "decent interval" in which to grieve for his wife. And anyway, he said, they'd been fighting for fifty years, and his feelings about her death were, at that moment, as mixed as he imagined mine were about him. With a single-mindedness that now makes me laugh out loud, he told me he didn't plan to waste a minute, because he might only have a few months. And for the next seven years, god love him for it, he didn't waste a second.

Watching him over the several years that followed my mother's death, it began to dawn on me that I'd been missing a lot of the nuanced stuff about him, as sons do when faced by a father with a strong streak of dominance and the vitality to make good on it. I began to see things about him that interested me despite myself, and they all contradicted the Oedipal fury of our lifelong conflict.

I hadn't, for instance, adequately appreciated his merry resistance to all forms of bullshit—except perhaps his own, to which he remained oblivious until the end. He'd always been able to see through other people with effortless clarity, maybe because he had utterly unsentimental instincts about human motives that stopped just this side of cynicism. When he was younger, he could cost out any man's suit a mile off, though he wore nothing but the cheapest suits himself. I'd grown up watching him gleefully cut visiting business executives down to size without their quite seeing how he did it or being able to stop it. He'd also had an admirable sixth sense about hostile intentions, physical or otherwise: he always nailed attackers when they were still in the windup, and nearly always, he made them pay.

Another thing I hadn't seen was that he was casually but profoundly industrious, which quality of his got things done even when all he had on his to-do list was growing African violets to sell at the local hospital-auxiliary booth. Even as he was heading into his late nineties, he remained perpetually busy and engaged, wrestling with problems that were how-to one moment, abstract the next. I think he was happiest when whatever he had on his mental workbench contained elements of both. When I thought about this industriousness, I began to recognize that a quirky mix of the practical and the quixotic had always been present in whatever he was up to, and I recalled, from my childhood, that even during the years when he was working fourteen hours a day building his business, he found time to plant gardens each year, including setting down a brace of rose bushes that he ordered each winter from the Sears cata-logue, and which never once survived the following winter. It was a ridiculous sort of stubbornness to do this year after year, but it was only part of the story. He also planted large, sensible and productive vegetable gardens, and he did it all with so little fanfare and ceremony that none of us really remembered he'd done it until he had us filling gunny sacks with potatoes and carrots in late September. He gardened pretty much the same way until he was ninety-nine years old—this time in a climate where, to his deep and abiding delight, roses and beefsteak tomatoes could thrive.

Until close to the end he took long walks most days, accompanied by the small mutts my sisters had given him before my mother died. The last of these dogs disappeared over the edge of his lawn in the mouth of a coyote about eight months before he broke his hip. He was heartbroken about it, but there was the new thing along with the sadness: thoughtfulness, and a tinge of resignation. "Life can be very cruel," he said and then before passing judgment on its cosmological significance, took the pause that was later to become so familiar. "I did have many hours of joy from those little dogs, so I have no regrets."

When I was cleaning out his house after the funeral, I found dozens of contraptions he'd invented over the years, nearly all of them created to accomplish some task no one but he would have even bothered with: a soaking device soldered from long fingers of ⅜-inch copper tubing so he could water five or six of his African violet clones at the same time; a 500-gallon steel tank in his basement designed to catch and store rainwater; a small electric fan screwed to a custom-welded base at an oblique angle to ventilate or dry god only knows what. His brain had been in high gear from the moment of waking in the morning till he parked it at night, but that didn't mean that he was an unreflecting production machine. He had a lifelong gift for thinking on the fly, and he thought about everything vigorously if not always deeply until a few days before his death.

The one thing he and I didn't talk about during his last years was the state of war that had existed between us for most of my life and for nearly fifty years of his. It seemed, I guess, prudent to both of us to let that sleeping dog lie. But in the hours immediately after his death, I found myself wondering exactly why, from about the time I reached adolescence, we'd disagreed over virtually everything except maybe the colour of the sky. Then, in a flash of insight, I realized that we'd disagreed on that, too. In fact, it was the root disagreement that precipitated most of the others.

My father, you see, fervently believed the sky was always blue, and I believed just as passionately that it wasn't. This disagreement had been partly substantive and empirical and partly Oedipal. For him, the blue derived from the openness of the vista: it illuminated a world of opportunities, and it was a vista without darkness or night shadows. For my part, I insisted, pedantically, that the blueness of the sky was light reflecting from dust particles in the atmosphere, and that once you got to the edge of space it was jet black—I wasn't about to let his perpetual optimism trample me or science. I splattered clouds and darkness across his permanent sunny daylight and tried to tell myself it wasn't just me contesting his alpha male status because I wanted his job.

The fact was this: when I thought over what he believed about the world and how a man ought to conduct himself in it, he just plain seemed wrong. Yeah, yeah, I understood dimly that his actions were often aimed at serving what he thought were my best interests. But I was in a world where in both very recent and more distant times people were regularly killed "for their own good." So his wrong-headed concern felt like a kind of moral undertow that might drag me under if I relaxed. I had to do things differently, see, and if I didn't, my balls would shrivel up and drop off and the screwed-up world would continue to fall apart.

It never occurred to me in the intellectual misery of

sorting between my Oedipal impulses and the practical, observable realities it was in both our natures to attend to, that my father truly, sincerely believed the sky was fundamentally blue—and growing bluer. Nor did I understand that I believed, just as sincerely, that it was grey and fading to black.

In my father's world, most things belonged to men like him. They had earned them by struggling through economic ruin and privation during the Depression, then winning an epic war against the real evil of Nazi-Fascism. They felt sure—correctly, as it turned out—that they would defeat the initiative-sapping global evil of Soviet Communism. For them, the world was a place of individual and collective opportunity, and they could reasonably expect their lives to get progressively better, collectively and individually, particularly if they were able to make and carry out practical, businesslike plans. Their sky really *was* blue.

My own generation of Canadians, which is the one that grew up after World War II, has lived very differently. We haven't had to survive or even experience privation or social upheaval, and we have fought no wars, heroic or otherwise. But as children, we were subjected to a political system and its educational apparatus that taught us that a final, ultimate war was in front of us, and that it was more or less inevitable. For a few years it had us regularly crouching beneath our school desks while air-raid sirens wailed through the hallways. They were supposed to be preparing us to survive the blast of an atomic bomb, but we understood that if an attack came we wouldn't survive, and that it would be the end of everything. I can't speak for all of my contemporaries, but I can testify that the experience twisted my outlook on human possibilities and human motives by convincing me that human beings are fundamentally unreliable and insane. It also infected the way I've been able to think of the future, then and since. Bouncing around inside my brain is the nine-year-old who once crouched under his school desk and still whispers in my ear that he was supposed to get blown up by the crazy people who ran the world, and that there isn't supposed to be any future.

Now, that dire radioactive future didn't come about, sure, although the evidence that we're all crazy continues to pile up, and most days it still feels like the end of the world is just around the corner.

Not very surprisingly, the nine-year-old who decided that his father was tangled up in the coming end of the world, because that father was the only one he saw able to make things happen, or change, or stay the same, is still here, too: a head tangled in childhood can almost never be completely disentangled, not by facts, futures, therapies or human kindness. And so the life manual and deeds of this child's father became permanently suspect. That's why the sky is never quite blue for me, and why even getting it to overcast, given the universe of blackened cinders I once believed was our collective human future, is as good as it gets.

I'm not whining about this, be clear, because I've had a good and easy life, and part of the reason is my father, whose hard-working industriousness made it possible for me to work as an independent writer for most of my life rather than at a nine-to-five job. But seeing dark shadows is a fact of the way I see things and I share it with a lot more of my baby-boomer contemporaries than is generally credited. We're just not optimists.

But look, it isn't all bad. The skies—and I remind myself of this from time to time—are grey, not black. This is a world with positives: civil and human rights have been widely extended, we now treat women almost as well as hetero-sexual male forklift drivers, gay normality is almost a reality, animals are treated better, and a lot of people in the developed world have become sensitized to the degree to which we're making our planet uninhabitable. See how this works?

While my father was dying, it happened that I was reading a book of essays titled *Stardust*. The essays had been written by Bruce Serafin, a Vancouver writer of great intelligence. I'd known Bruce personally and had admired him for many years, and it had struck me as tragic when he died of cancer about six months before my father took his last breaths. Bruce had been just fifty-seven, he died with a full intellectual agenda yet to be carried out, and his shy, obtuse and easily distracted nature made him about as unlike my father as a human being could get. The essay I read and reread over that twenty-four hours while my father hung on to life concerned the novel *Underworld*, by the American novelist Don DeLillo. DeLillo's novel is ostensibly a virtuoso regression in American time from the present to the moment of Bobby Thomson's famous home run that decided the 1951 National League baseball pennant race and which, in DeLillo's vision, was the last completely bright and heroic event in American history. The book is actually about the gradual darkening and descent of the psychological currents that made up cultural reality in the last half of the twentieth century in America. What Serafin spotted in *Underworld* was the degree to which that darkening has come to be seen as natural and without a credible alternative.

The thought that came to me as I watched my father dying was this: for him, the underworld that occupies large elements of my conscious and unconscious attention simply had not existed. He would have found DeLillo's depiction of American life utterly incomprehensible. "Underworld?" I could almost hear him say. "What the hell is that?"

In the *Stardust* essay, Serafin argued that the underworld is the strange sort of virtual simultaneity of things that has supplanted linear history and "progress" in contemporary social and psychological cognition. Ramped up by the immense penetrating power of modern mass media, past and future are crowded out by what is present, dynamic and actual, leaving everyone and everything in a claustrophobic, juiced-up here-and-now, with history and the future converging on each instant as threat, or seduction, instead of comfort and hope.

Nowadays we're marching towards Babel's oppressive totality, not the material Utopia my father imagined. In Babel, the Kennedy brothers were assassinated yesterday and tomorrow, the space shuttle exploded the same way because we had the lurid film-at-five forced on us by television over a hundred yesterdays and we can watch it tomorrow on YouTube at our leisure. Everything exists this way now, fused cognitively by media and culturally by the implosion of fact and ideology within a totalized present. And inside the totality nothing exists, because without a rectilinear past offering foundation and perspective and the hope of a better future offering frisson, meaning can't exist for more than a few minutes before it dissolves into competing voices, some shouting accusations, others murmuring, still others weeping. So that's one way to define the Underworld: the shadow that accompanies this fusion/implosion where nothing is exclusively what it is.

The underworld is also memory and cognition never quite freed from the violence of our parents and ancestors, the paralyzed future that belongs to everyone but us, and the guilt that burdens us, reinforcing our conviction that our lives, present and future, are not our own but the accumulation of the bad or thoughtless deeds of the past, the phenomena of the world wearied and stressed by a sense that visible politics and social life—even one's personal life—are a dumb show utterly manipulated by remote bodies: corporations, government agencies, the mob, space aliens as sanity begins, as it must in such a world, to centrifuge.

That's all very interesting in an abstract sort of way, but how to translate it for my father?

I sat in the darkened palliative care room and tried to come up with a definition of the Underworld that my father would have understood. Finally, reluctantly, it came to me. I would get him to imagine a world in which you couldn't make plans. As I went over how to make that real to him, searching for a way to simplify what I described above, in my head I could hear his voice saying what I'd heard from him a hundred times: "You've got to have plans. If you don't make plans, you can't achieve anything. I had a plan all my life. I always knew where I was going in the big picture. And every morning I woke up and made my plan for that day, and then I carried it out. That's the only way to succeed at anything."

But then his other voice, the more gentle one from the last years, broke in: "How the hell do you think I managed to live a hundred years?" it said.

I tried to explain to him—to the second voice—how we'd arrived at his future around 1975 or thereabouts, his generation believing they'd gotten as close to the Promised Land as they were going to get and my generation feeling depressed and defeated, and none of us could see anything good ahead of us. And it was around that time that Western civilization simply stopped making long-range plans. The governments stopped looking ahead, dunking their long-range plans in favour of "flexibility"—or expedience; corporations began pulling back their focus to the eighteen-month profit horizon; and individuals simply started thinking about what they wanted at the mall, or from the myopic marketplace.

Daily plans? Not a problem. Everyone needs to get through the day, the week, the month, even the year. But his generation's Chamber of Commerce Utopia ended with diminished expectations and the newly recognized public shadows of overpopulation, pollution, environmental collapses of one sort or another and self-inflicted public debt.

People stopped gazing into the distance because the vista was just too damned gloomy to bear.

It was fine for those like him who had everything they wanted from life: money, cars, things, the respect of others. That was good, a fine thing, and I'm glad he was able to enjoy it as he had. But I had to live in that future, which was his future, not mine, and that wasn't fine. For me, it was just "a" future, a place I hadn't chosen and had lost the power—or will—to influence.

Then I remembered that everything he wanted hadn't exactly been perfect. He hadn't been completely content with his marriage, a lot of people hadn't liked him for the way he spoke his mind, and by his own anecdotal account-ing, the everyday world was full of jackasses and politics, and business was overrun with blowhards and crooks, etc. I considered pointing out to him that just possibly things were getting worse, that there were more crooks and jackasses than in the past and that—

I stopped myself. Why take that away from him? Besides, he'd have come up with a thousand instances of how things were just fine, how people were terrific and hard-working, and we'd be back arguing over what colour the sky was.

So in that deathbed room, I stopped our imaginary conversation. The only way I could have made him under-stand was to blacken the sky, make him see that his life and his myriad goals were illusions. So I pulled back and said nothing, even in my own mind. He was my father and I loved him—at that moment, as uncritically as I had since I was a small child. I loved him partly because I was duty bound to it, but also because I'd grown to love the changes in him. He was remarkable: a man who'd taught himself, in his mid-nineties, almost deaf and nearly blind, how to care about other people in dozens of new ways. I wanted him to die with this newly acquired vision of things unchallenged, because in the moment I recognized that his vision had become sweeter and more encompassing than anything I had. And that's how, agonized, struggling to draw one more breath, his eyes and cheeks caved in, his big-boned arms at last like his hands had always seemed, too large for his body, he died beneath his big blue sky.

One more thing. I've spent a fair amount of time since he died bemusedly coming to terms with the idea that elements of my character—my irascibility, my tendency to trash-talk, to complain loudly but never more than half-seriously that the world seems to be full-to-the-rim with morons and self-serving irresponsible assholes—are adaptations of traits I inherited from him. It's as if, freed by his death, they've come clambering out of their hiding places in my brain, thus giving him exactly the kind of immortality he'd find most entertaining.

Most of these traits, I'm fitfully aware, are my private adaptations not so much to circumstances or events, but to the collapse of autocratic patriarchy, to the socially psychopathic evolution of entrepreneurial ethics, and other elements of the constellation of societal changes that have landed me in a world with more than my share of alpha male testosterone that has no safe place to go but out the exhaust vent.

I've never, as I've already said, wanted to be like my father or live my life as he did. His definition of maleness and authority are done, and even if the world I'm in operates without any substitutes and transformatives except "no," I like it better than his. I like being no better or worse than anyone else, and I don't want the privileges and presumptions his generation had. But still, I've spent much of my adult life suppressing the truth that most days I feel more like a sabre-toothed tiger than a man with a future and a mission. Like the sabre-toothed tigers, I'm dressed to kill, but have nowhere to go with it but the bone pile.

Then, just before I'm corrupted by the high/serious portents of this metaphor, I hear his cackle of laughter, identify it as not his at all, but my own, and feel the sky lighten above me.

June Callwood

HER

GREAT

ART

By Jill Frayne

A few weeks after my mother died, her friends took me to lunch, the ones who stand in for her, with grown daughters of their own. We sat by ourselves in the dining room with the good linen and dark walls, the trees outside in leaf, waving green light into the room. Dorothy looked me over. She said, Betty and I had good relationships with our mothers too and I'll tell you something. The thing you miss most now, the sense of protection, is the thing that will come back to you.

Is that what I was missing then, a sense of protection? I know there was a then and there is now, and they are different.

The way I'd put it, I know where to find my mother, now that it's been a year, more than a year. The state of emergency that came with her death has passed, and I have a sense of her again, not in the world, of course, but in myself, in memory and in dreams, but strongest in my body, in breath and bone, as if by physical feat I have incorporated her. More likely she was always there, in the way of mothers, in my marrow from the start, scribbling on my cells.

When she was dying and for months afterwards, there was just a kind of panic. And exhaustion, like the exhaustion I knew when Bree was born, only this time with a siren wailing under every sound, my speechless protest. She died so fast and so completely.

I came in to my parents' house from the airport at one in the morning, back early from my holiday, the porch light left on for me, the living room dark. My sister had stayed on from dinner and got up from the sofa like a spectre, already in the shock that looks like calm. An ambulance was coming in the morning. Mom's breathing had gotten so wild, so easily lost. She couldn't stay at home. Jess and I sat together in the dark, drinking water. Our parents were in bed on the other side of the wall, in the room they'd slept in for more than fifty years. Jess had heard them whispering a long time before they went to sleep, the old, easy volleys going back and forth.

There was an unfamiliar sound in the house. An oxygen

tank, like R2-D2, hummed in the dining room. When I went into my mother's bedroom in the morning, she had a thin, clear breathing tube in her nose. It's bad, she said, as though I'd just left the room a minute before, instead of two weeks. From that instant, I had no separate life. I was in the chute with her. It was as though my holiday and the night flight home had never been, as though I had no house of my own four hours away. Crisis blots out everything but its own details. It's the cyclone roaming over the ground, picking up all the buildings and furniture and lives, setting them in a slow spin, irrelevant and helpless. They land eventually— we landed—but not in the same place and not as we were.

My mother had a public life. People knew her. They'd seen her on television or read her articles or been at a talk she gave, or they'd worked on a committee with her or she'd helped someone in their family, or helped them. She had a long reach and a huge correspondence. She answered everything. She would read the morning newspaper, dress and get at it, be at her typewriter or off to a meeting. She was a kind of bearing point for many people, and for me too, but she didn't bring her work home with her and I didn't closely follow her career. She was my mother and that took up the room. In a certain way I didn't pay attention to the rest of what she did, or it was background. That seems incredible now, a lost chance. I think perhaps our parents don't live long enough to outlast their eminence as parents.

When the ambulance came, she did not dress. She got onto the gurney in her nightgown. The attendants unhooked the oxygen and we covered her in a vast blue shawl someone had knit for her. They wheeled her through the house and she did not glance around. At the door, I made a hat for her out of a corner of the shawl and she did not glance around, ignored her home of decades, her marriage and the keepsakes from her children, her honours on every wall. She had pared down to the present instant, living in her breath, the way we do at certain times—running marathons, making love, giving birth.

Jess and I rode with her, taking a long, roundabout route downtown to Princess Margaret Hospital and up the tower to the palliative floor with its dozen or so beds, an eddy of calm surrender on top of fifteen floors of cancer guns blasting away. She was glad to reach her room at the end of the parqueted hall, the cool blue walls and high bed, the new, efficient breathing tube. She settled back and sighed. We set her vitamins and magazines and newspapers on the stand beside her, and she left them where they were. When I called the next day, she declined her nighties from home. She wore the gowns the nurses gave her. I didn't understand. Her friend said, She's in the hospital now.

———

The twenty-four days until she died were my forced march. I could barely move. At night, I couldn't stay asleep. I'd get out of bed and make lists by flashlight, medication to ask about, phone calls to answer and make. The weather never changed. There's a name in literature to indicate when nature is in harmony with human affairs. There was no sun that April. The same wind battered the streets outside the hospital each day. I'd find a parking meter blocks away, trying for distance, and walk along Baldwin Street, then back again in three hours with more coins, the weight of the sky the same. Every day there were the same yellow faces in the lobby, cancer patients with their helpers, going for tea in Druxy's. I'd take the elevator up. The doors opened across from a bank of windows that looked down into a court-yard full of bronze figures, skinless, as though flayed.

———

What I think about endlessly, like a pool I'll be sponging up forever, is the time before the hospital, when my mother was ill and getting herself ready for her life to end. Why in her long life I go to that time in particular, I don't know. Because it was her death. Because I have to face my own, the next mother in line. I sit on my porch steps at home, the leaves of the trees lifting and sighing in the summer air, and try to figure how she did it, made death incidental.

———

There was a meeting at the house on a Sunday in early winter, when June's two doctors brought the expert. She served coffee in the Rosenthal cups, and we sat in the living room, the three doctors, my parents at two ends of the couch. Librach said that her cancer was a rare one, far along now, but not painful as cancers go. She said, What will I die of, and he said, Weakness. You'll die of weakness. The body can take only so much crowding.

———

My mother was content with that. There was a plan. She could go to the hospital if it got complicated, and she would not be out of her mind with pain. There was only all the signing off to do.

Later on she did an interview for *The Hour*, a CBC broadcast George Strombolopolos hosted. By then, she was running on nerve. It was taped at the house and the television crew wanted her greeting by the host to appear fresh. They kept her segregated in her bedroom for two hours while they set up in the living room. I went in to her several times while she waited, holding herself together. She wore the last thing that she still could fit over the tumours, a black jumper I'd never seen before. They called her out at last and she greeted George, giving it all she had, making it look easy, her great art. He said about the end of her life, Is there anything that comes next? She looked surprised by his naïveté. No! We get a life, she said, with slight rebuke.

So clear for her, the preciousness, the obligation of right now.

———

In the hospital, through the day, visitors pooled in the lounge beyond her room. They'd unwrap appetizers and

hand creams from canvas bags, wait to see her. She'd be bur-
rowed in her bed asleep, or propped up awake. Jess and I
were secretaries, working through her list. Who still to thank,
who to put in a word for. She was blithe, not estranged from
any part of dying, but not giving it much due. No part of
her clung; there was no bittersweet.

The mayor came and she showed him what tone to
strike. She said, What's a big, tall man like you with a wife
at home doing here on a Sunday afternoon?

When she'd worked through her list and made her spry
farewells, she was restless, wanting to be gone. Her eyes were
large and dark. I think she hated to detain us, keep us coming
every day, but her body had its pace. She had to wait.

The palliative floor was an island in the cancer building. It did not resemble the treatment floors below, where
there was a different endeavour, different rules and too few
staff. The palliative floor was a cocoon, well out of the battle,
and all kindness. The nurses made a loose lasso around us
all. When I passed the nursing station, any time of day, the
nurses would look up and smile a welcome. They never
woke my mother and they always came when needed. More
than once she fell, going by herself to the bathroom, unac-
customed to her weakness. Her hips were marbled in bruises.
A friend said, June will set the record for not calling the
nurses at Princess Margaret, and perhaps she did, but we
called them all the time.

———

Death is the bony birth, the inside-out of being born. In the hospital, June was Gulliver among the Lilliputians, pegged to the earth, having to yank up every stake one by one. There was a little knot between her eyebrows all the time. Even when she smiled, which she did every time I came into the room, or any of us did, there'd be that furrow between her eyes, concentration whirring. I'd hear it in her voice, her tone a little anxious, words humorously put, the way someone being brave in a startling landscape might speak.

Sometimes in her sleep she groaned, not in pain I thought, but from the effort to set down her life. Or keep her balance, navigate the hazards along the way, the emotion and the drugs and dreams, elephants and angels flying at her. She woke up once and looked around incredulous.

Am I still alive? Shit! .

She'd lie deep in the bed in the cool blue of the hospital room, flowers massed in the window, all the colours matching, the saffrons and oranges like prayer flags, the clock marking the stillness, the sibilance of the oxygen, the standing fan moving the air.

Her hands became beautiful. The swollen arthritis sank away and her hands were like small birds, the bones drawn together, supple and warm. She'd put her rail arms up and clamp them around my neck.

I can attest that she was queen of her last days, as she intended, greeting everyone with her accustomed aplomb, but there was something more. It came later, when she'd moved deeper and stopped keeping track. Her last stand was love. When the cancer had walked off with everything else, that's what she had. She was still funny and she loved us.

She'd like to know that.

Bending over her, moving her pillows around, I groaned all the time. My bones groaned and ground against each other. She led and I followed, having no choice. What could be more binding than to see her through?

I liked to sit in the room with her without talking. It was the only time I calmed down. We were by ourselves one time; she'd been drifting, but she was awake. I said, I don't like this. She turned her head and gave me a mild look.

Get a hold of yourself.

Or maybe I read her wrong. It might have been all right if I'd thrown myself on the floor and thrashed, the way I wanted to. But how could I, since she didn't?

My daughter came, from the other side of the world, my Bree. Dad and I met her plane, Dad a wraith, but you couldn't stop him. We drove straight back to the hospital. A policeman pulled me over for speeding on the Lakeshore. He said sternly, Do you know how fast you were going? My mother's dying, I told him. He bent and looked into the car. Go on, he said. Be careful.

Bree stayed with Dad and me at the house. She and I fought every day before visiting June. We pulled up every dragon in the pond. My girl, my bitter ally. And in the evenings we sat squeezed together on the couch, our heads rolled back, like exhausted athletes.

My mother and father floored me. She said he hated hospitals, but he came every day, and he hated elevators, but he rode them sixteen floors. One day was very bad. She'd gone through a change, her mouth set, her eyes fogged. I met Dad in the hall and warned him. He went into the room and sat beside her in his windbreaker and looked at her face for a long time. His eyes never left her. At last he leaned in and put his face on hers. You sweet woman, he said.

Both of them in their frail, slack bodies, the fierceness pouring off them like heat.

How did they know to do that, confect something between them that would be sustaining, a marriage that was springy and full of humour and quite easily carried? As if they'd said, at twenty and twenty-six, Oh, let's not say every-thing, or look for amends. Let's, if we can, amuse and comfort each other. (With the odd brick lobbed through the window.) How did they do that, skip the tampering and reproach and go for something that would hold?

———

She got more beautiful. Her lovely face, her hair mostly worn off, her body collapsed onto the bone. She had hard work at the end, pushing through the bottleneck, her chest crackling loud enough to hear her down the hall, the air in the room in turmoil. A day and a night of that, then she took a few slow breaths and died, and the room went dull and blank. At daybreak, they came and took her out in black velvet and my sister went home and I left the hos-pital and went out into the street. The sun was shining for the first time in weeks, light bouncing off the particles of air. She was everywhere, in the radiance everywhere. From no room at all, my mother had found her way to all the room in the world.

———

The now is this: absolutely she's not here. There's no semblance of her anywhere—no form, no body heat, no voice. It took me quite a while to find the subtler ground she'd moved to, somewhere in my breath or blood or memory. June used to say we live in each other, all of us, and if that's true, I reconfigure her inside myself. This must be what we do. The injured brain grows new cells, the damaged arteries construct new pathways to the heart, the atoms jump and spark when we lose each other. My mother transmutes herself. Instead of her being body-bound, filling the screen, I find her thin as vapour, boundless, somewhere in me.

I strain for it. I try to apprehend her life, find out about her, make memory palpable, as if that way I could keep her with me. It's like listening for the ocean in a conch shell.

She seems so grave to me now. I know that's an odd word, she was so rarely grave. But grave in her intent. Gravely, she decided to take death lightly. She didn't say, I'm frightened or I'm tired or I don't want to die—not plaintively or in a way that asked for help. She said, Let's get on with it.

How did she become that person, jaunty and purpose-filled? It seems as though she'd tell me now.

From my back steps I look up. With so much rain, my woods are a live wall around the house, the ditches stuffed with wildflowers. Down in the city, Dad stays on in the house. I dreamt my mother knew he had and was glad, and I dreamt her young, embracing him, leaning into him, the way she did, and smiling.

We're different without her. I mean the family. More exposed to each other, her granddaughter said. June was the centre and every distance out from her has shifted, every axis on a new tilt. It's not comfortable yet. We are tender and volatile with each other. And more vivid to ourselves. I'm a different woman with my mother gone. Less brave, more ordinary.

If this is grief, it feels like vertigo, a kind of motion sickness. I'm making myself over, without my mother. Now that she doesn't call me, or put flowers in my room, or settle an appraising eye on me, I'm not who I was. I'm someone changed, the floor under my feet still swaying.

Emily Jane Givner

ON PREPARING

MY DAUGHTER'S FICTION FOR

POSTHUMOUS PUBLICATION

By Joan Givner

My daughter Emily died in Halifax on a sunny July day in 2004. It was just five days after her thirty-eighth birthday, and she had walked downtown in buoyant high spirits. For the past two years she had worked with great intensity on her writing, often drawing on experiences garnered during her years of teaching in Korea and Poland. Now she had reached the point where she felt ready to find a means of support that would be compatible with her vocation. She was delighted to have been accepted by the Library Science program at Dalhousie University, and she was looking forward to starting in the fall.

She went to an instant-teller machine to withdraw funds for the deposit on her tuition fees, and then stopped at a food court to buy a sandwich. She had suffered from asthma and severe allergies since childhood, and she was always careful; but by some accident of miscommunication or cross-contamination, the sandwich contained a fatal allergen. She went into shock, and by the time help was available, it was too late to save her.

It was also an idyllic summer day on Vancouver Island. Her father and I had eaten lunch at a restaurant by the sea, watching the seals bobbing about on the water. That evening we received a phone call from a doctor at the Queen Elizabeth II hospital in Halifax telling us that our daughter had died. I still find it hard to believe that while I sat looking out over the sea and the mountains, I had had no intimation that my daughter was fighting for her life. After all, in *Self-Portrait of a Literary Biographer*, I had written of Emily:

> . . . we share the same temperament, the same genes, the same bone marrow, I'm sure. It does not make for comfort. When she is in pain, I hear her voice calling to me in my sleep. I wake, thinking she has come into the house. Sometimes I go on to the landing and call downstairs, "Emily, is that you?" There is no one there. The next day I hear from her. "I've

been having a terrible time. I didn't want to
upset you and Dad, but . . ."

Five days after that phone call, I flew to Halifax to
organize a small memorial gathering of her friends in a local
funeral home. After the reception there, I went directly to
the house where she had lived for the past year and a half.
The others followed, on foot and by car. They gathered tact-
fully in the back garden so that the house was very quiet. It
was a bright summer day like the one six days earlier, when
she had walked out of the house for the last time.

Her bedroom was just as she had left it—crowded
bookshelves, a desk heaped with papers and books, her
cello with Bach suites on the music stand beside it, books,
manuscripts, CDs and inhalers scattered all over the place.
I'm not sure how long I sat on the bed, looking out the
window at her friends below chatting in quiet groups
under the trees, holding glasses of wine. After a while, I
got to work. There was much to do, and only three days
before I had to return home to care for my husband, who
was in poor health.

There were manuscripts, documents, notebooks in
which she scribbled down ideas as she sat in cafés, drinking
endless cups of coffee, and drawers and boxes full of letters.
She had inherited my pack-rat habits, and never threw away
a letter. For three days I separated the irreplaceable items to
be carried as hand luggage from those to go as checked-in
baggage or to be sent by mail. Then I returned to Victoria
with her cello, and her precious legacy.

Emily had inadvertently provided me with a task to help me over that first period of shock and grief. For the next months I worked in my study, the curtains closed against the outside world, poring over, retyping and editing the stories she had written during her final surge of creative activity. She had sent me her stories as she worked on them, but when I urged her to submit her work for publication, she resisted. She quoted Katherine Anne Porter, my own literary foremother, back at me: "I think it is the most curious lack of judgment to publish before you are ready." Only a few weeks earlier she had decided she was ready, and had submitted a story to a competition. "Canadian Mint" appeared in the *Toronto Star* three weeks after her death. It fell to me to see the rest of her work into print.

"Don't do it," a writer friend warned me. "If the work's rejected, you'll feel mortified, and if it's published, you'll feel just as terrible."

I suspected there was truth in what she said, for nothing made Emily's presence so vivid and her loss so painful as her own clear voice speaking out of her stories. Yet I was determined to go ahead. My submissions of her individual stories to literary journals were successful, but placing a collection was a greater challenge. Publishers are reluctant to risk bringing out a first book by an author able neither to promote it nor to promise a second book. Moreover, a book by an author no longer alive is ineligible for the competitions that garner publicity. Many will not even read such a manuscript, but eventually I found one who liked the work well enough to take the risk.

Three years after her death, Thistledown Press of Saskatoon brought out *A Heart in Port*, containing a selection of Emily's stories. The launch was a magical occasion. It took place on an August afternoon at the home of friends—Penfold Farm, a heritage house with a beautiful garden and lake in the Cowichan Valley. Ninety people came, including the publisher, the designer of the book and Sean Virgo, the editor. The actor Paula Costain, Emily's childhood friend, did a brilliantly dramatic reading from two of the stories. Also among the guests was Sheila Munro, whose book *Lives of Mothers and Daughters* Emily had found profoundly moving.

When I welcomed everyone, I recalled my friend's words of warning. I assured them that while the process had been difficult at times, I felt only great pleasure and satisfaction in the publication. I said the same thing when the book was launched again in Regina. These were public occasions, intended to celebrate Emily's work, and I was determined to dispel any tendency towards the solemn and elegiac. What I said was only half the story, for the reality was much more complicated.

Around the same time, the editors of *Ars Medica* requested a short essay to accompany their publication of Emily's "The Bereavement Team." They asked me to describe what the editing process had been like for me. I wrote:

> Gradually . . . I move from being a reader with
> a maternal eye, much too conscious of the raw
> material and scaffolding behind the story, to

being a dispassionate reader. Since I've been
trying to understand and explain fiction for
most of my adult life, I slip easily into the role
of critic. Thus distanced, I begin to see the
story in a new way. I read, discovering new
patterns, appreciating the artistry, relishing
those mischievous turns of phrase . . .

Once again that was a simplification, a half-truth; the word
"easily" was a gross misstatement.

Any explanation of the complex process would have to
begin by taking note of my own life's work. A major theme
of that work in biography, literary criticism and fiction has
been a preoccupation—some might call it an obsession—
with the mother–daughter relationship. The following statement by Adrienne Rich was often my point of departure:

The loss of the daughter to the mother, the
mother to the daughter, is the essential female
tragedy. We acknowledge Lear (father–daughter
split), Hamlet (son and mother), and Oedipus
(son and mother) as great embodiments of the
human tragedy, but there is no presently enduring recognition of mother–daughter passion
and rapture.

In many lectures and articles, as well as in my fiction,
I tried to show that there was indeed an enduring record
of mother–daughter passion and rapture (rupture?). I studied

the autobiographies of Margaret Laurence and Eudora Welty—two writers who served as literary foremothers to a whole generation of younger writers. In my essays, I focused on their relationships with their own mothers. I found links between their attempts to explain how writers come into being with their own biological mothers' transmission to them of crucial knowledge about birth and death. Neither Margaret Laurence's stepmother nor Eudora Welty's mother could bring themselves to speak openly and clearly about childbirth. Their daughters had to find their own way to the necessary information. Nor are Laurence's *Dance on the Earth* and Welty's charming *One Writer's Beginnings* any more open and clear as guides to young writers. Both works are full of covert messages that demand skilful interpretation and decoding. Maternal discourse, I concluded, is a very convoluted process. Instead of being straightforward and helpful, it is riddled with anxiety, fear, denial and repression. It can be downright obstructive for one main reason: mothers know that gaining life experience is a very dangerous process, and their instinct is to protect their daughters from it at all costs.

I often evoked Virginia Woolf's famous remark that "before a woman can become a writer, she must kill the Angel in the House." Woolf's formidable being, who "would have plucked the heart out of my writing," bears a strong resemblance to Julia Stephens, her own biological mother. As a writer reading those words, I identified with the daughter.

Now as I studied Emily's stories in their entirety and subjected them to close readings, one fact was unavoidable:

it was I who was the repressive mother. To find myself thus
embalmed was an unsettling revelation, to say the least.

When she was a teenager, Emily had been dismayed
at finding what she thought were versions of herself in my
work. In "Private Eye," a runaway daughter says of her
mother:

> Before I left, she was working on a collection
> of short stories. *Mishaps* it was called. I found
> myself in several of the stories, transparently
> veiled by a different name. I bet she was spin-
> ning a story this very minute, and I would get
> caught in a mishap like a black fly.

Now, the tables were turned. I found myself in many of
her stories, transparently veiled by a different name. In
some stories that she spun, I was caught like a black fly—
a forbidding figure indeed.

In "Fast Food Families" (as yet unpublished), she
describes a girl who has a part-time job at a gas station,
while taking university courses in drama. Eventually, to her
mother's horror, she decides to become a full-time employee
at the gas station:

> "Carmen," her mother said, "if you're going to
> devote yourself to full-time work, why don't
> you find something more challenging? A gas
> station is hardly an ideal place. You're intelli-
> gent and reliable and you DO have skills."

"Why not a library?" her mother pleaded. "Why don't you apply to the Regina Public Library or the University Bookstore? I could put a word in for you, I know Esther who runs it. And there's always the Globe Theatre, you DO have theatre experience."

"Mom," said Carmen, as though she was addressing a small child, "jobs are hard to get, almost impossible, that's the reason I got robbed. Money's scarce. I hate to burst your bubble." She could almost hear her mother's bubble bursting.

As often happened, this particular story opened a door onto a vivid scene from my past. It brought back those Saturday afternoons in Regina when I went downtown shopping. After riding the bus back home, I would get off the bus and sit on the curbside so that I could see Emily in Neighbours, the convenience store/gas station where she worked. Sometimes the bus stopped outside, while the driver ran in to grab a cup of coffee.

It made me smile to see Emily behind the counter in her uniform, so pretty and animated with her long dark hair and broad smile, bantering with the motley array of characters who frequented the store—characters whose stories she regaled us with when she came over to dinner. But simultaneously I felt a great pang of anxiety. Working in a convenience store, living in a rundown apartment, taking university courses haphazardly and spending her evenings in the notorious Plains Hotel was not the life I had planned for my talented daughter. "Where will it end?" I asked myself in alarm, as I imagined all kinds of disasters. Already there had been a holdup at the store while she was behind the counter. I had assumed that she would get a traditional education, progressing smoothly from undergraduate to graduate work and to a career that would be safe and financially secure. It was a huge disappointment to me that she balked at that route.

Yet, as I read her stories, it became clear that the path she carved out for herself was the one that best equipped her for her vocation. That fact was dramatized by the use she made of her stint at the gas station in her one-act play *Shop Talk* (a winner in a 1992 *Grain* competition) and in her stories "Asphalt Angel" and "Fast Food Families." It yielded far richer material than a traditional middle-class job would have done. Quite simply, if she had taken my advice instead of rejecting it, it would have plucked the heart out of her writing.

Emily wrote with a poet's sensibility, creating fictions that work through a rich texture of figurative language. Within the story, she elaborates on the image of "fast food families":

> . . . a lot of people had the same attitude towards families. People like Ingrid and herself who ran away from home at an early age. They picked up surrogate family members wherever they went, in the same

way you'd pick up an order of fries. They enjoyed working at the kind of place where people were emotionally needy, but in a mature kind of way. Their emotional need had matured, so it was now deeply disguised. Their need was like good pastry; it was made with real butter, it had to be refrigerated and left at room temperature. That way, when rolled out, it wouldn't crack. . . .

Whereas Carmen harboured the concept of fast food families, the rest of her fast food family regarded their family ties in terms of a jail sentence. Somewhere along the line, she became considered a Lifer.

Fast food is contrasted by implication with the home-cooked variety, wholesome and nutritious, consumed around a table that is a permanent fixture, always ready for children to come home to. But those who sit down to home cooking bring plenty of ancestral baggage to the table—memories of old conflicts, grudges and rivalries, waiting to be reactivated.

In the final paragraph of "Fast Food Families," Carmen not only defies her mother's advice and takes a full-time position at the gas station, but she simultaneously abandons her drama courses.

"Samuel Beckett, Eugene O'Neill, Sophocles would have to wait." For the time being, she has become "A Lifer." Choosing life experience over upwardly mobile jobs and academic studies.

Taken as a whole, Emily's stories form a *kunstlerroman*, a novel that traces the awakening and development of an artist. "Fast Food Families" records a necessary first step in her development.

What astonishes me as I look back is that I should have been so slow to comprehend her needs. I know well that writers rarely live like everybody else, and that if they do, they generally pay a high artistic price for doing so. As Katherine Anne Porter said, "What I find most dreadful among the young artists is this tendency to middle-classness—this idea that they have to get married and have lots of children and live just like everybody else." Being a critic and being a parent are two different, possibly incompatible, roles.

Fortunately, in the last years of Emily's life, our relationship evolved from a parent/child one into that of writing colleagues—she at the beginning of her career, I at the end of mine. Letters and books flew between us, and we wrote e-mails, often daily. We could make light of our dovetailing fictions—hers describing a runaway daughter (imaginary, thank godness), and mine the mother of a runaway. She dubbed this habit of addressing each other obliquely through our fictions our "bizarre conversation."

One day, I was particularly impressed by her critique of the novel I was working on. The thought struck me that she really was an astute reader, and that she was going to be a very good writer. That thought was quickly followed by another—that when she was successful, I would not be around to enjoy her achievement. Quite spontaneously, I added a note to the letter I was writing:

> I can't tell you how much it means to me to
> know that you have turned into such an
> accomplished intelligent writer, full—it seems
> to me—of maturity about your work and full
> of wisdom about writing and with your own
> distinctive vision and sort of inner centre to it.

When I walked into her bedroom in Halifax on that
July day, I found that she had torn this note jaggedly from
the letter and placed it on her desk.

I was pleased to think that I had put into words the
approval that must have seemed to her a long time coming.
But I was also pained that the paragraph was so short—a
mere note at the end of a longer letter. There was so much
else to say. I should have said how wrong I was to try to
guide her along a traditional course, to urge middle-class
stability and financial security, when she had such a sure
sense of her vocation.

Sometimes I find consolation in thinking that the tension
generated by my maternal anxiety constituted a necessary part of her creative process, for that tension is the moti-
vating force behind several stories. And writers are produced
more often by the forces they resist and the conditions they
oppose than by favourable circumstances.

Another consolation is that most of what I wish I had
said had already been expressed in our conversations, letters
and the "bizarre conversation" of our fictions. She would
have taken special note of the paragraph at the end of my

story "In the Garden of Henry James." Here, a woman who has taken her elderly mother on an excursion to Lamb House in Rye thinks of destructive relationships within the James family and meditates on the relationship with her own distant daughter:

> She fills the kettle, thinking of Rifka, yearning to write her a letter. "Dear Inconnue . . ." she will begin. She will speak of families and their capacity to inflict deadly wounds on each other; of their blindness to one another's needs; of their congenital weaknesses of temperament and character flaws; of their shared susceptibility to the same physical diseases; of the impossibility of ever breaking the bonds that link them. She will say that the abuses are hidden in a past so remote that they are beyond human comprehension and she will urge the needs of the present . . . . She pauses, wondering what to say next. In any case, it doesn't matter for it is all unspeakable.

Today, as I recall my friend's words of warning about the pain involved in editing Emily's stories, I see that I embarked on an even longer and more difficult journey than she had predicted. It was a journey that did not exorcise grief; if anything, it exacerbated it. I might have known that it would do that, but we all expect too much in the way of easy consolation and quick healing.

In the event, I had no choice in the matter, for bringing Emily's fiction into the world was the only way I had to honour her life and her work, and to help her achieve what every writer most desires, which is to be read and to be remembered. In doing so, I added a final chapter (or a sad footnote) to my own work, and gained a deeper, more personal knowledge of my subject matter. Perhaps gaining a little wisdom from a grievous loss is the most any of us can hope for.

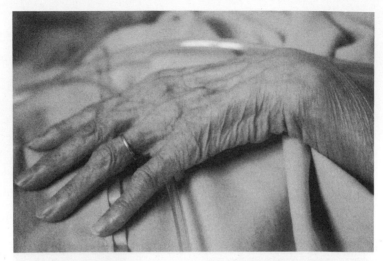

Naoe Kiyokawa (above) and Tiger Goto

WITHOUT

WORDS

By Hiromi Goto

Oba-chan was the one who raised me and my sisters while my mother and father worked immigrant-farmer hours, until we grew up, one by one, and eagerly left home as soon as we graduated high school. My mother and father continued working under an umbrella of debt, until my father's final year and a half with cancer, when he finally got to stop working. My grandmother's last two years were spent mostly in her bed. She did not like the radio and she did not want to listen to music. She did not want a television. She sat in the quiet of her room, hour after hour. Day after day, night after night. When I visited, there was not much conversation. She wanted company, but she also found it tiring. Oba-chan wanted something that I did not know how to provide. When it was time to leave, she always said, *Now it will be lonelier again.*

Sometimes I promised I would be back soon.

Sometimes I spoke crossly.

During what was to be her last summer, I lived with her in the trailer with my two children. She called out, all the time, night and day. How her voice carried, coming from such a wizened body.

Have you left, then? she would shout, every time she managed to shuffle to the bathroom. All day and all night long. My heart would bulge to my throat. Eyes blinking with fear in the darkness. Followed swiftly by impatience, annoyance, exhaustion, every two to three hours. *Have you left, then?* she shouted, a refrain, a skipping record of loneliness.

One time it was so bad that I drove in the middle of the night the 32 kilometres from Nanton to Claresholm so that I could see their facilities for patients with dementia. I lurked outside the hospital for a few moments, the engine running. I drove back without entering the building.

When the community nurse came to check on my grandmother that week, I asked her what it was like in Claresholm. She said that our grandmother had good care at home.

My Oba-chan died in mid-January 2005.

Some people carry guilt like a dead albatross. Some

people tattoo guilt all over their bodies. Some people carry guilt inside them as if it is cancer.

Often people conflate regret with mourning.

———

My father died in late November that same year.

I find it difficult to imagine any immigrant farmer, anywhere, to be a lazy person. Lazy immigrant farmers must exist, but I've never seen one and I suppose that their laziness would result in their inability to continue farming. Therefore, lazy immigrant farmers can't exist for very long.

Cancer allowed my father to retire.

Cancer made my father finally stop drinking.

I was thankful to cancer for finally allowing me to have a sober father. I was furious at my father for only stopping his drink for cancer, not for his own family. Cancer gave me something and took it away at the same time. Cancer fucked me up.

My family's tragicomedy is of epic proportions, with enormous dramatic potential: immigration, drinking, fortitude, madness, crushing farm debt, moments of symphonic exuberance and joie de vivre that invariably plummets into a great abyss. Think *East of Eden* meets *Otoko Wa Tsurai Yo* meets *Gone with the Wind* meets *Leolo* meets *Little House on the Prairie* meets *Gilligan's Island*. I'm sure that I could pitch the arc to NHK in Japan and they would love it. I would be a story consultant for their autumn TV drama series, making riches out of my family's personal tragedies. Let someone gain from these experiences, if not emotionally, then at least financially.

But it will not be me.

I am an asshole like my father before me. But I am not completely insensitive.

————

I don't know when the mourning began ("the mourning" sounds so contained . . . as if it has distinct edges); I think it was, at first, inert. I like to imagine myself as practical and efficient and consciously and subconsciously model my behaviour on my Oba-chan's before me. After the deaths of my grandmother and father, I carried on. The children needed to be fed, the groceries bought, the house insured, and the summer turned into autumn. They were dead. They were gone. We all die someday, I told myself.

Somehow, because my Oba-chan was ninety-four when she died, it doesn't seem such an unbearable thing. (Though I feel guilty about contributing to her life of labour, all those clothes and dishes she washed for a family of seven. The basketball, volleyball, softball uniforms always perfect for each game, folded and left in dresser drawers, all those stained socks scrubbed out by hand. My Oba-chan pressed my jeans flat beneath her mattress during the night. Her labour continued even while she slept.) My Oba-chan lived a long and labour-filled immigrant farmer's life, and I wish I knew then what I know now; then it would have been not such a difficult thing to have lived with her the last two years of her life.

What are two years to eighty years of hard labour?

Understanding is staggered. The trick of timing. Like a poorly written time-travel narrative with ends never meeting.

I will never be able to scroll back to that moment—the moment that asked for something that I could not give. It is only now that I see what it is I could have done, and I would most happily do it, but the recognition is too late. This is the dead end of understanding and restitution. In the darkness, in the incessant rain, this conundrum is enough to drive me insane.

I laugh, instead.

I was never one for self-help. I mean, I believe in helping myself, but I don't like the manuals and the chirpy cheerleader tone they often resort to. I don't like to be told what to do, I never have, and I don't like people who are making money out of other people's desperation. Too many improvement narratives have a step program, a technique, a game plan, a mapped journey, all leading to acceptance and growth, when all I want is two fingers of Bombay gin on the rocks with a twist of lime.

I have an X-ray of my father's liver. I feel an attachment to it, his liver, mine, how "live" resides inside the organ, the "r" modifying the quality of life. The liver has the capacity to regenerate. If there are enough healthy parts remaining, the liver will come back. Not like pieces of my broken heart. The liver wants to live more than anything else.

He was only sixty-seven years old.

"What a waste," my father said. "All those years of paying CPP."

Was he thinking of all of the books he could have bought? If he had known he would die before earning back his pension, would he not have bothered making the payments to support the retirement he would never have? Would he have bought more whisky instead? This crazy-making line of thought was more than I could bear. I turned away from the impossible question and poured myself a dirty gin martini.

At the hospital, when my father still had energy enough to walk to the washroom while leaning on my arm, he turned towards me.

"I've given you more research material for your writing," he said, a statement of fact.

I thought for a few long seconds. "Thank you," I said, "for this new experience from which I learn."

I meant it, and I think my answer satisfied him somehow.

I'm learning, still.

———

Was it mourning?

Look, my father could be a complete asshole and a sexist jerk-off. His sexism was worn down only by four strong-willed daughters. "Boys don't cry!" he barked at his crying toddler grandson.

I glared at Oto-san and he caught my look with the corner of his eyes. "Nor do girls," he added hastily, to neutralize the damage.

My father was sexist and misogynist, but he was also funny and introspective and had a dreamer's heart. He introduced me to Sasquatch and Stonehenge, kappa and ghosts, tanuki, UFOs and 007. I could talk to him about ideas and he could follow the fanciful thread. He showed me the beauty and humour of the absurd. He was absurd. He could be counted on to laugh when the night was dark and long and there were five more hours of immigrant-farmer work left before we could go home to bed. He'd be the one whistling, the one I'd want with me if I were stuck in a gulag.

What were the words to mark my way through the heart's terrain? My liver was missing and it was so difficult to decide between the jumbo bottle of gin or the one a size smaller. Everything was symbolic. I turned the mundane into ritual. Drinking from my father's cup, I didn't wish my father's death for myself, for my children to witness.

Disengagement, depression, denial. At the age of forty I had my first nervous breakdown, eleven months after my father's death. (I worry about saying *first* because I feel as if I'm setting myself up for a second and third. But I want to qualify that it was my first, because the first one is such a surprise. A holy-shit-it-can-happen-to-me moment I had never imagined I would experience.)

I couldn't sleep. Every time I tried to eat, foul oil coated my tongue, and the smell of the morning coffee turned into the smell of dog shit. I lost 20 pounds in eight weeks without exercising. I kept drinking water, but I was always thirsty. Cold. Always cold. My mind jittered and jabbed like fleas and knives, and I didn't know who I was anymore, what was going on inside my mind/heart. I felt as if I was going to fly apart.

"I'm not myself," I told my family and my friends. This was entirely true, yet it didn't begin to describe how I felt. I cried (oh-me-who-had-prided-myself-on-being-strong), I cried, I jittered in bed, the cold air whistling, my heart bulging, too much, too much, I couldn't take it anymore. Should I be in a hospital I wondered how do I know I don't know anything anymore should I be in a hospital I wondered how do I know I'm not myself and I'm trying to assess myself but I'm not myself how can I know?

But I knew enough to know that I didn't want to be given drugs.

I shivered and twisted, fearful and icy, inside my bed for many days. A sister and friends told me to go see my family physician. This was good advice that I listened to after several weeks had passed. My doctor was kind, and I filled out a questionnaire, and I was obviously not myself because I considered the rate-on-the-scale-of question with undue care when I hate these kinds of tests as much as I ridicule multiple-choice measures of immeasurable things. My doctor asked what I thought of medication. I said I preferred not to be medicated, and she said she agreed, and she told me about counselling services through Family Services. When I was able to phone Family Services, intake asked me more questions to assess my condition. It was government-funded budget counselling for people who couldn't afford to go private, and there is always a waiting list.

"Are you in crisis?" intake asked me, and I pondered the question slowly.

Crisis, I thought. Crisis.

What does she mean by crisis?

In my family, "crisis" meant practically dead. If someone had chopped off your arm with an axe and the stump was spurting blood, you could call it a crisis . . .

I looked inward and tried to measure my mental and emotional state:

Would I end it all? Would I jump off the Alex Fraser Bridge into the foul brown waters of the river (I thought that from the driver's perspective the lines and span of the Alex were more lovely than the Lions Gate Bridge, though Lions had the better view and possibly cleaner waters . . . I had thought of the bridges before, and wondered which would be the better platform for this kind of death. The graceful lines of the Alex or the promise of the open sea with Lions? Would wondering about something like this fall under ideation, and, therefore, crisis?)

———

No.

No, I would not.

Someone else might be ready to jump off the bridges, but it wasn't me.

No, I said, a sinking feeling in my heart. No, I'm not in crisis.

It was close to a year before there was a counsellor

who could see me. There was something of me left intact, because sometimes I thought it was funny.

———

I thought I would be the last person in the world unable to cope. How does a person know where to place the dividing line between mourning and exhaustion? Afterwards, I read that life-altering events can trigger depression. It wasn't as if my father and grandmother died and my life collapsed the moment after the funeral. Winter turned to spring and the summer led into an autumn that was a particularly economically pinched time. I was in my first motorcycle accident. I was running out of income and there was nothing on the horizon. The "check engine" light in the car kept on flashing, but I didn't have the money to get it fixed, so I was anxious every time I drove the vehicle. I had spent half a year struggling with the school system to advocate for my child's education. Someone broke in to the house while we were sleeping. I had written one hundred new pages of a choked novel manuscript, and I adopted a neurotic dog from the SPCA, thinking that he would at least bark if another intruder came into the house. These are some of the many things that added to my burnout. (The dog never barked at people. Only at the birds, the moon, bright stars, other dogs and evil squirrels. It would have been hilarious if everything else hadn't finally broken my spirit.)

All these crises were just manifestations of your

repressed mourning, some people might say. Does it matter what we call it?

The body grows tired. The mind grows weary.

The world is full of sharp edges and noises, and I couldn't bear it anymore. I desperately needed a cocoon, a cushion of soft stillness to absorb the barrage of worries and responsibilities and the pain of being alive. I couldn't bear the eyes of strangers. I couldn't cope with one harsh word. A tone pitched with the slightest edge drove me to my bed for three days. I wore a toque with earflaps, as well as earplugs to block the cutting edge of noise. Life was noisy. And I finally understood why some boys and girls wore toques indoors, in malls and in schools, probably even inside their bedrooms.

I was over the worst of my depression when I finally got into budget counselling. I got through the darkness with the support of family and friends.

———

Listen. Let me tell you. It can happen to you. It's okay. Even in our privileged lives, where we go through our days without the fear of exploding bombs or uniformed men breaking down our doors to whisk us away into the night, we can grow weary. Something deep inside us might break.

Listen. Let me tell you. When they ask if it's a crisis, say yes.

———

After my father died, I somehow felt compelled to scroll back through my childhood memories, the scanty ones that remained, to try to understand something that I think I might have missed. I spent hours on the computer, day after day, week after week, month after month. I googled grief, mourning, sadness, depression, good news, happy news, liver, love . . . ducked through blogs and websites and personal testimonials. I could relate to some of the stories that I read, but the spelling mistakes and slaughtered grammar on many of the sites also drove me insane.

I was suffering, but I was also a snob. I wanted to grieve with a certain level of literacy, with analogy and metaphor used in original and poetic ways. I wanted some helpful beacons along the uncharted terrain, but without the help of the good Lord(!) Jesus. I didn't want to inhabit cliché.

Let not my grief fall into cliché, I prayed.

I couldn't stop checking my email.

Get mail, I pressed. I was waiting for an important message that I needed very much to read.

Get mail, I pressed. Get mail. Get mail. Get mail. Get mail. Get mail. Get mail.

I was waiting for a message that would never arrive. I knew this, somewhere, inside my heart, but my liver would not accept it.

Get mail, I pressed.

Get mail, I beseeched.

Get mail.

The days stuttered with the routines of work, school, driving. Meals, dishes, laundry, dog, the body's reflexes of food and organic processes. Hibernation was what I longed for. Without the clatter and clamour of my children, who still needed me; it mattered little to them that I was a daughter without a parent. A girl without her grandmother. They do not really need to know this until I or their father dies, and then they will understand, the understanding, always staggered, a trick of time. Timing.

My bedroom was never warm enough. It is located above the carport, so that the cold winter air is beneath me all night long. Use a space heater, a dear friend advised. The cold is not good for you. Light a candle, she said. When you feel alone and afraid, burn a candle and the flame will remind you of bright things, it will provide warmth and hope.

The sheath of fire flickered in the night. I stared at the moving light. The impermanence. It burned and gave off a warm yellow glow. It also cast shadows upon the walls that writhed and shivered when the furnace kicked in. The light reassured just as surely as the shadows disturbed. That was the double gift of light.

This is the double gift of life.

––––––

Being a full-time writer is an economically unstable existence. Sometimes when I'm travelling, staying in hotels, drinking overpriced gin in dark and sexy lounges with my writer friends and I'm drunk and it all feels so very fine, a tiny part of my mind, the sober part, wonders at the disparity between the cycles of frugality and the moments of privilege. I am grateful for the travelling that my writing has afforded; I can't imagine having travelled to all of the countries I have been to without having been a writer. But the daily life of most writers in Canada is not a tale of economic bounty. Most of the bounty the writers measure is not on a financial scale.

I spend carefully, and, yes, with a certain amount of economic privilege, like a car and a mortgage that my ex-spouse and I have worked very hard to maintain for ourselves and the children. I understand, with the sensibilities of an immigrant farmer, the importance of working for the things I have, and I try to teach the children to be frugal but generous. Hard-working and playful. To enjoy their lives as well as apply themselves to making their way in a challenging world.

I approach my expenses with thought and care, such as choosing a lunch with a dear friend over a new pair of jeans. I don't need new boots every autumn just because the style has changed and people are wearing suede mukluks (in temperate rain forest country?!). I hang wet laundry instead of using the dryer (and it is also better for the environment and the longevity of the wardrobe!), turn down the heat and wear a housecoat, periodically force the family to eat everything in the freezer (thawed and cooked!) before buying new groceries. I make sure, though, that the groceries I buy are fresh and the best. Organic milk, free-range eggs, endives and occasionally prosciutto. Black cod, caplins, mackerel, extra-lean slices of beef. Asparagus, hakusai, arugula and gai lan. Organic tofu, apple pears, honey tangerines, avocados and Asiago. "We might not be rich," my mother always said, "but we eat well." This refrain has stuck to me, lodged inside my belly. My family and I eat well, and no one will take this away from us. I still go dining at restaurants, and sometimes I will buy cut flowers. But I am always careful; I am always thinking about my budget.

I stockpile undeveloped film because there is no rush to see the photos and it is a non-essential expense. Five, six, seven rolls will be on the bookshelf, waiting for the flush day when my income level rises. Tidal.

After depositing a much-needed cheque, I was finally able to take those films to London Drugs. I couldn't remember what was on them; they'd been on the shelves for months and months. I rubbed the dust off against my jeans and dropped the little canisters into my shoulder bag.

———

I opened the packets, the glossy colour photos brilliant in my hands.

I sank onto the bench at the mall. My eyes grew warm and wet with joy-sadness.

Photos of my father. In his straw hat. Photos of my father reading a book. He is watching a film, arms crossed and scowling. He sits with his arms tucked in his waistband, an odd habit that made him look like a perv when he really wasn't. He is posing in front of his house with his grandchildren grown big but not yet adults. My father's eyes are strained with the knowledge of impending death, edged with pain, both physical and existential.

And Oba-chan.

She is there.

In her narrow bed, in her narrow room, frail and alive. She looks so vulnerable, her eyes dark and, yes, childlike. Close-up photos I took of her hands, beautiful and transparent with age. Alive but so near to death. The cells, the pigment, caught on Fujifilm and developed by London Drugs. The moment, mundane, and oh-so-miraculous.

Oba-chan and my father were in my hands. A trick of timing, a life staggered, and suddenly I was allowed new images of them long after they were gone. They had come back for a surprise visit, and I could scarcely believe my fortune.

I stared and stared, lips slightly parted, partly a laugh and partly a cry.

Take photos of them, I wanted to shout aloud, to everyone in the mall who walked past me for a five-second frame of life. Don't use a digital camera. Digital is so blithely erased, so casually downloaded and altered on software. The tangible world needs more time to become significant. Take photos of them, then save the films for later. Be frugal. Forget that you took the photos.

How sweet the later.

———

I think I heard one of Philip K. Dick's children being interviewed on radio. (Philip K. was a prescient, intelligent and quirky American science-fiction writer. Many of his stories have been turned into seminal SF films, and as in all sad time-travel narratives, he died before they were filmed; he was broke for most of his life.) Or maybe the interviewer was talking to an interviewee who knew a great deal about Dick's life. Memory is inexact and subjective . . . and I'm no longer certain. In the interview, his daughter related (if we can set aside my relative lack of certainty around the irrefutability of detailed memories) the story that Philip K. left messages for his children to be read after his death. He wrote fatherly letters to his children because he knew that they would need something from him. He made preparations for their future needs.

Not long after our father's death, one of my sisters disclosed that she wished our father had left us letters. At that time I was feeling practical, I was in the mode of Life Applications and Organized Thinking. I don't feel the same way, I said, quite matter-of-factly. I don't feel like there's something more I wished I had.

I'm not so certain these days.

When I am out in public spaces, in Chinatown, the Nikkei Centre, Richmond, the public libraries, the malls and Hong Kong–style restaurants, I catch myself looking at people who would be the age of my father and grandmother before they died. (Funny, they are frozen in time now, and if I love my liver and treat it kindly, then at a certain point I will be older than my own father.)

I look at fragile faces, skin pale and delicate with age. The gaunt bones of their hands. The high brow and particular slant of cheekbones. In a gesture, a glance across a crowded room. They flit in the corners of my eyes.

I look at older men with interest and compassion, with a certain longing. (Stay away, W.P.! I don't mean you! Nor you, either, Woody Allen! I don't mean that kind of longing!) I don't know if I'm looking for anyone who resembles my father or if I'm looking for someone my father could never have been.

Maybe part of the mourning has to do with identifying the things I really wanted and didn't receive.

———

Almost three and a half years have passed since my father's and grandmother's deaths, and I have moved through pain and hollow into a new vocabulary. I am birthed a middle-aged woman. I cannot say that I am a completely new person. Perhaps my grammar has changed.

I am a little closer to death.

Somehow the idea seems oddly reassuring. Not that I am depressed and sad and weary of life. In fact, after a year of budget counselling, I feel that I see more clearly than I have ever done before. I am making sure I have time for fun, and in my practical way I am pursuing moments of joy with the same immigrant-farmer determination with which I pursued my writing practice. Maybe the idea of death is reassuring because that is where my foundational grandmother and my larger-than-life father have gone, and their absence from my life and their entry into death take a measure of familiarity with them.

———

The times when I have felt their absence most keenly I have found small consolation in the knowledge that they are always present with me. Not in the spiritual sense (though I carry a small non-scientific faith that this is so), but that a part of them is deeply entwined within my DNA and nothing can take that away. In more fanciful moments I have imagined winnowing the 25 percent of my grandmother out of me and my three sisters and reconstructing her . . . but I can just see her slowly shaking her head. She would not think it's a good idea.

———

I am given my coupon for my time-travel narrative. I clutch the precious ticket and thrust it into my pocket so I will not lose it. I rub the little yellow rectangle between my thumb and forefinger, worry the rough perforated edges . . .

You may travel back in time, I am told, but no one will see you.

Good, I think. That's a good thing!

No one will hear you. You cannot alter the past.

Yes, I understand. Time-travel paradox, etc. It's all very complicated. I won't touch or break a thing.

It's a one-way ticket.

My heartbeat is overloud in my ears.

You can't come back, they explain gently.

Hot blood surges up my neck. My face is hot, pressure growing in my head. What's the point, then! I just want to see them again! I just want to really see them, because I know what it's like not to be able to. Who would go back if that's the deal! There'd be no point.

Many people accept these limitations, they say.

My hands are tight fists inside my pockets. The coupon is crushed and wet with sweat. Please, I beg.

One-way passage. Next.

There is someone behind me. There is a lineup. Move on, the woman behind me says. She gives the small of my back a little push.

I can hardly feel her touch.

She wants to go back so badly she is already on her way before submitting her coupon, stepping through the portal.

I blink and blink.

And step to the side. The lineup shuffles past me.

The children need to be fed and we're out of organic milk and we need more apples. Tonight I will grill mackerel dusted with coarse salt. I will light candles in front of my Oba-chan's and Oto-san's altar. I will pour them hot sake into little cups. I will burn incense, and the slight musty and bittersweet smoke will curl upward and disappear.

———

Things that helped:

1) Counselling. Go before the nervous breakdown. But if you don't, better late than never. Just go.

2) Music that nourishes your spirit. Jacques Loussier Trio's *Satie, Gymnopedies/Gnossienes* and *The Essential Dave Brubeck* have helped me stay connected to my feelings without intellect getting in the way (the absence of lyrics was key).

3) Hydrotherapy, i.e., swimming, Jacuzzi, sauna, has had enormous impact upon my sense of well-being. (Thank you, Ayumi, for forcing me to go when I was floppy.)

4) Care for yourself as you would like to be able to do for the one who is gone.

5) Ask for help.

6) Accept help.

Things to avoid:

1) Any major life changes, such as moving house, etc.

2) Adopting a neurotic dog.

3) Benders.

Clyde Bruce Jackson

JUST

CREMATION

By Marni Jackson

The director of Just Cremation was vacuuming when I happened by. It wouldn't do to have dusty surfaces in this line of work. The shop was a small storefront affair, handily across from the Egertson Funeral Home, where my father now reposed—or so I thought.

"I'll be right with you," the director said. He had large, liquid brown eyes. I sat down in one of two winged Victorian armchairs that faced his gilt-edged desk, furnished with a leatherette desk blotter and a faux-granite pen set, and took one of his business cards. *Armand Alazzi.* A Lebanese or Armenian name, still unusual for the small lakeside town in southern Ontario where I had grown up without encountering a single dark-skinned person. But cremation was the sort of necessary, hidden and slightly janitorial job that someone named Alazzi could expect to do well with in Burlington. The director had a full brushlike moustache and smooth, thick, springy hair. He directed an apologetic smile at me as he moved the vacuum back and forth over the broadloom, and we shared its high-pitched, indignant noise.

For years my mother had made it clear that no funeral service, no fuss, was to be made of their deaths. Always in the plural; having done everything together for sixty-eight years, they assumed they would die together too. It would be like the two of them finding a parking spot at the mall—she was the spotter, he was the driver. Whenever I came home to visit, my father would open the bottom drawer of his mahogany pull-down desk to point to "the arrangements," as he always called them, filed inside a brochure from the funeral home.

"You only need to make one phone call. Call Egertson's, and they'll take care of everything." In case we couldn't or wouldn't open the brochure, he had written the phone number, using his engineer's mechanical pencil, on the front, under the little drawing of the funeral home, Burlington's oldest. He knew that tidy business arrangements and planning for the future were not our forte.

"I don't want any strangers gawking at me," my mother would always add at that point. She had a horror of funerals with an open casket, and of trays of crustless sandwiches passed among the curious. She had already embarked on a course of electrolysis because, as she put it, "I don't want to have a stroke and be lying in some hospital bed with hairs sprouting out of my face."

"Just send us up the chimney and come home and have a glass of sherry," she would say with a kind of gay irritability whenever we tried to protest that the three of us would at least want to get together with family friends afterwards. She had bad memories of funerals when she was growing up in Saskatoon, where they were considered a social event and an occasion to gossip. But now that some of my friends were being picked off by cancer or suicide, I began to find the conventions of funerals reassuring. Someone thought to make sandwiches, someone could be counted on to say the wrong thing, so-and-so would get drunk and stay too long—it all kept you clasped in the present. The mundanity of funerals said that life with its pots of tea and mixed motives would go on.

But burning a person, it turned out, was not as simple as a phone call. There were laws about human remains, and the question of scattering or interment, and then the business of what to put the ashes in, and who in the family would keep them. As murderers and widows come to learn, it takes surprising enterprise and a certain amount of work to truly rid yourself of the body.

I think my mother was in shock. My father died in a matter of minutes, slipping to the floor of the bathroom with a gastric hemorrhage—the result, we suspected, of the drugs he had been prescribed for an arthritic shoulder. He was ninety-four. He had just driven my mother to Sears, to pay a bill—he liked to pay in person. He had been weak for a number of days, and had asked my mother to cook a steak and potatoes for dinner—no more tinned salmon, he said. So my mother bought the groceries, and when they got home, she said, "Oh, let's have a drink." Because of his medication, they hadn't been enjoying their usual pre-dinner cocktail. My mother poured him a weak gin collins and went into the kitchen to prepare dinner. She heard him go into the bathroom, and the door close. Then the sound of him falling. She rushed in to him.

As she put a pillow under his head, waiting for the ambulance, he looked up at her, and his eyes widened; she knew he knew it was goodbye, and by the time the para-medics came he was dead.

———

That my father would leave her side forever and ever, just as a hot dinner was about to be served, was not something my mother could quickly grasp. So instead of weeping and falling apart, she applied herself to the immediate practical problem—the recipe, as it were, for her husband's ashes. It was like a casserole: first, we had to choose the appropriate vessel. So my mother and I undertook a potential-urn tour of the house.

The hand-painted porcelain jar brought back from Asia by their first grandson, Jake? Lovely, but not my father.

We fingered the crystal candy dish that always sat on the living-room coffee table. He would fish salted peanuts out of it as he passed by, popping them into his mouth with a kind of exaggerated, faintly theatrical aplomb. He did many things with a jaunty flourish, like a man signing a painting. He was an artist, at one time, a gifted cartoonist. He was a good whistler.

Onward with the urn tour. Gripping both banisters, my eighty-nine-year-old mother laboured down the basement stairs and we opened the door to the cobwebby fruit cellar, with its lone bulb. This is where my mother's old ceramic creations—bowls, cups and clay figures—were kept, along with Mason jars, ancient flashlights, fondue pots and broken-handled Christmas baskets. She had made a number of ceramic cherubs out of clay, which she eventually sprayed gold, to use as Christmas accessories. These lounged pudgily on the shelves. We stared into the past as cold cellar air flowed off the objects and over us.

"I suppose a Mason jar wouldn't do," my mother said with the blend of annoyance and gloom that her husband's bolting through the door on his own had caused her. With trembling hands—not just from grief but from an "essential tremor," her doctor called it—she fiddled with pitchers, jars and vases, some of them droopy or misshapen, others marbled and swirling with cracked glazes. We began trying stray lids on different receptacles.

"A lot of these were experiments," she said, picking up a large ceramic pea pod, one of my favourites, quite clitoral in aspect. She took down a tall cylindrical vase, bevelled like a banister, with a free-form blue and green and white glaze. The mouth of it was a bit asymmetrical, but it had a certain verve and energy. Zero pomp, though. It didn't in the slightest resemble a funeral urn.

"This could work," I said, sighting down it in a professional way, as if I had become an expert in funeral urns. "But it has no lid."

"Oh, do we need a lid?" my mother said querulously. "They wouldn't give it to us loose, surely."

"What if it falls off the mantel? And you don't want to depend on some inner plastic liner, like a box of cereal," I said. We gazed glumly at the shelf of jars.

"We can improvise a lid, don't worry." I sensed my mother's formidable imagination rallying to the challenge.

"I think this vase is perfect," I said to her firmly. "It's something you made, and he'll be there inside it, just like he lived inside the home you created."

Relieved to have this decision over when so much daunting business—banks and wills and lawyers and pensions—lay ahead of her, my mother closed the fruit-cellar door and made her way back up to the kitchen. I brought up a broken basket full of lid candidates—clear glass ones with handles, a woven one, an array of orphaned stoppers.

"This could work," I said brightly as I stretched two wide blue elastic bands around a glass lid, so that it snugged down into the off-kilter mouth of the vase. We looked at it and knew that my engineer father would not approve of such feminine, hairpin jerry-rigging. We needed the proper equipment here. An ill-fitting lid would be an insult to his whole meticulously lived life. And yet . . . the non-regulation, the amusing, improvised lid was a Jackson thing too.

"Leave it with me," I said. "I'll zip off to the craft store right now and find the makings of a perfect lid." On the second day after my father's death, this project filled me with a little crest of usefulness, of dad-like ingenuity. My mother, her mouth drawn down in the bitterness of being left alone—he had died so secretively, in the bathroom, while she was cooking steak and potatoes for his dinner—laboured into the den and poured a glass of sherry.

I drove to the craft store, a vast warehouse of buttons and wires patronized by industrious, well-cared-for, unhappy people who haunted the aisles looking for meaning. I toyed with asking a clerk for help—*What do you have that would make an appropriate seal for a crooked-mouthed cremation urn?*—but what if I wept? I made my own way down the aisles. So many potential things in the craft store, so many unborn ideas. Objects about to be made, not burnt or buried. I considered using a layer of hot melted wax, the kind used for sealing preserves, to seal the urn. Or whittling squares of cork flooring into a thick plug. But a cork in an urn seemed too insouciant, like a flagon of picnic wine. At last I settled on some thin, round plywood discs that were the right diameter; I had the vase with me in a plastic bag and tried them out surreptitiously. Close. I could sandpaper them into shape. Then I went searching for paint in a French blue that would match the glaze on the jar. I bought a small brush, and a bottle of glue to stick four or five of the discs together. All this gave me a kind of handle—or a lid—on the situation at hand, of losing my father.

My sister is better at crafts and so she took the materials home, assembled them into a lid, painted it and even added the decorative knob that I had impulsively bought as well. But she welded together all the lids, and in the end the lid was a few centimetres too thick. It rose above the lips of the vase, as if something was bubbling up within. But my mother was happy with the choice of vase, so we went with it. I put the vase and lid in a plastic shopping bag and drove down to Just Cremation to see what came next.

When Armand had finished vacuuming, he sat down opposite me. His movements were gentle and tender by habit. I took the vase out of the plastic shopping bag and placed it on his desk. He handled it carefully, hefting it, and said nothing.

"My mother made the vase," I offered.

"May I ask how big a man your father was?"

"Not that big. Five-ten, medium build." He squinted down into the vase.

"You may find that this is not quite adequate for the cremains." That is the term, cremains. "I'm not suggesting you need to buy a fancier model—you can spend an awful lot on them—but you might want to look at the range of available urns. Just to determine the . . . volume we are working with here."

I didn't want to look at the urns.

"Let's just go with this, Armand, and we can divide up whatever is left over between us. There's no lack of vases in our family."

"Certainly," he said. "And do you wish the cremains to be interred or scattered? We use a very nice scattering ground down by the lake if that appeals to the family."

"We haven't thought about that," I said. "Up the chimney" had always been the family phrase. And why the fuss over the urn, if the ashes are only going to be scattered? My father was always the one who did the vacuuming in the house, so that came into my mind as a possibility. If he was grit, he would want to clean himself up.

I went back home, and my mother and I enjoyed a brief lacuna of time when everything seemed to be in other people's hands. "The nurse at the hospital said that Egertson's would take care of the body and give us a call," my mother said. It was amazing to me, the discretion with which all this was happening, my father's body travelling from the corridors of the hospital or a shelf in the morgue, through the familiar streets of Burlington, which my parents had navigated together in their gold 1978 Buick, both steering wheel and front seat lined with sheepskin; his body being conveyed to the funeral home I had passed a thousand times, a house that stood like a formal blank on the main street, a place you never noticed until someone you knew was dead inside it.

Four p.m. came. We sat with our sherry. "Wouldn't you think the funeral home should have called by now?" my mother said. I picked up the old rotary phone beside her and dialled the number. A low female voice answered. I asked after the preparations for Mr. Jackson, my father, who was currently in their care. A long, thoughtful silence followed. I repeated his name.

"I'm afraid we're not aware of a Mr. Jackson here," the woman said in mournful tones. "There must have been some mistake."

The vertigo of imagining my father already buried, or lost in the bowels of the hospital, or divided up into useful scientific bits swept over me. He was well and truly gone! I put down the phone. I told my mother that I had to check a few details with the hospital and went up to the bedroom, shut the door and called Admitting. I explained the situation to them, and the same gratifying, horror-filled silence ensued. "Let me make some inquiries," the voice on the phone said. It was a small hospital, thank god. Downstairs I heard my mother move to the sherry tray on the old stereo and pour another, clinking the decanter on the lip of the glass.

"I'm terribly sorry, Ms. Jackson—you are his daughter, correct?—but there seems to have been a miscommunication. Your father's body is still here, waiting for the coroner's release, and the funeral home was not notified. We'll see to that right away, and they will call you when he arrives."

My mother stood stricken in the doorway, her face white and the glass sloping in her hand. "They don't have him?"

"Well, it seems they lost track of him for a while, but it's all sorted out now. It's just that nobody called the funeral home, and they had to wait for the coroner."

"Why would they bother with a coroner? Do they think I hit him with a frying pan?" she said angrily.

"It's standard procedure, I guess. So much for the simple call to Egertson's." I shepherded her back down to the kitchen.

"When people get this old, they should just go into the garage and turn the engine on," my mother said, flinging a tea towel over the edge of the sink. "All this fuss is ridiculous."

But the image of my father on the floor of the bathroom, trying with his hands on the vanity·to haul himself up would not leave my mother, so despite the prior arrangements to burn him immediately, she decided that "one more look at him" might be a good idea. Alarm ran through me. Maybe the deed had already been done. Maybe he was molecules now. Explaining that I needed to go buy a heavy-duty antacid, I drove down to Egertson's, where I was taken into a side parlour curtained in maroon, by a man no more than nineteen, with gelled hair, wearing a dark suit that sat too widely on his shoulders.

"My parents made arrangements for 'direct to cremation,'" I explained, hoping the correct jargon would endear me to him, "but my mother has changed her mind, and would like to arrange a private visitation, for the family only."

Mr. Gel looked a little troubled and excused himself to speak to his father, the owner of Egertson's. In his absence, I studied a portrait of an English riding party hunting to the hounds.

The maroon curtain whisked back again and Mr. Gel appeared. "Ms. Jackson, that will be no problem, but I feel I should discuss with you the choice of container involved here."

"My mother doesn't want any fancy casket," I said, like someone in a John Wayne movie.

"I understand, but in the case of direct to cremation, we use the least-expensive receptacle, which some people find a bit of a surprise in the case of a public visitation."

"What, is it a FedEx box or something?" His glassy manner was getting on my nerves.

"Cardboard, essentially. I only mention it because when the family comes into the visitation suite, it can be a surprise."

"What's the next model up?"

"I suggest we go upstairs and you can see for yourself."

The upper floor of the funeral home, reassuringly like the furniture section of a department store, was filled with caskets of hierarchical splendour. Ruchings and drapes and swags—window treatments for the departing. It was true, the cardboard model did suggest sound equipment or a Loblaws patio chaise about to be unpacked. The high-end caskets were lined in puckered satin. They disgusted me, like the mouths or reproductive pockets of underwater mammals. In the corner I spied a plain pine box.

"This is perfect," I said, running an appreciative hand along it as if it were an entertainment unit.

"I'll see to the invoice then, and we'll set up a visitation appointment."

Although I vowed not to tell my mother any of this, when I walked through the door at home I immediately said, "We can't have the cardboard, Mom, it's horrible. The next one up is only ninety dollars more and I ordered it. You don't want it to stick out."

"All right, but no flowers. They're so . . ."

"Funereal?"

"Yes! People should make donations instead. Flowers are a waste."

"Some people will want to send them anyway," I said wearily, "and the room will look bare without them."

"We'll only be there a few minutes," she said. It seemed clear that my mother was not in a mood to face up to the enormity of losing her husband. All of this seemed a nuisance to her, like a distant relative's fiftieth anniversary.

The visitation was closer to half an hour, in the end. The ten of us—the three kids and spouses, the three grandchildren and my mother—went in two vans, entered via the discreet back door and filed past the casket. My father lay in the clothes he normally wore: a beige Eaton's short-sleeved shirt, a brown cardigan with criss-crossed leather buttons, and grey wool pants. His big square hands were folded on his lap, just the way he would watch TV, stretched out on the couch, his hands clasped. Except in life, he was a fidgeter. Now his hands looked the most like him, square and big-knuckled, still vital, even at ninety-four, and dead. His mouth was twitched down a bit, and his hair didn't look alive anymore, but otherwise my eyes took him in gratefully. I covered his hands with mine.

Each of us spoke about him. "Whatever good qualities I have, I owe them to Grandpa," his eldest grandson, Jake, said. "He only got mad once," Jake said. "When I rented a tux for the formal instead of borrowing his." I remembered him going to four stores on a Saturday, to fit the right size of kickplate for my skis: his care. My mother thought he should have talked more to us. But as far as I was concerned, my father had said all the important things, and was unreservedly proud of his wife ("oh, she's a smart one!") and all three of us.

"Well, that's that," my mother said on the way home.

But that wasn't that, at all.

The next day she had a photo propped up on the den shelves—a slightly blurred snapshot of my dad, looking down with delight at a Black Forest cake she had made, which he was about to cut and serve. He always served the dessert with surgical precision as to slice size and equality of toppings, standing at the head of the table. The carving stance.

"That was just how he held his hands," my mother said, looking at the photo. His face was blurred, but her own eyesight was blurred as well. It was the gesture that contained him.

———

The undersides of bridges tend to feature graffiti, debris and stray condoms. I had forgotten that. Before my father died, I had made a long-delayed plan to drive through the prairies and see the bridge my father had helped build in 1930. It was one of seven bridges that span the Saskatchewan River as it runs through the city of Saskatoon. My father graduated from the University of Saskatchewan as a civil engineer just as the Depression began. But the dean of engineering, C.J. Mackenzie, initiated a relief project that would employ as many men as possible and build something the city could use—a "bold, simple" bridge made of cement, with nine graceful spans. My father was one of the team of engineers who worked on the bridge, which took eleven months of twenty-four-hour labour, sometimes in the 40-below winter weather, to complete. It was a job he often talked about, with undisguised affection for "Dean Mackenzie," as he always called him—something of a father, I gathered, to my dad, whose own father had died of tuberculosis when he was twelve.

The completed bridge was more lovely than anyone could have predicted, and it eventually became the post-card icon of Saskatoon, its horizontal Eiffel Tower. I still have a photo of my dad in a dapper news cap, smiling as he walks beside the tall, patrician Dean Mackenzie. When Dad died, I knew I had to make a trip back to the bridge and walk over it.

I flew to Saskatoon, where it was clear that the Broadway Bridge is the grandest thing about the otherwise modest, pragmatic, farm-circled city of Saskatoon. Close by was the Bessborough, a CPR hotel built in the days when their hotels still resembled Scottish castles. I prowled through the corridors of the Bessborough, and then walked by the river to the base of the bridge. I had originally planned to scatter the ashes off the bridge itself, but it was too high above the water, and the wind blew too steadily. The ashes might simply waft over to the forlorn parkette on the other side and coat the single empty park bench there.

Down by the pathway that wound along the riverbank I found a bronze plaque, almost overgrown by foliage, saluting the engineering triumph of the bridge. That would be the official spot, and perhaps I could scramble down the bank beside it and surreptitiously pour the ashes into the river there. Eyeing the current, I calculated that they would be carried under the bridge.

I had left behind the vase, thinking that a woman with a vase on a bridge might draw attention. The ashes, in a plastic bag tied with two garbage twists, were as heavy and big as two bricks. I had had to decant the ashes from their original bag, which kept springing open, into another one, a task I did as quickly and unthinkingly as possible. The ash was a light grey, very fine and clinging, except for the bits that were bigger, and honeycombed like bone marrow. Not like, but were. What does it matter if these are his ashes, or just whatever was on the bottom of the crematorium, I thought, but I continued to address the vase as "Dad." Then I put the new plastic bag inside the dark blue velvet bag supplied to us by Just Cremation. It had a drawstring opening and reminded me of the old Seagram bags we used to keep our marbles in.

The river was wide, milk-chocolate brown, with a steady, powerful current. The Saskatchewan wound itself down through the province and ended up god knows where. In the Pacific? The river gave breadth to the otherwise timid city, and had dictated the scale and ambition of the bridge. In the public library I had found black-and-white photographs of the construction of the bridge, the supports of which were sunk in clay, a design that had to compensate for the ferocious cold of winter, and the shrinkage of the materials. "Only four men died in the construction of the bridge," said one news item. I found a picture in which three men stood behind the rebar skeleton of the steel supports for the curving piers. One man, not the tallest, wore a cloth cap that did not hide his ears, which stuck out, just like my dad's. The face was obscured, but there was a certain jaunty eagerness in the posture. I told myself it was him.

My cousin Margaret Anne, from Colonsay, stood behind me. She didn't know my father well, being from my mother's side of the family, but she was kind enough to tour me around Saskatoon and witness this increasingly odd ritual. The moment was as awkward and unceremonial as I could make it, but still, when I squatted by the riverbank and looked up at the rib cage of the bridge, my mind filled with thoughts: of my father and mother skating on the river in the evenings, which they loved to do; of my father working at the YMCA, typing the witty, flirtatious letters with which he wooed my mother; of my mother in the white frame house on Tenth Street, wondering when my father would come home for dinner from the bridge-in-progress. Of my mother quitting her job as a switchboard operator because the relief project hired only married men, and married couples could hold only one job, so that no one would hoard the work.

Traffic gleamed on the bridge, and my good shoes slipped on the stones at the water's edge. I untwisted the ties and tried to shuffle out the ashes, but they had been too tamped down, and I had to dig them out. They sank, except for a few small clumps that snagged on weeds, clinging like frog's eggs. I shook and shook the bag—it took a long time. My cousin clicked her disposable camera, although I had originally snorted at the idea of documenting this furtive act. The fine grit got under my nails, and when I had emptied the bag, I saw that my hand was grey, cadaver grey, gloved with the dust. I clambered back up the riverbank.

"Well, that's that," I said to my cousin. She smiled and said nothing. Sentiment is not a prairie thing. We walked back to her car and drove past the city limits to the RV campground that she ran with her husband, in the great curving nothingness west of Saskatoon. Farmland, it had been, until the farms failed. Colonsay's grain elevator, one of the classic old wooden ones, was scheduled to come down in the next year. My hand, with its grey, ghostly coating, lay radioactive beside me on the handle of the car door. Like something stuck between my teeth, I keenly wanted the grit out from under my fingernails. There was nothing to be done until we reached the campground, where I was staying in the guest trailer, a perfect, surreal bubble of shag-rug domesticity up on cement blocks.

Margaret Anne went back to the house to prepare dinner. Inside, I went to the sink. I watched the water wash the last filaments of grey dust off my hand and down the drain as the trailer rocked a bit, buffeted by the soft, strong, constant prairie wind.

Dorothy James

FURIOUS

HUNGER

By Linda McNutt

The day before my father's funeral I woke up ravenous, again. As casseroles and small food on platters arrived with the neighbours, my mother and my brother sat in the living room and refused food. I, however, rushed through the den to the kitchen so I could open plastic lids and peel back cellophane to feed.

I'd been eating church-cookbook carbohydrates since our friends found out about Dad's death on the basement stairs three days before. At first I thought it was the business of answering the door and finding photographs and writing the eulogy that was driving the aching need to consume. Usually I can opt out of any frantic response to the busyness Olympics by making a picture of a peaceful moment I'm going to reward myself with when the stress is over. This never fails to make busyness feel temporary. I tried to focus on my plan to sit in Dad's airplane model–building shop with a bottle of his single malt and his Count Basie albums playing. But eating pasta out of cold containers kept creeping into my image of the next evening's anticipated peace.

When my family doctor called to see if she could do anything, I asked her to set up a pregnancy test the next morning.

The day of the funeral I was up before the July heat set in, eating potato chip–covered noodles and then driving towards the hospital for a blood test. Before I made it to the end of the street I saw a huge stag and his doe cantering along the sidewalk. Although there are occasionally early-morning deer in my hometown, they are almost always down beside the river. I pulled over and watched them run along my parents' street, around the court's grass circle, and then past me again, a tribute to a completed life together. I knew watching the tawny creatures that the power of their run and their obvious symbolism of fidelity were beyond my ability to use without making them sound trite. The image suited my dad though. The detail of the real moment was something my father always encouraged me to write, but he clearly emotionally embraced the romanticism of "The

Highwayman" and *The Lord of the Rings*.

When I pulled into the hospital parking lot, I assumed the spaces around me were clear because it was so early in the morning. I took a moment to think about the deer because it was too soon to think about my father without the undoing fondness that kept catching in my throat and making me helpless.

I remember noticing the light of the fire and hearing the sirens at about the same moment, but I'm not sure how much I have shaped that over the years. To my right, completely consumed in flames, was a Volkswagen van. I watched it flicker beside me, realizing it was not a remembered vision of the orange van in which we drove across Canada, but a real burning camper. The second symbol, the pyre to our adventurous past, was overwhelming.

I didn't think to move the car until a fireman knocked on my window and motioned me to another part of the parking lot. It turned out that some electrical kitchen appliance in the van had been left on. Someone standing in the doorway of the hospital told me that as I went in. I told her that my hippie parents once had that van in that colour, and knew again that it was a detail from a story that was too neat and too well made to use.

When the nurse confirmed my pregnancy, she made the day more complicated because I would not be drinking, but she also made the structure of the story perfect. The deer, the burning camper and the pregnancy test.

I liked the story that way. I liked the simplicity and the way it was balanced by the slight oddness. The natural world intruding, the vessel of travel set free by Viking torchlight, and a baby that was a gift from the dead.

I also liked the awkwardness when people told me it seemed as if my father had sent me the baby and then registered the nearness of the taboo. I didn't feel that the baby was a gift from Dad, but I knew he'd appreciate the symmetry of death and life. The great wheel. We go to nature and we come from nature and the world goes on. I tend towards more postmodern structures, but death in proximity to life is a closet favourite and Dad raised me on redemption songs. That day, even missing my best editor, I felt better. I felt compensated. All the clichés about doors closing and windows opening seemed briefly true and my lupine hunger at the reception was less humiliating.

If they couldn't tell by my sandwich gorging, people found out I was pregnant at the reception because my mother told everyone in the receiving line that night at the funeral home. After the first mourner passed through the line, from my aunts to my brother to my mother and then from me to the urn, she felt that, in practice, a receiving line with ashes on the end was anchorless and anticlimactic. After I motioned the first man in the line on to the Raku pottery retirement present my father had designated during his lifetime for the purpose, the strangeness was palpable. People are used to moving from the family to the pink body and then on to the food. We looked at each other. "I don't like sending people to look at the pottery," I told my mother. "They don't know what to do." She took a breath, stepped forward so that the line curved in front of the urn and announced my pregnancy to the next six hundred people.

I became the last image, the comedic beat. Ferdinand's Tempest-tossed father does not lie full fathoms five below. The lion has come back to life. The ring has been destroyed. Since my father had been a mixture of Prospero, and Gandalf, and Aslan to me, this ending burst of life at the funeral home was perfect. I really, really liked that draft.

Still, you don't always get to tell the same stories you grew up in.

In October, at Thanksgiving, I spent three days in the hospital, waiting to give death to Dorothy James, and the final element of the story shifted on me. The symbolism got ironic. Curse of my generation. Stories are not allowed to be happy. It makes them shallow.

I missed the ease of the earlier version, but the longing for a quiet moment and the hunger stuck around. When a baby dies in the second trimester, it takes a while for the hormones to catch up. So, along with the shattering knowledge of my failure to allow life to develop, I got to keep the round, hard belly and the ridiculous appetite. The hunger, vicious and mocking, was hard to bear for two reasons. The first is that in the maternity ward people are allowed to bring in various outside and aromatic foods because women who have just had live babies are healthy and voraciously hungry. So, while I waited to go "naturally" into labour, an increasingly savoury bacchanal of dressing, fresh rolls and pie danced past my open door. The second reason the hunger was tough is that I had to eat lighter hospital fare in case someone took pity on me sooner than

Tuesday and agreed to perform the surgery. Finding a doctor for the procedure was tough. One man chose not to participate in something so much like a late-term abortion. A second doctor had living-baby emergencies to deal with. So I waited.

The smell of the visiting foods got worse over the weekend, as Thanksgiving-dinner leftovers made their way in, carried by beaming grandmothers and tired new dads.

Through all the long days, food came in and I stayed hungry. During the nights, the sound of babies being born woke me, reaching in to claw me up from the mild sedation prescribed.

I remember that when I wasn't weeping and apologizing to the little one I was uselessly still carrying, I was salivating over the smell of food. My hunger was impervious to its own futility, and I love the root-vegetable holidays. I salivated so hard the tranquilizers under my tongue dissolved like ice in cups of tea. The longing for a living child and a sated body were acute.

To distract myself from yearning and to please the first social worker they sent in, I chose the name, Dorothy James. I used my first name and Kevin's second because I still thought we'd have other babies and because it seemed wrong to use the name we'd chosen for a living child.

At twelve weeks, when I thought it was safe, I'd agreed to Beatrice, though I'd wondered if she'd forgive me for a Shakespearean name. I love names from the plays when they are given to cats, and thin, eccentric rescue dogs, but I'm always slightly anxious when I meet a human

Perdita. I'd thought about something Gaelic, but Morag Gunn was too much alive for me and still using up the name. In the end my four-year-old, Maeve, had offered up Beatrice, after her doll. The name settled in with the fluttery kicks and soft, sweet turning under the skin of my belly.

I still remember each turn in the palm of my hand. I remember holding still and feeling my cool skin fluttering. An eyelash, a flipping string of bones, a butterfly.

During that naive pregnancy I let Maeve and Kevin feel the tickle growing stronger until we could feel a spiral turn or a push against my side as the baby swam across the inside of my skin. Maeve would lie in the bed with me, hovering with her soft cheek against my hip and her blue eyes staring into mine, listening hard for movement. "Beatrice," she'd occasionally pronounce, and Kevin would mutter, "Really? Beatrice? You're sure?"

I was still reaching for a middle name during the ultrasound when the technician left and came back in with Kevin. Odd, I thought, they are tetchy about dads being there. When she left again and the radiologist was paged, I told Kevin that it was not a good sign.

"It'll be fine," he said, and I stopped trusting him and in things being fine.

When the technician came back in and said I could go to the bathroom, I knew. Comfort and fertility are not linked in hospitals. "It's bad," I told Kevin when I came back. "The best it can be is something that needs surgery."

"You don't know that," he told me.

He was right. I knew it was something other than the less-good options listed in the last chapters of the pregnancy books. I knew it was something other than the living issues we could adapt to and love our way through. I knew it was something darker.

When people insist that I must have known something was wrong during the pregnancy, that women always know, that's the moment I think of. I may have been a dead loss as an intuitive pregnant woman at close to six months, but when I was allowed to pee at the ultrasound, I knew.

I don't know why people want me to have known something was wrong before I went to that ultrasound. I didn't. People at my dad's funeral reception had wanted him to have known his aneurysm was coming too. When they insist that he knew, deep down inside, I tell them there was no warning until his head hit the floor. The things people need to tell me about death are myriad, but the instinct strangest to me is their desire to make those in its proximity retroactively understand that the Grim Reaper was coming. I suspect there is an atavistic need to think they will have a moment to understand their death before it pulls them under. It may be a distancing technique, the way blaming the other driver in car accidents makes people feel safe for another heartbeat. I suspect when we took up nihilism, we lost faith in the accident.

Whatever drives the need to tell grieving people that there must have been a detectable and dark epiphany, this is not a helpful statement. Just to be clear, I don't want to think of my father fearing his end and keeping it quiet. I don't want to taint my memory of our silly optimism as a pregnant family with some sense of impending doom that wasn't there. I need to believe in the accident. You're fine and then, crash, you're not. Survival is hiding inside the acknowledgement of the unpredictable.

I think I understood, by instinct, the importance of believing in the disaster in the dark green room where I found out about the relatively rare occurrence of "second trimester infant death." Although the radiologist spoke to Kevin and looked at the watch in his lab-coat pocket several times, he did give me a term I've found useful. I like "infant death" better than "miscarriage," which feels to me like finding fault with the carrier.

After giving us the name of the situation, the radiologist told the technician to help me get dressed. "I got her pregnant, I can get her dressed," Kevin told him, striking out with enviable masculine and misdirected fury. The radiologist looked startled and we watched him look for his golden pocket watch again as he turned to bolt out to meet the Queen of Hearts.

"But what happens now?" I asked his back, and he paused for a beat before turning around. I'm sure he didn't actually sigh and tut, but I remember it that way.

"What do you mean?" he asked me, looking still at Kevin.

"Just that." I remember forcing the words out. "What happens now?" I suspect he thought I meant something existential, or something womanly and emotional, because he had that I-didn't-go-into-OB/GYN-I went-into-radiology-for-the-unconscious-patients look, but I wanted details. I have a calm, numbing practicality that settles in the face of death. I meant, How will I have contractions if the baby is dead? How will the hormones start the labour if it's living babies that begin the process? How will she leave me?

Neither Kevin nor the radiologist seemed to understand what I was really asking. Possibly because all I could say was "What happens now?" I remember asking again because I could not get any other words to form.

"What happens now?" as a mantra seemed to be the final indignity for the radiologist, because he shook Kevin's hand to restore equilibrium and then darted, as if pulled by a bungee cord from another room.

Eventually, the technician told me to go home and contact my doctor on Tuesday, since it was the long weekend.

I remember getting out, going past the pregnant women waiting for their turns, making it into the car and stumbling across to the chesterfield at home. When I'd been there a while, I realized that this was actually the third element in the story. I was not the redemptive note in a comedy. I was something else. Gertrude was not going to understand in time. Cordelia was not going to come back. The narrative was not going to work out happily. The deer would collide with traffic, the travel dream was extinguished by flame, the baby died before birth. As I realized that this was the real conclusion, a keening came up from me, rattling so hard it hurt my skull emerging.

I don't know how long that sound of grief entering in lasted, but I know I've never made a sound like that before or since. I think of the sound and the feeling of it in my body as a link to the anguished and an absolute separation from the hopeful. Although I know I was still shocky when my body stopped resonating, I knew what to do. I think the things we understand about ourselves in moments of loss are the truest guides. I'm not sure why we doubt ourselves so profoundly in sorrow.

"I'm going to the hospital," I told Kevin.

Kevin, tough on others, soft on me, was troubled. "I've called the doctor's answering service, and Maeve's at the daycare until three, so you should sit."

"Friday, long weekend. It'll be five days until I'm seen." In five days, I knew, I'd just climb down into the pit with Ophelia and give up. It would feel good, it would feel right. I couldn't afford it.

By the time I got to the car, Kevin was with me, taking away the keys. "I'll walk," I warned him, but he put me in the passenger seat and drove.

At the emergency room there was a pregnant woman with a feverish toddler. I waited a while, but I wasn't able to hide. "When are you due?" she asked me.

"Spring," I heard Kevin say as I moved past her to sit in front of a desk. I heard him explain that we'd been sent home. Mistake, I remember thinking, mistake. I also remember trying to look up at the fluorescent lights, the way you do at funeral homes to keep your eyes from filling fast.

The triage nurse looked at me, took my temperature. "I need to be admitted," I told her. "Admitting" seemed like the right word. Not in the sense of responsibility, or fault, but in acknowledgement. I have a huge need, dating from that Thanksgiving, to avoid evasion.

"Normally, we like you to stay at home, let nature take its course." Nature has, I thought. Styx is just not the river I was expecting. I remember thinking about expecting and feeling that the grave-pit was very close. I concentrated on not quoting Hamlet, understanding that it wasn't going to help me here. I remember taking a breath, concentrating hard on the words: "I need to be here, I can't be at home. There are baby things at home," I told her, "Thanksgiving food." I saw her shoulders stiffen for a difficult-patient moment. I was in shock and she had protocols. I tossed a fraudulent mental coin: domestic abuse or suicidal thoughts.

"Cramping," said Kevin from behind me, "lots of blood, and I have to get our daughter. There's no one else free." There was a brief beat. She looked at me with whatever humanity had led her into this business twenty years ago, nodded and sent me to the cubicle. "Cramping," I kept saying, "no support system."

Eventually, I made it to the maternity ward, where they place the baby people, living or dead. I ran the gauntlet of walking women, women on balls, women wet from birth pools and showers and into the mixed blessing of a room alone.

I waited alone for three days to give death to Dorothy James. On the final day they let Maeve come and watch movies with me in my bed. I told her the baby was not going to be born, and we watched preadolescent magicians learn to fly.

On Monday, after I had failed again to do anything natural, like go into labour, they sent another social worker. We spent an hour getting me ready to see the baby, to hold it and to look at its hand. She showed me photographs of other dead babies' hands and told me I'd feel better if I held mine. Better was good, I thought. Better was vital in the maternity ward, with its white halls smelling of ginger cookies and resounding with the life cries of other women bearing living children.

At least holding the baby was a way of doing something properly. Touching its hand was the least I could do. I remember telling my hard little belly the way it was going to happen and realizing that one of the nurses was watching me. She apologized for intruding. "Even the dead need a heads-up," I explained, feeling foolish. She was young and came forward fast, holding my hand and crying. Before she took my blood pressure, she apologized for being unprofessional. She helped, though, with those sad tears. I meant to thank her. I hoped she'd be on duty after I held the baby.

When I came to, there was nothing to hold after all. I have the cervix of a supermodel and the baby could not be retrieved in a way I could touch. I remember thinking how useless I was, not even able to force out a dead baby properly.

After Dorothy James we had six more failed attempts and then we gave up.

Because we stopped trying, I'm not certain about the utility of my story. I am not the mythical woman who had lots of trouble and eventually succeeded. I know that my story is of no comfort to those who are still trying, and should not be repeated at cocktail parties. Second, it feels wrong to tell it to women who have tried and have no living child at all. When I feel like a note of realism intruding on an anticipated comedic wedding feast, or as though I am only a tragicomedy playing next door to Lear, it makes me quiet.

When I am silently swallowing bile with the anniversary sweet potatoes or hitting one of the seven due dates, and someone who hasn't been through it tells me I was lucky, I tend to binge on rage less silently. I know I'm lucky because I have a living daughter. People don't need to point that out. The implication that she nullifies the losses makes me growl and bite. Of course she does. Of course she doesn't. When Maeve is around for baby questions, I open my mouth and my father speaks: "She's the happy ending." I'll say, "She's the one who stayed."

I know that if Maeve had not come to walk me out of that place, I would have given up. She saved my life. Absolutely and entirely. Saving me is her superpower, but I don't want it to be her undying responsibility. Because I owe her so much, I am furious when people ask me fertility questions in front of her. She gets very still when I'm asked about other babies, and her quiet breaks me open.

When I am alone with someone who insists on stressing that one child is much easier than a big family, presumably assuming that I wanted more time to sort designer handbags, I point out that casual statements about only children and their longings for siblings and normality force me back into a come here/go away game with the grave

and my duty to try again. When told about the importance of siblings, often by people who disliked their own,
I say that Maeve had seven unborn brothers and sisters die
at various stages and that pregnancy, death and family planning are intrinsically linked for me. When asked why I don't
try one more time before it's too late, I explain that after
so much death, I stopped expecting and that I have actively
purged hope as if it were invented in a carnival.

Despite being embarrassed about frightening people
with my black hood and scythe, I know that anger saved
me and that it continues to do so. It seems odd that it is a
stage of grief that mourners are supposed to pass through
and release before true acceptance sets in.

Rage is my truest guide. It helps me alienate people
who want to make sense of my story for me, leaving the
way open for the intuitive and the compassionate. Rage
devours my useless hopes. Rage allows me to complicate
and retain aspects of the narratives my father loved: deer
leap madly in the city traffic, campers burn out and never
fade away, and my lost babies leave me pregnant with a
guiding fury that was not there before.

Instead of letting anger go, I work hard to keep it close.
It keeps me alive. It feeds my hunger.

Mary Irene Moure

A YEAR LATER,

I AM IN

LILAC NOW

By Erín Moure

escuro, sscuro, nai:
no escuro alzo a miña torre no ar
desde o claustro húmido onde o agarimo
abre a súa flor, e eu te amo.
—*Antón Avilés de Taramancos*

I.

Even now as I write this, over ten months later, I am staggered by memories, they enter me as shards of electricity or
glass or light, I pick them out of my skin, I put them together
into a cord and device, I am the human toaster, handle held
down against the machinic *pop*, the bread long turned to
cinders. I am red glow, refractory. And hard on the surface, so

hard. My mother, my mother. Who can know anything, even a spark, of who she was, of her is-ness that is-not anymore.

In the first days after she died, I would go into her walk-in closet and stand among her clothes, they too also standing, thin, touching each other, uninhabited forever— but for her smell. And the small ghosts of her posture. Where the elbows were, deflecting the weave, where a button had been worn by fingers. Where she'd left Kleenex in the pockets, or elastics. And I'd stand in the closet, it was so quiet there in the suburbs of Calgary. I was gone too. I'd inhale her smell, push sleeves to my face, and cry for each bit of her left alive in the world: this smell of her in her clothes, this smell was tremendous to me and I was going to lose it too, for I was losing everything. I'd smell too in the blue toque she'd worn, I'd push my face into this hat, the cancer hat, and breathe in the smell of her head, that smell of a child. Of a kind of light.

It was a month before I could move her clothes at all from the closet. Even smell, this part of her aliveness still with me, had to vanish before I could perform any act with the things that she had left.

Gone.

Oh yes, I had had friends who died. Had already seen the world stripped away, the veil of it torn irrevocably. I knew I would get "better" in "time." I knew that the world would come back to me. But nothing, nothing in my past prepared me for the death of my mother, nothing prepared me for the death of this person from whose body I emerged into the world and whose values and ways of seeing and expressions were woven into my very DNA. The clarities and the secrets (for who can know all of another person), her "right and wrong" and her "who I am" were part of me, and it was like unwinding every strand of DNA and pulling the sides of the ladders apart, as if my mother who was dead one time only, and in her own way, was now dying over and over again, in me. I had to let her go where she had gone. She was already there.

I was torn open. I probably looked normal to most people, I walked and ate, I smiled, I stopped looking so tired when I no longer had to spend long vigils in the hospice, long hours in the ice and traffic of winter Calgary, far from my home. Yet I talked incessantly about my mother, and did for months. It was as if I had to relate every aspect of my life to something my mother had said, to some memory, before I could move on my own again. And no one around me was immune: ten months later at the book fair, the foreign writer asked what I did at Concordia (University) and I said, startled, "Nothing," and it came out that he had been told I teach there. But no. I end up by telling him what my mother said: if you wear clean clothes and finish your sentences, people will think you have a bachelor's degree. And that was years ago, I add. Now they think you have a master's. Or they think you teach there.

Later I felt stupid. Why did I have to go on and on about my mother?

My mother. Her very qualities that drove me mad— relentless focus on an irrelevant task, insistence on each gruelling step that could in fact be skipped to reach a goal, her independence (she'd left our father at sixty-eight)—had all turned in her illness of twenty months into purely marvellous qualities of endurance, patience with the smallest increments of progress, focus and, after the first tumour paralyzed her, no anger at her now-corrected diagnosis: she relearned to sit up, learned to use the sliding board to get from bed into wheelchair on her own, the victory of getting into the hallway, of the bathroom, of getting, blind, to the kitchen to make a piece of toast on her own, learned to stand up and walk with the walker, had relentless patience with eating when she wasn't hungry, when her mouth was full of sores from the radiation, with, with . . .

Oops. I am going to start talking to you about my mother. I am going to stagger you too with these memories. I get up. I am going to stun you again. I am going to shock you. But it is me I shock. You, reader, friend, have already stopped listening. It is 4:30 a.m. I write these thoughts down instead of sleeping. It is almost eleven months later. I don't care how you feel about what I do. I will never see my mother again and if there is one fact in life I cannot bear it is this one.

coyote. mère.

2.

I don't feel angry, but I feel sad. As sad as loam, as heavy as the felled trunk of a tree. Everything in me knew it was time for her to go, that she had assumed this time as hers, in going. Yet, the hole. Time changed, when I wanted it to go on forever. Time didn't leave me, though. It only left my mother. But for me it changed unutterably. How did it change? How can I describe it?

I was here, still here. *Time wasn't.* Time had not left me but had turned into a "wasn't." I found myself in time's negative, which—I only realize, writing this, a year later—is still time. Time isn't, that's all. And time doesn't heal. What isn't, can't heal. It seemed completely absurd to think of healing.

I felt like Émile Ajar's orphan Momo, in the novel *La vie devant soi* (*The Life Before Us*), faced with the death of his beloved and outrageous Madame Rosa, the only mother he'd ever known: "I don't give a shit about the laws of nature. I don't even want to know what they are."

3.

I tried to translate one language into itself, English into English, staring at a friend's translations of Paul Celan's Romanian poems, which she'd sent me in letters, one at a time. I had kept myself alive in these translations during my mother's sickness and my stays away from my home. Words had become impossible to me on my own. They were pulses of light, fragments of snow, burnt bits of darkness. I could not use them. For months, I could only use language to make poems by pretending I was translating from the poem of another. If the original of this "other" poem was already in English, then so be it, I was defiant, I translated it just the same, out of sheer stubbornness, into English.

Nothing had been blunted in me, but everything had.

4.

Strangely, I had fallen in love about a year after time first altered, when already Mom was able to walk again, with a walker and with a cane, after the cancer that had returned in force while she was getting up again had been stalled by chemotherapy. We knew it was only for a while. My mother was still frail. I was with her more than half the time, for I had made the choice to go to Calgary to be with her, to laugh with her, to make sure she had what she needed.

And I fell in love. With language, a language. With the sounds of a language. And the love sustained me. Buoyed me onward in ways I did not even suspect till much later. Then everything changed in this love, it deepened and altered: I started to understand some words and they moved away from me. I felt them moving. The beauty of incomprehension, perhaps, had sustained me. In some ways, then, the death of my mother became a double grief for me for quite a while. I struggled to understand and accept the love I'd received as a gift for a while, a precious gift from language, its mystery and purity, while I accepted and honoured the love I had always been given, from a person who was further gone than gone. Much further gone. Knowing even as I accepted and returned love that a gift of such magnitude may not always be given again and again.

The gift. There were so many gifts. Precious to me. And then none.

(But that's not even true.

Love was still given, everywhere, just differently. A full-

ness such as the fullness of love cannot be measured, as meas-
urement itself is a form of parsimony.)

5.

I think of the last time I saw my mother's body before she
was cremated. The peacefulness in the small room. The fact
that this body was no longer her and she no longer needed
it. That she was gone. There was no more "her." The white
garments of the priest, and my brothers' calming presence.
The way each of us went up to her, to what remained of
her physically in our world, in her blue dress in the simple
plywood open box, with twine handles, covered with paper,
and spoke in our hearts to her, our mother. We were siblings and we loved her with a mightiness. We had come
through all this with her, because of her. It was so peaceful. We couldn't remember the Catholic prayers, so the priest
said our parts too, quietly in his pact of belief. We were there
together, the way she wanted, just us. We were at peace.

But what is it to have lived a life? What does a life mean,
lived? Who will remember my mother forever? Where will
my memories go? My memories, so clear, of air light sights
smells the woman in her concentration and her supreme
dignity, in her love of the birds sticks trees light coffee? *On
porte en nous la mémoire de nos parents*, the writer said.

What is in my body that is suffering so much?

My head knows that my mother lived a long life, that
she accomplished much, that she fought for her life with
everything possible when it was under threat.

What does it mean to die?

I know from my mother's own acts that each person invents their own death, creates it, creates it by living. That there is life in dying, much much fierce life. My own mother gave me a fierceness, and a patience. A long time ago. Before I was born, she gave it to me.

Mère, coyote. Which is to say: I know too from my mother that each person who is dear to us and whom we know intimately is also a secret person we can never know, whose forces are a mystery to us. Whose past is not just a tale but a lived thing, we cannot know it. Whose time away from us too is a lived thing: and we cannot know it. What I remember of my mother is a fullness, but it is not all her fullness. Part of that is inaccessible to me now. It is hers. She is gone.

To leave this world is not only to vanish, I realize in these months. It is to leave a terrible and beautiful bond, not in the sense of a promise but in the sense of a ligature. My mother's bond with me is that I lift my coffee in the morning and rejoice.

And yet, I will never see this person again, and that matters. Today, almost eleven months later, it matters and it is 5 a.m. now and I am still up and it matters.

6.

Steps of grief. I read all about them. I recognized none of them. Steps? I knew my mom had to die, I supported her in doing it her way. Absence? We'd spent time together so fruitfully. We hadn't wasted a minute. It was full, replete. Still, there was the bodily pain. It woke me up at night. I had an injury. I had it again. The steps of grief were utterly foreign to me. That there could be *steps* to this? Like falling onto the knife again and again and again.

I wanted nothing to do with steps.

It was the steps that made me angry.

I'd dress in her clothes, the few ones I kept for months after giving away the others. I told no one. The sleeves were too short for me. I'd dress in them and stand and sing. Satchmo's "What a Wonderful World." Lhasa's "La Frontera." "Shenandoah."

I'd examine her photos: in Cuba, in Constanta, in Cairo, and place my own photo beside hers, looking for any trace of a resemblance. I wanted to resemble her. I wanted her eyes, her eyes of the steppe, her own mother's eyes, Slavic. Eyes of the East. The way the bottom of the eye folds into the top when I smile. There it is. There. See? I told you so.

I'm a European, she said to me, one day, near the end, through the brain tumour, as I was helping her walk to the bathroom. *O. is European*, she said. She stopped, stooped and small, and turned towards me. *What are you?*

I struggle to answer that question. That day I said, "I'm a Canadian, Mom."

We were both saying that it matters to be born some-where. That it matters to be born. The rest, after this impos-sibility of birth, is sheer gift. "I'm European too, Mom, because of you," I'd added. I think she was satisfied with that. She had turned back around, away from me, and was

moving forward again past the mirror, I saw her in it, concentrating, hairless, blind, and I was holding her shoulders
from behind as she walked slowly forward, oblivious to me,
autonomous in the gift, and focused on her own secret goal.

So now, when I'm not satisfied, when I ask *What am I?*
I think of her satisfaction. That we could be satisfied, with
a bit of an answer, and let the rest be a mystery, while we
get on with living in the midst of it.

7.

Fragments come back from before she was ill, too, incessantly,
for months. They console and frighten me at the same time.
Especially this: she is standing in her garage on the steps, and
I am backing out in a rental car, heading to the airport to go
home. We wave. Pang. I drive off through this pang as if
a road could be cut through it, and she stands there in
the garage, not closing the door, watching me. And me,
in the rear-view mirror, watching her. It could be the last
time we ever see each other. We did this for years.

And fragments from when she was ill. The soft fuzz
on my mother's head after the chemo. Her neighbours in
the retirement home where she lived after the hospital, who
exclaimed on seeing her: *Your hair looks nice!* And my
mother lifting the wig off and saying cheerfully: *But I don't
have any hair.*

There's light coming in the window. I get up. Sun's
going to dawn soon. Hard pellets of snow and ice hit the
glass of my apartment in Montreal. In five days it will be her

birthday, November 27. I did not buy her a birthday card
this year. It has felt so strange to walk past the card section
in the store. She so liked greetings cards. I could not go get
my prescriptions filled for a week: I could not walk by the
card section (vision of pink) and I could not *not* walk by
the card section. Thus, I'd leave, without prescriptions.

But as my friend in Vancouver said so wisely, anticipa-
tion is often the worst of it. After her birthday, I went in. The
card section had gone silent. It just looked falsely cheerful. It
was all pink. I walked past it. It was meant for other people.

8.

On our mother's birthday, I fought with my brother. Or we
disagreed. Or we didn't. We were just not able to speak to
each other as intelligently as usual for a few moments, and
the thread broke. Or it didn't break, but there was a sound
like breaking. Inside me, perhaps. Did he hear it? It scared
me, even though I knew it was momentary. It threw me
into despair for days. I reminded myself that he's affected
by this birthday too, maybe without realizing it.

But why should I take care of him? I want these feelings of tenderness I feel for him to be for me. I want
someone to take care of me! He's silent.

Then the birthday passes and I realize we've taken care
of each other already. The tenderness. There is nothing to
patch over, for we are listening to each other, with our usual
respect and joy.

So what happened?

It was as if there was an accretion, an excess, in me. I
wanted him to take care of my own accretion, which I did
not want to acknowledge as my own. Then it dissolved. Its
stone was limestone, not granite. Take care of your own
wound was the lesson, and love as you have always loved.

9.

At times, what's hardest is that others think I should stop,
and I don't intend to. Perhaps it's that my place or existence
is still untimeable, asynchronic. "Remember the good times
instead," my good and cherished friend writes from Spain.
But that's not it. I do remember the good times. I laugh at
them every day. They are tremendous and feed me and I
know my luck in having so many of them. But my mother's
still dead. Time is still apart from her. Who is anyone to me?
Who are you?

Then the phone rings and I answer. My friend, the
poet, has phoned to talk about Walter Benjamin's essay "The
Storyteller." She reads to me about modernism: " 'A generation that had gone to school on a horse-drawn streetcar
now stood under the open sky in a countryside in which
nothing remained unchanged but the clouds, and beneath
these clouds, in a field of force of destructive torrents and
explosions, was the tiny, fragile human body.' "

That's it. The tiny human body in the "field of force."
It's me there. Or my mom. One of us. But my mom went
to school *on* the horse, not *in* the carriage. The horse King.
The horse whose mother had been killed by the train, and

my mother, tiny, had fed him with a bottle. But this, yes, I knew: *the clouds, and under them, the tiny, fragile human body,* and all else utterly changed.

This is the friend who helps me. She never says "Remember the good times"; she phones to say "Nothing remained unchanged but the clouds." And under them. The fragile body.

10.

"What are you so upset about?" she asked me once from her bed, detecting something awry in my presence.

"I'm mad because I can't cure cancer." The absurd surprise of such a line.

"No one *asked* you to cure cancer," she said.

I still hear that voice now. No one asked me to do what I could not have done.

11.

In the days before my mother died, restless I had read the rituals of mourning from her old etiquette book, howling at the ridiculousness of it: "The ladies of a bereaved family should not see callers, even the most intimate friends, unless they are able to control their grief. It is a source of discomfort to the visitor, as well as to the mourner, to enact a scene of semi-hysteria in the drawing room. Yet, at a time like this, one can hardly be expected to be in full control of one's emotions. Therefore it is always wise for the women to keep to their rooms until after the funeral."

And: "For three weeks after a bereavement, women seclude themselves and receive no visitors except their most intimate friends. After this they are expected to be sufficiently resigned to receive the calls of condolence of their friends and acquaintances. They themselves do not usually make visits until six months after the death."

And: "One can easily see in this custom of crepe-hanging a relic of that custom of ancient Patagonia that required all belongings of the deceased to be painted black."

But what *did* make sense: that it didn't just last a year, that for a year you wore black, and then switched to lilac or lavender. That it was up to two years before you let the colour back into your wardrobe, gradually. To let others know, to keep yourself knowing. To acknowledge to others that it was still with you. And the respect that ensued from that, the tolerance. That tolerance doesn't exist in the same measure in society since we dropped our ways of wearing these clothes, dropped all the Victorian mourning rituals that contributed to this publicizing of personal grief, that resulted in public acknowledgement of personal grief. Even writing paper had black borders that decreased in width as distance from the time of death grew.

Of course, I didn't wear mourning clothes or write on black-bordered paper. One can't reinvent a tradition that is gone. The lilac, when its time came, appeared inside me.

———

12.

Other books did help me in the months after my mother's
death. At my brother's urging, I read *La vie devant soi* (1975,
translated by Ralph Manheim as *The Life Before Us*), written
by French writer Romain Gary under a pseudonym, Émile
Ajar. And Romain Gary, too, was a pseudonym. I love those
layers. The book is narrated by Momo, the orphan looked
after by the retired madam, Madame Rosa, all his life, who
looks after her when she is dying. When she is *éteinte*, he
brings her downstairs to the grotto she'd created for herself
as a place of safety in the basement of the seedy Paris apartment building where they live. He hides her and makes a
ritual site for her there for days, lighting candles and putting
makeup on her to make her look alive. Finally, his way of
admitting she had died: he goes to see the transvestite pros-
titute upstairs in their building.

>   —Oh my God, Momo! What's the matter! Are
> you sick?
>   —I've come to say goodbye for Madame Rosa.
>   —Have they taken her to the hospital?
>   I sat down because I hadn't the strength to
> stand. I hadn't eaten since God knows when,
> I was on a hunger strike. I don't give a shit
> for the laws of nature. I don't even want to
> know what they are.
>   —No, not to the hospital. Madame Rosa is in
> her Jewish hideaway.

I shouldn't have said that.

—What?

—She's gone away to Israel.

And his words of defiance at death and grief and everything that so resonated with me: "I say fuck the laws of nature, they're no good, they stink on ice and they shouldn't be allowed."

Polish poet Adam Zagajewski, born in the mythical place of Lvov (which changed countries to become L'viv mere weeks after his birth), 30 kilometres from where my mother was born, and his poem "Airport in Amsterdam," written for his mother, also helped me with mine, who so loved travelling:

The old priest will garble your name.
The train will halt in the forest.
At dawn snow will fall
on the airport in Amsterdam.

Above all, I held to Jacques Derrida's *Work of Mourning*, the collection of eulogies for his friends, the philosophers I admired and those I met for the first time in these very pages, already dead, already beyond mourning, already words. I learned so much of friendship, and of mystery and gift from that book.

And at the Salon du livre in Montreal in November 2007, I heard Rita Gombrowicz speak. Her husband, Polish playwright Witold Gombrowicz, died in 1969, and she has tried to make sense of him and preserve him in the world as memory ever since. And she spent but five years with him, the last five years of his life, before he died at sixty-four. This loyalty astonishes me and gives me courage.

I open up Derrida's rich book at random, for on every page I find something to alight on. In his talking about Max Loreau, I hear myself talking about my mother: "He knew, to be sure, that what separates—divides and cleaves—by the same token also gives, and that it is not necessary to know, indeed that it is necessary not to know, and thus recognize, restitute, or identify: he knew that the *without return* is necessary in order to give."

13.

Without return, *mère*. At times I'd be talking to my mother in French, outpouring feelings and frustrations in French to her, and she'd say, talk in a language I can understand.

First I have to let language come out of my body, I'd tell her. Then I can translate it for you, but only after.

So she'd wait.

As I wait today. For at times I feel more easily abandoned and alone. I forget the lesson. Or I can't enact it (of course, I remember it, for it is written here, just a few pages back: T.C.O.Y.O.W.A.L.A.Y.H.A.L.).

At such times, I go look at Calgary on Google Earth. Today, over a year later, I did it. Google Earth takes a few months to catch up to reality. Today, in its pictures, the overpass at Crowchild and Nose Hill Drive is still under construction: they've just laid the bridge deck. The surface shines, unasphalted, disconnected from the teeming roads around it. I plunge in. If this is Calgary, I am still there. Perhaps one of the cars is mine: I am bringing her clothes down in the rental car to the charity depot. I move along Nose Hill Drive north, coaxing the cursor. I go left at John Laurie, then across and upward to the right till I pass her house in Arbour Lake to make sure I've shut the garage door. But this time I don't stop or go in. I continue up and out again to Nose Hill Drive higher up, then head south, turning left on John Laurie till I reach the fields of Nose Hill on the way east. I soon cross the high spot where I was at the moment she died. Between field and city. The lights spread out below me and far in the distance.

What is abandon? What is grief? In some sense, we are all made of griefs. Some learn to go forward.

I go forward. I send you, reader, this image. The clouds are over it. It is a body. It is outside on a hill, walking into the storm of snow light high above Calgary. It is fragile. *The secret will remain. No one will ever know anything essential about it.*

It is my mother and my feeling. It is lilac. It is a poem.

Mary Ormiston Quarrington

THE

BLUESMAN

By Paul Quarrington

On my first day back at school, I was approached in the hallway by Paul D.

I can remember that I was doing nothing in the hallway, going nowhere, standing still and staring at my feet as though they might contain some hint as to where I should be headed. It was midafternoon, and my inaction was causing traffic jams. Some kids were moving quickly, trying to accelerate the journey of the sun across the sky, others were benumbed and simply placing one foot in front of the other. What neither current needed was to encounter a boulder. All around me were angry little riffles, near- and full collisions. Ordinarily—only a few days previous—I would have been trampled underfoot, but I had acquired a kind of contagion through personal tragedy, and no one wanted to go anywhere near me.

Except Paul D., who slapped a hand on my shoulder as he said hello.

Paul D. was a couple of years older than me, and I'd known him from early childhood. We had grown up in the same neighbourhood, only a couple of kilometres away from the high school and its feeding area, but somewhat more distant on the class level. The houses surrounding the high school had big bay windows and two-car garages. Paul D. and I grew up in houses built just after the war, and the architects—if indeed there were certified architects involved in the process—seemed to add windows only reluctantly, perhaps thinking that they weakened the facade in the face of nuclear storm. And there were no garages at all in my first neighbourhood, although some of the more enterprising fathers constructed carports out of raw timber and corrugated metal. In that neighbourhood there were single mothers, and fathers with no visible means of support. There was a crazy lady whom we could provoke into fairly advanced craziness—pursuing us down the street with a butcher knife, clad only in her nightgown—merely by appearing on her lawn. Mind you, we did often appear there in the middle of the night, and we would stare bug-eyed into the little windows grudgingly provided by the architects, and I dare say the effect was more than a little creepy.

It was a neighbourhood that could produce trouble and troubled children, and Paul D. and his brother, John, were the most notorious ne'er-do-wells the neighbourhood had produced thus far. His brother was worse; at least, his brother got into more trouble—although perhaps he simply got caught more often, Paul having a half-step on him in a foot race—and spent a lot of time in reform school. (They don't seem to have reform schools anymore. What happened to them? I imagine derelict buildings perched high upon barren hills, the sounds of lashes still echoing.) Paul D. was a greaseball for most of his youth, although with the British Invasion he let his hair grow long and started doing vast quantities of drugs. His association with drugs was no secret; in fact, I was somewhat surprised to see him in the school hallway, because it was common knowledge that should he be spotted by the vice-principal, the authorities would be summoned.

Paul D. had always liked me, which I reciprocated, because he had a sunny disposition and a good sense of humour and if I was friends with Paul D. it meant I couldn't actually be the lard-assed wimp that I appeared to be.

"Hi, Paul," he said. "What's news?"

"My mother died," I informed him.

"Oh, too bad." Paul nodded, momentarily sombre. Then he asked, "What on the bright side?"

———

When I remember my mother, I remember her with a book. A distinction I would like to make: my father had books— the walls of the den (where he'd hide many days, smoking his pipe and furrowing his brow professorially until there were deep grooves slanting down either side) were lined with scholarly tomes—but my mother had a book. It changed on a daily basis—she could read astoundingly quickly—but she always had a book with her, juggling the book and a cigarette and a drink as she wandered about the house. She was often looking for something, or so it seemed to me. Her brow would be stitched with annoyed conster-nation, and she'd move things out of the way and overturn cushions, and finally she'd either find whatever it was or abandon the search, at which point she'd recline on the chesterfield. She'd prop herself on an elbow—the drink on the wall-to-wall carpeting beneath her, the cigarette roost-ing on the lip of an ashtray as big as a chip bowl—and she would begin to read the book.

She would not get up until she finished the book.

Then she would set about making dinner. If the book was of a reasonable length, my family would eat at a rea-sonable hour. If the book was an epic—and they were very fashionable in those days, I remember, *Exodus* and *Hawaii* and *The Agony and the Ecstasy*—then we would eat after most of my friends had gone to bed. And, I should mention, the food would be awful. My mother seemed to believe in the tuna casserole in much the same manner that George Washington Carver believed in the peanut, i.e., that it was a wonderfood that could satisfy all of a human being's nutritional needs. She would occasionally augment the basic recipe, always with disastrous results. For example: once, before putting the casserole into the oven, she crushed a box of corn flakes and sprinkled it overtop the grey, gummy fish meat.

———

"What on the bright side?" Paul D. asked, and I laughed; at least, something like a bark of laughter ripped through my body and shot out of my mouth. For an instant I felt relief from the stiffness that had possessed me for the past few days, a stiffness that came from being hugged repeatedly by family and family friends.

It was my hope that my manner—straight-backed and silent—would be interpreted as inner strength. Really, though, I was blocked and clogged, unable to allow myself demonstrations of mourning because, well, I had wanted my mother to die. You see, she had suffered a cerebral hemorrhage and gone into what they called back then a vegetative state, and after a few days the thought occurred that her not waking up was probably the best thing that could happen. This thought is not usually welcome in the hearts of fifteen-year-old boys, certainly not in the heart of this particular boy. And when she did pass over to the other side, my first and strongest emotion was relief. My second emotion—which was, come to think of it, way stronger than the previous one—was guilt. Tears were banished to the nether regions, an edict decreed by the despot in charge of my emotions—*if you can't cry over this,* the warning went, *then you must never cry about anything, ever again.*

This is why, at the funeral and the subdued affair afterwards, I only exhibited physical discomfort, my buttoned collar and necktie biting into my neck, depriving me of air.

———

Suddenly Paul D. began to look around, his hoodlum senses pricked. "Let's go," he said. At the other end of the hallway, the vice-principal wheeled around a corner, his slate grey suit sweat-stained and chalk-pocked, as it was the only one he owned. Paul D. and I pushed through the doors and walked through the parking lot, across the football field. We were long gone before it occurred to me that I had become a truant—there were a couple of periods left in the day, and I needed to catch up on my classwork. But I said nothing. That particular argument would hold no truck with Paul D., who had achieved, the year previously, an average of 38. He was rather proud of how his average had been dragged down so dramatically by attaining, in arithmetic, a grade of 11. "Anyone can get a 1," he'd proclaimed disdainfully. "You just don't go to class. But to get an 11, you have to work at it. You have to go every couple of weeks, you have to take the occasional test or pop quiz."

They hadn't finished building Toronto when I was a kid, and the tracts in the north end of the city were endless and empty except for the hydro towers that marched across the horizon. Everything was white, because all this—my mother's illness and her death—took place in December. Christmastime.

As we walked, Paul D. told me about how he had been arrested the week before and thrown into a cell at the Don Jail. He told me that there had been some sort of formal inspection that night—he made it sound as though an illustrious eminence, the Governor General or someone, had been escorted down the corridors—and keepers labelled the inmates aloud. "Arson," they said. "Break and Enter. Theft Under." But when they came to Paul's cell, he said, they only allowed a dismissive "Common drunkenness."

———

I remember announcing to my father that I was not going to cry, as though it were a decision I'd arrived at, like dropping German or getting an after-school job. He was hiding in the den, surrounded by his books. The largest volume on the shelves was bound in a tooled cowhide jacket, a present given to my father by some friend who had taken a course in leather working. This tome sat upon the shelves with the heft and majesty of the Bible, but it was in fact *The History and Social Significance of the Potato*. This is significant when trying to understand the emotional makeup of the men in the Quarrington family. When I entered the den, my father was on his feet, leaning over his writing desk, his huge hands squared around either edge. My father's pipe hung out of the corner of his mouth, cold and unsmoking, and I guessed that he'd reared up from his seat, meaning to fill and tamp it, but had been stilled and stayed by sadness, regret or run-of-the-mill bafflement. He appeared to be holding on to the desk for dear life; he was squeezing so tightly that his knuckles had whitened.

I told him that I was not prepared to cry about this.

My father looked and there was a moment when he couldn't seem to remember who I was. He nodded. "Well," he said, after a moment, "I suppose you know best how you're feeling."

This was mighty wide of the mark for a psychologist.

―――

Paul D. and I walked north on Victoria Park until we came to its intersection with Lawrence Avenue. There was an apartment building there, twenty storeys, painted white but made dingy by bus exhaust. For reasons that I can't explain—I mean, I don't know the explanation myself—he and his brother now had their own apartment. Perhaps their mother had inherited some money or something, and had happily installed her children as remittance men in this high-rise, sending them a small stipend every month.

The apartment wasn't actually a pigsty, which was startling and oddly impressive. Mind you, there wasn't a lot there, a dining-room table and some mismatched chairs. I sat down whilst Paul went into the kitchenette and fetched refreshment.

"Where's John?"

"Oh, well, you know," answered Paul. I heard a small *pop*. "He's gone away for a little while."

Paul D. returned with a bottle of wine, two greasy arti-
cles of stemware threaded through his fingers. "A fine
Beaujolais," he announced, pouring me a glass. "Cheers.
Sorry about your mom."

They say that an experience shared by all alcoholics is
that with the first taste of hooch a tremendous sense of well-
being descends. I did not have that experience, not at all.
The first two sips were bitter, and I barely managed to
swallow them back. With the third sip, though, I was
enveloped by a cloud of fluffy, muzzy contentment.

I telephoned my father and told him I wouldn't be
coming home for dinner.

————

Above, I described my emotional state as "blocked and
clogged," and while I don't want to belabour the somewhat
distasteful metaphor, you might imagine that the wine
worked as a kind of Liquid Plumr. But that isn't what happened. Rather, the alcohol seemed to supply me with a kind
of alternative bloodstream, one that kept me perfectly func-
tional but went nowhere near my heart.

By the way, that first bottle of wine wasn't really a fine
Beaujolais. I don't know what it was. My drink of choice,
for the next couple of years anyway, was something called
Four Aces. I suspect that the truth-in-advertising board
would insist, nowadays, that Four Aces label itself as a "wine-
like beverage." Maybe even a "beverage-like substance." All
I know about it is, it had alcohol and it was cheap, namely,

a bottle cost one dollar and five cents. "Come alive for a dollar five," was my constant refrain. Then, of course, came beer and tequila, and with middle age came Cabs and Pinots and single malts, and that's pretty much how things have proceeded for the last forty years. You might wonder where grief, grieving, plays into all this. I'll admit, I'm not certain that it does. With alcohol I achieved a fluid stasis, although occasionally, especially in my twenties, I howled at the moon and slammed my fist into brick walls.

———

A source of some little comfort, back when I was fifteen, was the fact that both Paul McCartney and John Lennon had lost their mothers at the same age. As all of the biographical bumpf mentioned this sad fact, I could only assume that it contributed somehow to their musical genius. I single-mindedly strummed my guitar and awaited the Muse. Curiously, though, I grew less enchanted with the Beatles' music. Perhaps it was that I couldn't really belong to the proper demographic; because the coolest kids at school were Beatles fans, it somehow seemed to me that the entire fan base was way cool. I was overweight, pimpled and bespectacled, and I suffered from a severe fashion deficiency that plagues me to this day. The other kids liked me well enough, I realize in hindsight, but though they tried to be kind following my mother's death, there was some ancient alarm sounding within them all. "Stay away from this kid," their inner voice warned. "The gods have singled him out. They fucked with him and they may not be done yet." So I felt abandoned and monstrous, and somehow couldn't really muster high-test enthusiasm for the Beatles. There was another reason, too, admittedly inchoate, that had to do with the lightweight nature of many of the Beatles' lyrics. I was not in the mood for "Ob-la-di, Ob-la-da, Life Goes On." For a couple of guys who had lost their mothers—this was the thought that was lurking backstage—Lennon and McCartney were putting out some pretty lightweight drivel. (Yes, there's "Julia," and as soon as I heard that John Lennon had written it for his mother I put it on the player and bent my head to it. But it's wishy-washy, the girl in the song could be anyone, and . . . you know what, I guess I was looking for someone else to do my crying for me.)

One day my older brother, Tony, fetched home a record album, a sampler from a company called Elektra. The label was largely dedicated to folk artists, and very good ones, too, people like Tom Rush and Tim Buckley. They were also making a stab at the new young audience of hippies with The Doors and the Lovin' Spoonful, but what really intrigued me on that Elektra sampler was the Paul Butterfield Blues Band. That was music unlike much else that was going on. The rhythm was funky and insistent. Really insistent, a "you owe me money" order of insistence. The rhythm grabbed me by the collar and shook me back and forth. And over top of that rhythm there was this electrified keening, a young man named Mike Bloomfield pulling teeth out of a beat-up old Telecaster. The harmonica, as played by Butterfield, didn't sound like a human voice, it sounded way more human than that, the howl of a beggar outside the Pearly Gates. Not only that, but photographs of the band showed them to be pot-bellied louts, with greasy hair and nicotine-stained fingers. Some still retained their Brylcreem-sculpted greaser-dos. A couple were even black. This seemed a reasonable alternative—musically, fashionwise, even as a lifestyle—to a pudgy young anti-social fellow like me.

And so I became a fifteen-year-old hard-drinking bluesman from Don Mills, Ontario.

I wish I could tell you what happened to Paul D. I know he started hanging around with the Para-Dice Riders, a motorcycle gang with a clubhouse that seasonally announced, "Merry Christmas from the Para-Dice Riders!!" Then I heard that the bikers were angry with Paul D., and he disappeared. But I'd like to thank him for that day—with very major reservations, of course—and wish him well.

Stephen Reid and Paddy Mitchell

THE ART

OF DYING

IN PRISON

By Stephen Reid

His last letter was less than half a page on a small piece of
yellow paper, more of a Post-It note, really. The handwritten
words closed in on themselves the way his life was closing
in on him now. He was weakened as much from his knowledge of the inevitable as from the disease.

I longed for his letters of old, those bulging envelopes,
fifteen- and twenty-page raves on anything from "the amazing
salad bar here at Leavenworth" to the joys of "running an
8-minute mile! Before chow line!"

After the diagnosis he wrote heroically about beating this thing, how he was responding to the chemo, but every passing month the envelopes grew thinner. Then they became more infrequent. It was as if he were slipping away from me one page at a time. In this, his final kite before falling into a coma, the grit, even the imagination, was gone from him. He knew he wasn't going to throw some knotted sheets over the wall or tunnel his way out of this one. The letter ended with, "We've had a life, haven't we. God bless. Your friend . . ."

Pat and I had been friends and partners for the last quarter of the twentieth century, even turning the corner into the new millennium. The first time I ever laid eyes on him I was young, just turned three times seven, and was holed up in a basement suite in Ottawa, fresh off a prison break. The unofficial mayor of the local underworld had come to take the measure of the new kid in town. Pat's strong suit was charm and he carried it off with the smile of a little boy and the manicured look of a Las Vegas pit boss. When he peeled me off some "pocket money" from a thick roll of hundreds, I knew right then and there that this was a guy I wanted to get busy with. When he mentioned a "piece of work you might be interested in," I leaped at the offer.

Pat introduced me to the big leagues. Within months we had robbed millions in cash, jewellery and gold bullion. He was usually having tea with his mother or driving his son to hockey games while I was doing the robberies. Our M.O. was established. Pat planned and I carried out the work. It was a perfect arrangement. We became like

Jack Spratt and his wife: we licked a lot of platters clean.

Over the years we became known as The Stopwatch Gang, outlaws and fugitives. We robbed banks and armoured cars from Ottawa to San Diego to St. Petersburg and back again. Later, there were others who entered into the crew, with names like Skywalker, French Danny and French Gilles, The Iceman, and chiefly a little fellow named The Ghost. These were guys, with the exception of The Ghost, who parachuted in for a particular score, then left again. But Pat and I remained together. Between the two of us we have notched seven escapes, robbed hundreds of banks and served sentences so long they look like telephone numbers.

Throughout we have remained bonded by deed, consequence, nature and friendship. Even his last letter, which left North Carolina in a canvas mailbag marked U.S. Bureau of Prisons, arrived in a canvas mailbag stamped Canada Corrections. Our friendship, often separated by iron bars, always found its way through the spaces between.

I'm not sure if anyone can truly know another human being, but I knew more of Pat than anyone could. That is to say, I knew him in ways that friends, girlfriends, priests, policemen, cellmates, bosses, even brothers, sisters, wives or children, could never know him.

Pat was a man of a thousand and one faces. A natural-born con man, he possessed an uncanny ability to sense whatever he, or you, needed him to be. He was able to make the transition to the inside of an alias and live behind a mask with ease. I've watched him take a name off a tombstone and breathe life back into the long-buried deceased. He didn't just assume the guy's driver's licence and social security number, he exhumed the persona. Pat could invent a history, then inhabit an alias so consistently, that it became somehow more real than the flesh. Yet, in all the roles he played he never lost who he was in the act of who he wasn't.

In the years in prisons we put on masks for the same reason people put on survival suits. As fugitives, we changed identities the way most people change their socks. New town, new history, new habits, values and beliefs. Because I helped to gild the puppet personas, I got to know the man behind the strings.

I knew Pat when he smoked cigars and heaped sour cream on his baked potato. I knew him when he ate raw carrots and ran five miles a day. I knew him as a Democrat and as a Republican, as Catholic, agnostic and Southern Methodist. I knew him when he liked black people and I knew him when he pretended not to. I knew him when he wore white shoes and pressed the pedal to the metal of a beige Cadillac. I knew him when he wore horn-rimmed glasses and drove a Volvo station wagon under the posted speed limit.

Somewhere up the middle of all our tomfoolery a truth ran through. These were the versions of ourselves that emerged time and again despite our well-constructed roles. As in all things human, there were often contradictory traits. I got to see Pat when he was kind and generous and humble to circumstance. I've witnessed him churlish and insufferable. I've seen him act bravely and heroically. I've looked on sadly when his nerve failed him. I've seen him as selfless as a monk and as selfish as a two-year-old. I knew him as honourable and less than honourable. He has been disingenuous to my face, and honest behind my back. He has demonstrated a loyalty beyond the capacity of most human beings, yet he betrayed me in the most petty of ways.

The only reason any of these things even bear saying now is that Pat also saw all the same facets of me. Disappointment, as much as self-sacrifice, defined our friendship. He went on being my friend. He punctured the piety of my expectations. He taught me that friendship is not built from ideals. Most relationships in the underworld, although at times intensely sentimental, seldom deepen beyond camaraderie. Maybe it was because our lives were played in such high dramatic notes that there was no time for judgment and sourness to congeal. Perhaps because our lives depended so much, and so often, on instinct and intuition we were able to become less dependent upon the construct of personality. Or maybe it was just our sense of heehaw, laughing at ourselves above all else. It could have been simply the weight of time that allowed us to see that there was no one truth to the other person. Whatever the reasons, our relationship endured and deepened, at times because of, and at other times, in spite of, ourselves.

In the beginning Pat was my mentor. He taught me about good wine, musicals and how not to think in nickels and dimes. By the time I was thirty, and Pat thirty-eight, Pat was as much student as teacher. I taught him the joys of cocaine, the language of poets and some on-the-job training—how to throw his first bank up in the air.

In those years we may as well have been Siamese twins, the way we stayed connected. Shoulder to shoulder coming out of the same bank, seated side by side in the same cars and planes as we criss-crossed the world's atlas. We holed up in the same apartment after every score. He rolled the enchiladas while I tossed the salad. We shared chateaubriand in hotel dining rooms and lived together in rented houses far away from the action. We borrowed each other's ties, double dated and drank whisky from the same bottle on the edge of a cliff in San Diego. In prison we have been cellies or lived on the same range, even played on the same hockey team. When in a tight spot we double-teamed our opponents. Once, after an unsuccessful escape bid, we were cuffed, waist chained and shackled together in the same cell in the hole. One steel bed. Only the food slot opened twice a day for eight days straight. We had to eat, stand, roll over in rhythm. We almost held hands as we took turns going to the toilet.

We were as competitive as race-car drivers. We sat for years on the floor of a cellblock, playing Scrabble through the bars. I frustrated him with superior word skills, but he always took the win with a more clever board strategy. Later in life I wrote a book, and later still, when he began to write, I encouraged and helped edit his work. But when he published a series of articles in the newspaper and I felt demeaned by some of what he wrote, I fired off a scathing review. My words danced around his on the page in a way a Scrabble board would never permit. It was our only public spat, but our friendship, as always, found a way through.

More than any other way, I knew Pat through the intimacy of risk. The stakes were high when we sawed our way through bars or robbed banks with stopwatches around our necks. Time was eternal when we bluffed our way across borders or held our breath passing through roadblocks.

Pat had once, after making a clean getaway, returned through buckshot and hot lead to take me out of a very dicey spot in the parking lot of a big-city mall. Another time I dressed up as a surgeon and threw down on four guards, just to bust him out of a prison ambulance.

Pat and I were present in the kind of moments known only to the blessed or to the damned.

We shared a long contract with loss. Arrest was as inevitable as death, and in fact, is a kind of small death. We had a throwaway phrase, that prison was "just an occupational hazard," but in the privacy of our thoughts we both knew it was the house of losers. Freshly recaptured, we would sit on opposite benches in the back of a caged van, smiling weakly at one another across the dim space, waiting for the jaws of the penitentiary to swallow us once more.

———

On January 14, 2007, Patrick (Paddy) Mitchell died in prison in Butner, North Carolina. There was no one there to fluff his pillow or hold his hand. No family or friends, no flowers at his bedside. No witness to his final breath. Pat died alone, locked in a cell, far away from everything and everyone he knew and loved, even the country he called home.

When I first got the news, I was at William Head, an 80-acre minimum-security prison on a peninsula, closed off by a quarter-mile of razor wire at one end and the cold waters of the north Pacific at the other. I remember the words simply drifting through me. "Paddy died yesterday." Words I had been expecting, yet once out of the box somehow unexpected. The freight they carried felt as heavy as the train they came in on. One disembodied telephone call, three words, and he was gone.

I must have hung up the phone, walked out of the community building, past the sounds of washers and dryers, background conversation and the click of pool balls over on the corner table. Life moving on around me in the ordinary ways of a prison evening.

I must have cut through C Unit and crossed the darkened yard, because I found myself sitting on a stump out back of the carving shed. I stared across the black and hammered surface of the sea and let the enormity of death, his, but also of death itself, sink in. The intellectual abstractions left me. The news of Pat's dying continued to drift through me, like fine particles of dust falling, accumulating on a phantom outline, gradually made visible what was formerly unseen. The shape of death became as distinct as the engraved granite on a headstone—the moment we are born the end date is in the mail. I sagged a bit and stared into nothingness. The second-to-hardest part was knowing that there was not a damned thing that could undo Pat's dying. The hardest part was sitting there in the shadows, constantly reminding myself to keep my back straight.

Sorrow is a softening, not something to readily display in front of other prisoners. Truth was, I didn't feel any teeth-gnashing, breast-beating kind of grief. I felt more numb, bereft of something. It had to do with relationship and history and memory. Our relationship had defined so much of my adult life, of his, of our mutual identities. What did it mean now that he was gone? Did the concept, the idea, of "us" die also? Where did his memories go, and what does it mean when there is no future to create them again? It felt as if the part of me that had joined with Pat in that long-ago basement suite in Ottawa had ended the moment his heart had stopped beating.

I have grown old in prison and seen more than my share of death. I have stared into its emptiness and known its finality, but Pat's death brought with it the absence of possibility, the end of the way I lived my life.

I'm not sure I even know grief, nor the intense anguish of it. I have felt everything from deep sorrow to an almost total indifference towards death. Being behind bars for so much of my life has taught me that everything is bearable, that sorrow must be kept close, buried in a secret garden of the self.

My mother, then my father, have both passed during my current sentence. For each I felt shock, then an ache, the sorrow and loss, the emptiness of a world without them in it. Only the intensity of sorrow has changed. They were my parents. I have never stopped loving them and I will never stop missing them.

I have had friends and peers and a little brother die,

some of natural causes, some accidentally, and some needlessly and violently.

I learned early and well the harsh lessons of not concealing sorrow while in the carceral world. In 1966, in Oakalla prison, I was taken to the solitary-confinement cells below the old cow barns for something I didn't do. It was Christmas Eve and I was all of sixteen years old and naked, save for a quilted "baby doll" gown that stopped about midthigh. A guard opened my door slot late that night and what he saw was a kid with his knees drawn to his chest, sobbing his face off. What I saw when I looked up were the eyes of an avuncular old man, maybe a chance for sympathy, or even an open door. What I got was, "Boo effen hoo." Then my slot slammed shut like a shot down the hallway and the guard announced to the rest of the guys in the hole, "This kid down here is crying." I was exposed as weak, cut from the herd of my fellow cons. The ridicule and abuse lasted until I made bail in mid-January.

There is an eternal grief in the nature of prison life, accompanied by an unwritten law that we must not dump more on the landscape. Like men in times of war, we cannot afford to sing the songs that may weaken us. Even the language of prison forbids it. If a person is caught crying, he's said to be "bitching up" or "sucker stroking." A teardrop tattooed under the eye signifies that a guy is doing a ten-year bid. Pat, who had fifty years in the States and twenty left from his last escape in Canada, could have tattooed five tears falling from one eye and two under the other. He didn't, but as he said in one of his near-to-last letters,

"At least I'll cheat them out of watching all seven drop."

Pat and I were often defiant but never hardened or calloused by prison. There were times, especially in the American jungles of maximum security, where we had to set aside some of that which makes us human. I remember making chit-chat about the weather with a guy as we waited for the gates to the big yard to open. Unknown to him, there were half a dozen guys out there with homemade knives waiting to put Xs on his eyes. He had broken the rules. If I had tipped him off to the play, they'd have buried me alongside him. In the heat of the jungle you can sweat but you can't cry.

I was walking a max joint on the mainland of B.C. the day I was paged over the loudspeakers, told to report to the chaplain's office. I was informed that my mother had died. I recall later that day standing in the chow line, face numb, eyes set straight ahead. The guards were leaning against the far wall, weighing me up. They knew my news; it would have been sent in an earlier Observations Notice to all staff. Not hungry, I carried my tray to the table and chewed mechanically until the food was all gone. I was determined to present no differently than any other night in the chow hall. My mother's death was too intimate, too private, too much of a loss. To show a crack in the armour, to give a face of grief to the guards lined up along the wall, would be a way of sharing. I had to play a hand of solitaire: my mother didn't belong to any of this.

My case management officer informed me that I was eligible for a leave of compassion to attend her service. I was tempted to go. The funeral might give me some solace, the permission to grieve openly. I might see something, a sobbing aunt or the courage in my father's face, or hear a cousin's joke, something that would touch me, connect me communally, make me not so alone, so unsure of what to do. Then I was told I would have to go under escort with two guards and I would be wearing leg irons. I chose to stay in my cell, to participate in the rituals of bereavement through memory and my most familiar companion, imagination. I conjured up old man McNalley wearing his grey felt gloves, driving his black hearse that would carry my mom over to the little red-brick United church on Imperial Street. My five sisters in dark, muted dresses, supporting one another. My two brothers, uncomfortable in suits, directing the traffic of mourners towards their pews. Most of the citizens of our small town would gather later in the graveyard under the whispering pines. Our family would stand nearest the damp mound of earth, the clean rectangular edges of the freshly dug hole, my father leaning on his cane and probably on one of my brothers, Mom's casket being lowered, a handful of dirt, and another.

I would have chosen not to go because of the leg irons alone, but there was another complication. I was estranged from my brothers and sisters at the time of Mom's death. They had phoned the prison chaplain, asking him to let me know. They were stingy with details. I was being punished for not being there for Mom when she was alive, for all the times I had let her down. Their consensus was that I had lost the right to be a part of their mourning for her.

I accepted without argument their consensus and their anger. I loved my mom as much as any of them but knew I had to live with the consequences of my actions. I gathered up what scraps of dignity I could and laid shame atop of sadness. I let it all sink down to that place where those things go to exist, the place where we don't hold grief, it holds us.

A few years after my mother passed, when I was still in prison, I was called to the phone. My brother told me that our dad wouldn't be coming out of the hospital this time. A week later he died. I wrote my brother to thank him for that courtesy. When we were both quite young, whenever we fell down, banged an elbow or scraped a knee, we each, with all the fierce determination of little boys, tried hard for Dad not to see us cry. Which in a way was curious, because if tears did spring forth, as they sometimes would, Dad was never harsh about it. But I think I would have done anything, bit clear through my lip, pinched the flesh until it was black and blue, anything other than having to make him look away. My father, born in the thirties, brought up in a working-class family, was silent, wounded by war. Like too many men of his generation, imprisoned by circumstance, he was deeply afraid of tears.

I have carried grief throughout the years, kept it close, like precious cargo, never letting a drop spill. Coast Salish women will sit in a darkened room, long before the sun rises and the household stirs, and there they collect their tears in a bowl. Once the day breaks they won't be seen crying. This is to allow the spirit of whomever they are mourning to pass over to the other side, not to be held back by the sorrow of the living. I, too, have kept my grief in a darkened room, but for much less noble reasons. I did not want to appear weak in front of others, to be seen as less of a man. In doing so I fear I have become in some ways less of a person.

Pat's dying was different; it changed in me the way I saw death, and that in turn changed the way I held grief. For the first few weeks after he passed, I walked the big track every night, kicking stones. I would feel the familiar loss, accompanied by the odd, inexplicable flash of dread, as if something was wrong, then I would remember. I read books and essays, texts on loss. I sometimes wondered why philosophers and holy men often anguished so much over the purity of their grief. All grief is pure, all grief is self-serving.

Other times I would cloud over with anger and indignation that Pat had to die in that place, that sick as he was, Stockwell Day, justice minister, would not sign his transfer papers and allow him to return to a Canadian prison via the Prisoner Exchange Treaty. He could then have been visited by family during his final days. I soon saw through these thoughts disguised as feelings. They were a way of invoking pity for Pat, along with a dose of self-pity, a sentiment we both hated.

At the bottom of my feelings was the presence of death that Pat, like no one before him, had brought home to me. It had begun on that stump behind the carving shed. My own death had formerly seemed a foreign and vague thing, a nagging surety that I somehow postponed facing. It was a date not on my calendar, an event that happened to others, not me, not for a long while anyway, long enough not to have to entertain for now. Even the deaths of my parents seemed natural progression, but for them, not for me. I had spent my life in wilful non-engagement with the knowledge that I would die.

Pat and I shared a life so intertwined that his death seemed to open a way for me to begin to reconcile with the inevitability of my own dying. I began to fear death a bit less. It became possible for me to hold my gaze on the end of life. Through Pat I became curious about how it all ends but stayed just one step back of letting this persuade me—like the one bad habit of all gods and all religions—towards romanticizing my notion of his death, or even my own.

When Pat was first scheduled for surgery and there was still hope, he was transferred to the federal medical facility in Butner, North Carolina. I suspect that even then he carried a homemade handcuff key under his tongue as he passed through the gates of what would prove to be his final penitentiary.

He was also looking forward to his son Kevin's coming down from Canada for a visit. Kevin kept his promise, appearing with his two sons. It was the first time Pat was able to see his grandchildren. They were allowed two, two-hour visits on two consecutive days. Pat was shackled to the bed throughout, and four guards stayed present in the room. Kevin wrote later that Pat never uttered a word of complaint, about pain nor circumstance. "But Dad has never complained, has he, Stevie?" No he hasn't, not in a lifetime of it. Kevin had to return to Canada with his sons, the surgery was ultimately unsuccessful, and Pat was alone with his imminent end.

It took a long time for me to see his dying in that place clearly, but finally his death made a perfect poetic sense. It was honest to his life, completely unsentimental. In a barren cell, uncluttered by comfort or distraction, he had to lie there on his back and stare up at a concrete ceiling. There was no dodge, no escape, no new identity to slip into. The only tombstone in the room had his own name on it. He was made to acknowledge that he was dying. I feel certain that he did it with dignity and grace, and without illusion.

"We've had a life, haven't we." It wasn't a question, it was his way of introducing the end. He taught me there was no hope or value or wisdom in death, only death. No more tunnels, no more banks and no more letters. He left me with only the inescapable gift of grief.

Jeab holding Cherie

Noah Meyer

GOOGLING

THE

BARDO

By Renee Rodin

In 2002, Noah Meyer, my son, gave up his job as a
Manhattan computer programmer to live on the beach in
rural Phuket, Thailand. There he met and fell in love with
Chompoonut (Jeab) Kobram, who had moved to the more
prosperous south from her home in Burriram, Thailand, the
most depressed part of the country.

Jeab had a daughter by a European man who'd
returned to his homeland without acknowledging paternity.
As is common in Thailand, a country high in poverty and

low in prospects, Jeab left her baby, Cherie, with her parents in order to find work; after rigorous training, Jeab became a certified scuba-dive master, a good job in Thailand, where aging parents depend on their grown children for support. Noah adored Cherie, whom he got to know through visits, and intended to adopt her.

Jeab and Noah had been living together for almost two years, and were engaged to be married, when her former boyfriend, Sam Van Treeck, a Belgian expat, reconnected with her. Van Treeck and she had split up before she met Noah, whom she told, "I'm glad he no longer hates me." Van Treeck was phoning mainly for advice. Jeab said Van Treeck was having trouble with his wife, a woman from Laos.

Jeab's scuba-diving diploma arrived in the mail in June 2004, while she was away on a trip. In the middle of the afternoon on June 25, she phoned to tell Noah she was returning home the next day. He was to call her early that evening to make arrangements to pick her up either at the bus station or at the airport. His calls to her cellphone went unanswered and he spent a frantic night trying to reach her by phone and email.

The following day, Jeab's uncle came from Bangkok with the newspaper; Noah saw Jeab's lifeless, semi-nude body sprawled out in a photo on the front page. She was in Van Treeck's condo in Pattaya. Police estimated that she was killed soon after she and Noah had last talked. Though the article reported 48 wounds, we were to learn from the autopsy that she had been stabbed 134 times, her throat had been slashed, and there were signs that she had been tortured.

Newspapers reported that nothing had been stolen from the apartment and that police believed the murder was not the result of a robbery gone bad but was more likely a murder committed during a fit of rage. It appeared that Jeab had fought her attacker; hair found on her hands and blood and tissue from under her fingernails was sent for forensic testing. Newspapers also reported that a building security video showed that Van Treeck was in the apartment building at the time of the murder and that this information was confirmed by witnesses.

A few days later, Van Treeck was arrested as the prime suspect. He said that he discovered Jeab's body once he got home from his job as a tourist guide. He maintained his innocence, but police remanded him in custody to face charges of murder.

Later, in July, while Noah was staying with me at my home in Vancouver, we heard that after Van Treeck had spent seventeen days in jail the Belgian embassy in Bangkok had helped him make bail. We read in a Thai newspaper that Van Treeck's father, Marc, a well-known Belgian musician, had made a champagne toast to his son's freedom and declared, "The bail proves he's innocent."

Then I received a private phone call from a case manager for Asia at Foreign Affairs in Ottawa. She said she thought that Van Treeck would be allowed to escape, because such is the privilege of Western murderers of Thai women. Thailand has never been occupied, but it has been colonized by the West, upon which it is dependent for tourism. She said our only hope was to get as much media attention as possible, because it would bounce back to Thailand and might embarrass the government into detaining Van Treeck. Before Jeab's death and since, newspapers have reported incidents of Western men finding ways of leaving Thailand after being accused of killing Thai women.

My main concern was for my son, who was focused but traumatized. Even so, he continued to work hard to bring attention to the case. But with the call from Ottawa, I suddenly felt that I needed to get involved.

We were grateful for immediate coverage by Vancouver's weekly *Georgia Straight* and soon afterward by the *Asian Pacific Post*. But all other media I approached were indifferent to what they construed as a "Third World story."

There had already been a lot of publicity in Thailand. Jeab was beautiful and the murder sensational. Jeab's mother, Sa-nga Phanbuatong, told the *Bangkok Nation* that Van Treeck had been asking her daughter to get back together with him. "Chompoonut turned him down as she was in a new relationship. My daughter said that he was very upset about the refusal and he had tried many times for reconciliation. I think Sam Van Treeck might be the person who killed my daughter out of jealousy and anger as my daughter did not want to get back together with him."

Jeab's family, impoverished rice farmers, has neither resources nor voice in their own country; they considered Noah their son-in-law and relied on him to obtain justice for their daughter.

My family is Canadian, so I appealed to authorities in Canada, as well as those in Thailand and Belgium, to have

Van Treeck put on the Interpol list to stop him if he tried to cross a border. Canada's minister of foreign affairs responded with platitudes and the statement that it was "a matter between a Belgian and a Thai citizen," as if Jeab were alive to sue Van Treeck. The Belgian consul sent me an email warning me not to talk with the press.

In the fall, just before evidence in the case was to be presented in a Thai court, Van Treeck fled to Belgium. A major trading partner with Thailand, Belgium has a one-way extradition treaty with Thailand; they can have criminals returned to them, but they never send their own citizens back to Thailand.

As far as I know, except for the *Phuket Gazette* and *Pattaya News,* no Thai press covered Van Treeck's escape nor its aftermath. A warrant effective for twenty years was issued for his arrest, but it is only good if he returns to Thailand. A series of hearings was held without him.

In Canada the *Asian Pacific Post* published another large article, which was followed eventually by an extensive feature ("Justice Delayed, Justice Denied") in the *Vancouver Courier.* With the silence by all other media in Canada and the censorship in Thailand, the media in Belgium made do with Van Treeck's side of the story.

Van Treeck's parents organized a press scrum and a hero's welcome for their son's arrival at a Belgian airport. For weeks he was on television and radio, in newspapers and magazines, boasting about having survived seventeen days in a Thai jail. Van Treeck never said how he had left the country, but he did thank the Belgian embassy in

Bangkok for support. Thai papers said his passport remained in the possession of the Thai government.

One of the many Belgian journalists who wrote about him called me to say that Van Treeck had brought his Laotian wife to Belgium to appear as a "good family man" for the media. Some newspapers reported that Van Treeck's wife had arrived in Belgium a week before he did.

In November, his family held a benefit, raising over 75,000 euros, during which Van Treeck announced, "Everything is for sale in Thailand. I'll use the money to pay back my bribes for escaping." Around the same time, he sent Noah an email advising him to "keep looking for Jeab's killer, he's out there."

Several Canadian lawyers told me about the complications of international law. In the end it seemed that our only recourse would be to sue Van Treeck for "wrongful death" and that would mean hiring a lawyer and paying for a trip to Thailand to investigate. It was all prohibitively expensive.

When, in November 2006, two and a half years after Jeab's murder, Thailand sent evidence and transcripts to Belgium and petitioned them to prosecute Van Treeck, a Belgian journalist called me to say, "Until now we were sure Van Treeck was innocent, because naturally we stand up for our own." Belgium accepted the Thai petition and agreed to prosecute, but Van Treeck remained free.

The more time went by, the more muddled things seemed. As reported by the *Vancouver Courier*, "Even setting aside the intricacies of bail procedures and extradition treaties, the murder of Kobram is surrounded by puzzles. Early press coverage from Pattaya indicated that the police had a wealth of forensic evidence, including blood, finger-prints, hair and tissue. But as early as September, stories about the case featured police spokesmen refusing to comment on the forensic evidence, and more recent stories suggest the evidence was inconclusive."

Jeab lived to be twenty-three, but it's as if she never existed. If demographics are destiny, Jeab was devalued to nothing because she was a woman of colour with no money and no power. Her erasure was not an isolated incident. All over the world more women die due to domestic violence than war. Countless women have been killed. Countless numbers of their murderers have gone free.

In December 2005, a British tourist, Katherine Horton, was murdered in Thailand. To avoid discouraging tourism, Thai authorities apprehended, tried and convicted her killers in under a month and the news was publicized internationally.

In the summer of 2006, another Thai woman was killed. Her accused British boyfriend was given bail and went on the lam. There was little publicity. The only dif-ference between him and Van Treeck is that no one knows where the British boyfriend is.

Jeab's death no longer defines my life. But it is as close as yesterday when something triggers me into thinking about it. No amount of scar tissue can cover my anguish about her terrible death, or my anger about the grinding injustice that followed.

No amount of time can eradicate my anxiety. Such evil does not fade away. It is hard to let go of expectations of justice, of any kind of justice. It is hard to get to grief.

———

The news spread through me sickeningly. Noah was on the phone, telling me in a voice so flat it was airless that his fiancée had been stabbed to death. "No," I shrieked, but then gathered myself up to concentrate on my son, who told me, "I'm sleeping like a baby," and I knew he was in deep shock.

He didn't want me to go there. He'd be home in a couple of weeks, after organizing a memorial for Jeab and a trust fund for her daughter, Cherie. Schools are free in Thailand, but uniforms and books are not. Her future was now his focus.

I'd recently spent a month with Noah and Jeab in Thailand. She was strong, proud, a feminist, exceedingly bright and very attractive. People gravitated towards her.

Before going on the trip, I had experienced inexplicable dread. I'd had to take anti-anxiety medication just to get on the plane, and needed it the whole time I was there. The dose, enough to topple an elephant, only took the edge off, and even after I returned I remained afraid but didn't know why. As soon as I heard about Jeab, I stopped taking the pills; they had prevented nothing.

Violence is the spine of news—the Montreal Massacre, Vancouver's Missing Women, B.C.'s Highway of Tears. It has surrounded me, swarmed me, in movies, books and songs, but this was a direct hit. A thousand times I have heard the story of possession and destruction in the name of love, of a man destroying a woman rather than letting her go. Yet this was the first time I'd really heard it. It was unreal, unimaginable.

I went about my daily life, returned a tool to a neighbour and told him, told others too. Very matter-of-factly, I said, "My son's fiancée has just been murdered." From a distance I watched as people gasped, as if I'd delivered a kick to their solar plexus.

Soon Noah was home and I held him in my arms, held back my tears. He needed me to be strong for him; I wanted to rock him as if he were a baby. If only I could soothe him. "It was just a bad dream." But he could not awaken from this nightmare.

I am his mother. I was supposed to protect him, but I had no idea how to guide him through this wanton waste—I struggled for words. All he wanted was that it had never happened; all I wanted was to make his hurt go away. The shock that had been such a blessing was wearing off. The pain was getting in.

Noah's sister, Joey, and his brother, Daniel, who live in New York, came to Vancouver. Our family rallied around Noah. At times we fell apart. It's difficult enough to cope with natural loss due to sickness, accident or age, when there is no one to blame. How were we to grapple with the knowledge that some person had deliberately caused such suffering?

In the warm air I felt old and cold. I pushed my leaden body out of the house only when necessary. The sunlight was too bright for my eyes. The slightest breeze battered my skin. Social events were out of the question; I didn't know how to make small talk, could only talk about the murder. Small violations became huge to me. I felt hideous, as if strips of flesh were hanging off me. I was crazy with grief. To be shunned. Stay away. Stay away.

Jeab's daughter had just turned two years old when her mother was killed. Noah told me after one of his many trips to Thailand that even months later, every time Cherie heard the phone ring she asked, "Is that my mother calling?"

I kept going over the details of Jeab's death, wondering what her last minutes were like. Was there a point at which she realized she was losing a battle for her life? We know she fought back; there was skin under her fingernails. I vacillated between disbelief and disgust about the freedom of the man accused of her death. Injustice really is burning; it released corrosive acids that swilled around in me. I lost trust.

Some people were creeped out by me, as if I were carrying a contagious disease. Others pretended that nothing had happened, out of their idea of politeness, and so the burden was on me either to bring it up or to join in the pretense. Some prescribed how long it would take "to get over this" or what to do "to feel better," as if I were ill. Their reactions came from simply not knowing how to respond and their fear that I might spiral out of control. All strong emotions are frowned on in our society, but especially anger and sorrow. Restraint and control are the order of the day.

But there is no correct or incorrect way to grieve. No right or wrong way, no timeline, no limit. Nobody can tell you how to feel or when to feel it, or for how long. Grief is totally individual, totally personal. Emotions can't be legislated, are not subject to logic; they are their own universe. Closure is a myth. You learn to live with the hole in your heart.

Waves of grief came at me at unexpected times, in unlikely places. I went down, under, then resurfaced. It happened over and over, only the intervals and intensity varying.

Old friends extended themselves in soft, sensitive ways with words and gestures I could absorb. New friends came to me. Secrets were revealed as if previously kept in shame; I was amazed by the number of people who have been touched by violence to their close friends or family members.

Because I couldn't stand being so self-absorbed, trapped in my own misery, I forced myself to go downtown for a demonstration about the plight of Afghan woman. After the bus ride, while walking over to the protest area, I spotted someone I'd just seen as a subject in a TV documentary on homeless people in Vancouver. She'd changed her hairstyle and I thought she looked good. As we passed each other, she punched me hard in the belly. I doubled over and screamed, "Fuck you. Why?" while she sauntered away. But I knew why. She'd seen something on my face that showed I was too vulnerable to be out in public. I jumped back on a bus and hurried home.

My one ritual for the newly dead is to light a candle— I have no spiritual framework, nothing to bolster me. Jeab was Buddhist. I googled the Bardo, which means "gap." It is a description of the journey you take, the transitions you make, right after you die. I clicked on "violent death," "enlightenment" and "rebirth" for a person who has been killed. Then I explored what happens to the killer. Buddhism is pragmatic; it has an answer for everything. But blinded by "an eye for an eye," I could find nothing of comfort to convey to my son, and his comfort was the only thing that would comfort me. The umbilical cord is a magical material, a substance that lies dormant, ready to stretch when needed over time and distance.

I carried the murderous stranger with me. Someone else's child had become part of me. I abhorred him, wished he were dead. Somewhere, very deep inside, notions of forgiveness skittered resentfully through me. But I expelled everything that threatened to dilute my sorrow and rage. These feelings I had to hang on to, or I'd disappear.

Explanations were meaningless, experience nothing. There was no sense to Jeab's murder, no way to understand Van Treeck's actions. I knew only that the shape of my son's heart had changed forever. I could promise him only that his life would go on. On the radio I heard another mother and son discuss the Yiddish term *kine-ahora*. It is meant to ward off the evil eye, to protect those you love. I berated myself that I'd never said it too.

I put on the bracelet Jeab had given me, an exquisite amber bead on a braided rope. I wore it constantly, its consistency and weight a reassuring presence. Every time I thought of her, a hundred times a day, I held on to the bead.

———

My three kids are close in age and close in spirit. After spending time with me in Vancouver, Noah joined Daniel and Joey in New York. There he was able to find work to pay for lawyers in Thailand to represent Jeab's family.

Though he was holding down a full-time job, going back and forth to see Jeab's family, stopping en route in Vancouver to see me, he remained solidly involved with the case. But I took on the full-time job of dealing with the media, politicians and authorities.

I researched law, fielded phone calls and monitored e-mails from different time zones in North America, Asia and Europe. This meant staying up late into the night and waking up early the next morning. Always I received opposite messages from those in the know about international murder cases. Some advised me to continue seeking media coverage. Others urged me to leave it to quiet diplomacy. The only consistent message from everyone was never to use "emotional" language, state only the facts. Otherwise I was likely to provoke and alienate authorities. All my writing, my press releases, my pleas to politicians, my requests for legal information and help from international agencies became an act of repression.

Along with being concerned for Noah, for two years I tangled with officials in Canada, Thailand and Belgium. The stress, frustration and exhaustion built, and one day I ended up howling in the bathtub. I was overwhelmed by helplessness, in despair at the tragedy of Jeab's death and the futility of all my efforts to bring the accused to trial. I had failed to reach the "right" politician, failed to reach the "right" press.

As a temporary measure my doctor put me on anti-depressants, and the first time I smiled, after about a week on the drugs, my cheeks ached—it had been so long.

Slowly my energy for life returned. Our family danced with joy at Daniel and Kelly's wedding. Joey and Craig's new baby, Henry, has brought all of us great happiness.

Noah continues to support the Kobrams in every way possible. Cherie lives with her doting grandparents and her aunt Jah in her own culture, rich with tradition, and she is thriving. She is being raised to honour her mother's memory and will grow up knowing that Jeab counted.

Noah has found new love with a woman in New York, and they recently went to the remote village in Burriram so that Sarah could meet Cherie and the Kobrams.

Mostly I accept that there's little more within a legal framework that I can do about Jeab's murder.* Part of me still resists letting go. I wonder whether I'll retain the lessons I've learned about grief or if I will disappoint people in the future as I've no doubt done in the past. It is hard to be consoled and it is hard to console.

---

* In June 2009, Belgian law enforcement finally arrested Sam Van Treeck.

Rob Allen

WHAT

WILL NOT

BURY

By Anne Stone

I expect you to appear
at the threshold of a tabagie in the plateau
and explain what it means that you're not here.
Explain your protest against the heat death
of your universe, explain in severe
terms the flavors of the waters of lethe.
I write because some things will not bury

—*Jaszon Camlot, "I am writing just because I can"*

Last night, I opened the yellowed pages of one of Rob's books on wildflowers, and ever so briefly, there was the faint smell of his American cigarettes, the very breath of one of those quiet nights when the world blanketed itself away, and became something unguessed at beyond the cedar trees. On such nights, our wood house was folded into the sounds of sashaying branches and his face, outside the cast of the wood stove, was soft with darkness.

Sometimes, I think that grief is the last connection I share with Rob, its shape and dimension known only to him and to me. Known to me, as I remember him. Known to him, as he dreams the place we once lived: a little house on the edge of a cliff, bordered by a cedar swamp. That's what ghosts do, it seems to me. At peace, sleeping, ghosts cast their dreams into the realm of the living.

———

The night that Rob died, my world shrank down to the size of one suitcase.

Long after our romantic relationship had ended, Rob had been my home in Quebec, the place I shored up, and with him gone, outside of my home in Vancouver, I didn't have a place in this world to be. Not one that felt natural, unquestioned. There were plenty of people to "put me up," but with Rob, I'd had a home. The night he died, that home died with him.

I should backtrack. Explain. Rob was a much older man who extracted me from a terrible eddy that had caught me in my early twenties. One night, I caught his eye, and he asked me to come home with him. And I did. I "came home" with him, and that "coming home" was more profound than the casual invitation suggested to either of us. Over the next six years, we built things together, stone fences and concrete ponds, pine bookshelves and dreams of things we'd do before we quit this earth or it quit us.

Idle, with all the hubris of youth, I'd ask questions by way of planning for exigencies that never came: What would we do if you lost an arm? if I lost an eye? if we won big at the lottery? had a cerebral hemorrhage? gave birth to a child? Both of us were writers, and we spent a lot of time alone together in a cabin bordered by a cedar forest on one side and a swamp on the other, in the company of deer and squirrels. After two thousand nights of talk, there wasn't much we hadn't imagined ourselves living through.

Rob dying slowly of cancer was one thing neither of us had imagined.

————

When Rob found out he had cancer, an aggressive melanoma, we'd not been together in a long time. For half a dozen years, I'd been living with my new sweetheart in Vancouver. But there was a connection between Rob and me still. A real and felt obligation to care for one another. So when he asked me to be there at the end, I promised him I would.

I didn't guess what it would mean to return to L'Estrie, the Eastern Townships, and find myself exclusively in the company of people from an earlier time in my life. I didn't guess that Rob's dying would· cast a recursive line backwards, leaving me unsure which time frame, exactly, I belonged to. I looked up from his bedside and saw faces from the nineties, a decade past. Did I belong, still, to the immediate past? Everything that surrounded me now was both urgent and historic. Or did I belong to my distant present, a life that lay some 3,000 miles from here? As Rob lay dying, time slowed to a crawl: time moved more slowly even than it does for a child. Moments spent leaning next to a bedside, touching hands, grew into hours. These were days spent in an endless gathering of breaths. Time was not large and plotted out, but small and infibrillated, each moment content to reach tiny cilia outwards, gathering minute sensations from the present, sometimes tapping rich veins of meaning from the past.

When Rob died, his breathing slowed.

Time slowed.

The world paused, stood still, and, slowly, began to revolve once more under a new sky.

It was like this: the time between each of his breaths grew longer, and there were pauses, too, between the breaths. As Rob was dying, these pauses were like a diver's just before he breaks the surface, and I never knew whether Rob was in between breaths or at his very last, and each breath that did come, each gasp, pulled me down with him into an oceanic darkness, and he slipped away from us that way, between breaths. At the end of one breath, I waited and waited for him to surface with me, but he was gone.

———

The hospice nurse told me that there was a tradition. We would be given coffee and cookies in the solarium while they washed and prepared the body, and then we could see him one last time if we wished. I leaned over the bed and closed Rob's eyes, or I tried to, but his eyes were so dry it was more difficult to do than anything I'd seen in the world of film had suggested it could be. I wondered if they'd be able to set his mouth right—it'd been gaping for days, as if to drink in the air his body could no longer possess.

A few moments later, while they prepared his body, I stood outside of the hospice with his son, Cary, and his friend Jon. I was surprised the sky was there. It was a new sky, a child's sky, and I wondered, entirely, what the sky was still doing above us at all. I remember that as we walked into the night, someone joked, likely Jon, and we were all so relieved to laugh that we laughed hard, and our laughter sounded very alive and reassuring, and obscene. The three of us were moving, breathing, laughing, aware that the world outside the hospice walls had held together after all. All the old familiar nouns were out there waiting for us: tree, sky, earth.

I looked at a sky that was indifferent to us, and inside of me, I knew, there remained a strong connection to a dying man. In that moment, I knew I couldn't yet go home to the living, to the man I shared my life with now. I was standing at the threshold to some other place, and I couldn't yet turn back.

———

In the solarium, they served us coffee and cookies. I don't think I ate, don't think I could eat, but the presence of food was comforting, and it occurred to me that this wasn't a "solarium," as it was nighttime and there was no sun. If anything, this room where they'd placed coffee and cookies was a "lunarium," and similarly, I was no longer the person I'd been before Rob died, because some self that existed only in conversation with him was now consigned to memory and was no longer a thing of the present. Some subtle thing about the light in the sky had been replaced, and I was someone who lived under this new, strange sky. I looked at the black walls of the lunarium, the glass in darkness, and wondered what I would do now, what this world with the sky still in it had to do with me at all.

———

Soon, Rob's sister Viv arrived to see her brother one last time, and to take me to her home.

Some people, when they grieve, develop an increased tolerance for alcohol. At least, this was the case with me, and I needed more alcohol than Vivienne customarily had on hand in her house. Jon and I both. After Viv and Rob's mother had both swallowed sleeping pills and gone to their beds, Jon and I wondered at the quiet, and talked. We were pretty much strangers to one another. Our connection was Rob, and Rob had been extinguished. Our relationships with him had, for the most part, taken place at different times and in different time zones. That night, we talked easily.

Rob had been a drinker. We drank some after Rob died. And it was companionable. And the blurriness drinking offered me was a good prosthetic for skin, because on this night, and on many nights to come, I had none.

———

The memorial for Rob was held at his sister's house in Lennoxville one week after he died. That afternoon, while preparing, Jon and I accidentally let Vivienne's dog out, and spent an hour or so racing through the neighbourhood's yards, trying to catch the little black furball. Vivienne's dog was one of those small ones: yippy and unnaturally fast. It was both comedic and terribly sad at the same time.

I was glad to see people I knew from Montreal and my life with Rob, and was glad to greet them, but I didn't know what to say about Rob's death. If asked, I entered into a long loop that described Rob's death, from wherever my head was at that moment. I hadn't manufactured a cliché to hand out, like a Hallmark card, to somehow relieve the people around me. Not that anyone expected anything of the sort. I was still seeing Rob then. I mean, he'd come and lean up against a tree and look at me, sort of gently grinning the way he did, even if only in his eyes, and look to see if I was doing okay. He wanted to hang around and see that I managed. It's hard to speak of someone like they're dead, when they're dead to everyone but you. His ashes were in an urn and the urn was wrapped in a burgundy velvet sack. Vivienne had handed the sack to me; it was surprisingly heavy, and she'd said: "I thought you might want to spend some more time with Rob." Though unsettled by the arrangement of nouns, I put Rob on the table next to my bed. The grammar of death undid me. The intractable past tense. The strange bedmates made by nouns.

When Rob and I were together, I'd made him a little keepsake: a lock of my hair, braided around a small knot of wood. When he was incinerated, he'd kept that with him. It was one of the few things he'd taken with him to the hospice. I wasn't sure if I was entirely here, or partly there, with Rob. That night, I was aware that a lock of my hair was on the table, next to the guest bed, burned to ash inside a red sack.

A lot of people spoke that night. Talked about Rob, read his poems. I stood at the back and quietly drained a bottle of amaretto. I don't usually like sweet stuff, but on this night, it was smooth enough to go down fast, and this grief had a thirst all its own.

Vivienne's shut down at about ten, but a lot of Montreal folks walked over to the Lion's Pub. Nora, a young woman Rob had lived with after me, David and Jason, whom I will always love for the way they were with Rob when he was dying, and some other friends. And we drank until the Lion shut down, then went back to the hotel.

That night, I felt like I was up for adoption, pulling my suitcase along the streets, pulling it through the slush on creaky old wheels. All of us went back to one of the rooms, where more bottles were pulled out of suitcases. This was right. It was how Rob would've had us do it. If he were here to oversee things, he would have approved. The night was good, but then, of course, the body gives out and you sleep and the morning has to come, and what do you do with yourself then? When the memorial is over and you're still remembering?

———

David was grey. That's how much we'd drunk. Because, as far as drinking goes, I think David could have held his own with Rob, and for David to look grey meant we'd done some serious liver damage. I smiled at the sky, which was blue and sunny, though the air was cold and there was a grey pallor to the clouds. That day, we'd head back into Montreal. Always, whether in the Townships or in Montreal, Rob was my home, my place to come back to. Now, I was drifting. A friend had invited me to stay with him, and so I vaguely headed up to Mile End. On the way, I called my old friend Grant, to see whether he wanted to kill half an hour till my friend got home. Grant asked me to meet him at their place. Elsie was home, he said, and he'd be there soon.

Grant and his wife, Elsie, had been great friends with Rob and me those years we were together. A lot had happened since then. Rob and Elsie had grown much closer, and she and I had grown apart. For the last couple of years, Rob had rented one of the rooms in their apartment, a place to stay when he was working in the city. Like Rob, Elsie had been struggling with cancer.

In the last month, I'd learned how to take care of Rob. I'd learned a lot of things about dying and about cancer. As I pulled my suitcase towards Jeanne Mance, I carefully composed the face I'd worn for Rob, the one that looked into his eyes and saw him there, and didn't pause on the ways that cancer had profoundly changed him. I pulled my suitcase step by step up Grant and Elsie's walk-up and stood at the door to Rob's old *pied-à-terre*. Then I knocked.

———

Elsie was changed by the cancer the way people are changed by cancer. Everything goes. She was so bent on survival that things like how her head was half-shaved no longer mattered. Later, when I accompanied her to the hospital for radiation treatment, she'd laugh and put on her pink beret and say, "I have to, so I don't terrify children."

Elsie and I sat down at her kitchen table. At this moment, she was where Rob had been a few months before I'd arrived. Her skin was grey and so was what remained of her now-curly hair. She sat down in her blue bathrobe, lit a cigarette and offered one to me.

Soon, Grant was there too. He'd start a sentence and sometimes his blue eyes would fill with tears, though he gave no other sign that he knew he was losing Elsie, just this crying in the midst of ordinary speech.

You're welcome to stay here, they both told me. You don't mind staying in Rob's room?

I don't mind, I told them, and I didn't. It would be comforting to be around his things.

I had drifted into a house, you see, where nobody had any skin and everyone was so immersed in grief that no one was confronted with the strangeness of it all. In their home, I didn't have to pretend I felt otherwise. In the midst of a sentence, I would sometimes get tired, and here, I could simply walk to Rob's room, curl up inside his covers, bury my face in the old pillow I knew so well, and sleep. Here, I could get through it all. Or so I thought.

———

Before Rob died, I'd read that grief comes in waves. When the first terrible wave hit, it didn't feel possible it'd ever pass, it felt *forever* bad. I could find no way out. So it was good to have read in a book that this feeling might pass, and know that if the book was right, there might be moments in which I could breathe between this and the next wave that, again, would feel forever bad. But when the first wave happened to me, it came at me harder than I'd expected. It washed down hard. The wave pulled me off my feet, and when I was upside down, suspended, there was nothing to do but *whatever* I could. Period.

(*Whatever* as in absolutely nothing, curling up in a ball and dimming into sleep when my brain started that old familiar roll. *Whatever* as in grieving with those among us who were still dying, but not yet dead—fitting company to bear, with not a shred of skin between us. *Whatever* as in conjuring up what there was between Rob and me, good and bad, searching for something to make his death an easier thing to stand. *Whatever* as in drinking and smoking, my mouth a dishrag, while speaking of the dead.)

There are things I learned from this time that I don't know I want anyone else to learn. What it means to be dying of cancer, for instance. What it means to have time to grieve in advance of a death. What it means to be scared, to look at an IV bag full of blood, dripping down time, and wonder if you can outrun it. How some of the clichés are true. How, when someone is dying, people really are their best selves— or their worst. As Rob died, I wonder if it occurred to him that he was surrounded by exaggerations of the people he'd once known. Sometimes regrettable. Sometimes offering kindnesses I know I'll always be grateful for.

I found it hard to see the difference between love lost and grief, if that subtle distinction exists. And I found it hard, for some time, to find my way back to Vancouver, to my love, to the living, to my life. So I stayed on a month after Rob died, with Elsie and Grant. It was easy to stay. Their lives were rough, filled with crises, and such crises both made sense to me and meant I couldn't dwell on my own sadness for too long. But then one day, and it was as immediate as this, I telephoned my sweetheart, and I heard the present tense in his voice. I heard something that reminded me, urgently, of where I lived now, and I hung up the telephone, explained that I had to go, bought a plane ticket for a day after the ash ceremony, and began to find my way home.

That Sunday, I stood among those old cedar boughs for the last time. Rob's family and oldest friends had gathered to spread, as Rob had wished, his ashes on his land. I still have Rob's old jacket, which I wore on that day, though I am getting closer to giving it away. To some soul who needs its physical warmth more than anyone can need a symbol. We stood, and we read his poems, and his ashes were passed between us and into the land, and though I was clumsy, and though the ashes blew back onto the jacket I was wearing, and though these gestures were messy and flawed, they were also perfect, because here we were, Rob's imperfect friends and family, who had been loved by him as we were.

———

A month after Rob died, I arrived back in Vancouver. At home, I checked my phone messages and there was one from Rob. I was elated. My first reaction was pure celebration. After a wonderful pause, and as the seconds ticked down, the smile slowly left my face. I knew better. The call was months old.

A year and a half has passed since Rob's death. The sky is an old and familiar friend, and I've grown back into my familiar skin. Rob lies more comfortably in the past now than once he did, though still there are times—as when I opened the book of wildflowers and drew in a breath of the past— when I am shocked by his loss, and he is newly mourned.

Tiff and Bill in their only mutual stage appearance

GOOD

GRIEF

By *William Whitehead*

There are things you need to know.

Most of all, you need to know about Tiff.

In 1962 I was co-producing a season of repertory theatre in Toronto. My partners and I had hired a young actor named Timothy Findley, known to his friends by his initials, Tiff. We had barely met before, but he had the reputation of being a troublemaker. Well, in a sense he was demanding, especially when it came to the fit of his costumes. But—a superb actor. And an impressive person.

He would turn out to be deeply caring—about any kind of creativity, about people, about nature. He had a way of connecting immediately to children, to animals—and to love. All that I was to learn later—long after I met him as an actor in 1962.

He came to my office one day after rehearsal—with a favour to ask. He had taped a CBC television drama a few months earlier, and it was to be aired that evening. The trouble was that the room he was renting from friends had no TV. Could he possibly . . . ???

I was delighted to invite him to my place, but after he was gone, I realized that I had absolutely nothing to offer in the way of refreshments. And, having invested deeply in the theatre project, my pockets were just about as empty as my refrigerator. A quick check revealed just enough to acquire some crackers and cheese—or a six-pack of beer. Hmmm. Timothy Findley. So I slipped out and got the beer.

When Tiff arrived, I welcomed him in and headed for the kitchen, confidently calling back over my shoulder, "Can I get you a beer, Tiff?"

"Oh, Bill, I'm terribly sorry," he replied, "but I've just started taking a drug that would make me desperately ill if I touched anything alcoholic."

Ah.

"But I'm absolutely starved, if there's anything to eat."

Well.

We watched the show—with Tiff in the title role of Jules Pfeiffer's *Crawling Arnold*—and we talked. And talked. And talked.

And for the next forty years, on a certain date in February, I would turn to Tiff, smile and say, "Tiffy—isn't ,it time you went home?"

Forty years. Over half my life. Years filled with wonder, laughter, a lot of travelling, six dogs and over a hundred cats—and even a little glory, given Tiff's successes as a writer. Years also touched by excess (which for me meant eating— and for Tiff, occasional bouts of drinking) and inevitably, a fair share of loud and even violent disagreements and bitter disappointments. But still—forty years of being together and loving it—at our place in the country northeast of Toronto (always with two dogs and as many cats as might turn up), and on countless book tours and eventually part-time at a little writing retreat in the south of France (with still more cats).

That was our life together—until the first day of summer, 2002, when—in a sense—Tiff finally went home, to dwell in his books and in the hearts and memories of those who knew and loved him.

It was a midnight fall in the bathroom of our house in Provence. A pelvic fracture that caused undetected internal bleeding, a spreading infection and finally, after two hospitals and six weeks of induced coma—death.

My world had been filled with so many wonders for over forty years, and now it was empty and I was alone— or so it seemed. Off in a foreign country, trying to cope in a language I barely spoke—and dealing with the countless friends back home who wanted to give or receive some kind of help.

How would I survive? How would my sanity survive—my sense of humour? My sense of self.

And so we come to more things you need to know. ,

First of all, I made no attempt to suppress my grief. And even had I wanted to put a damper on it, I would have failed. It was too deep—too insistent. In France—back home in Stratford—even recently—I punctuated my days with bouts of uncontrollable sobbing. All I managed—with only two exceptions—was to keep it private.

Among my friends in France were a restaurateur and his wife. They hosted the lunch that followed the low-key "service" that a few close friends and I shared at the crematorium. And a few nights later, when eating alone at their restaurant, I suddenly rose from my table, dashed through the kitchen and out into the back lane and stood at a fence, literally howling my grief into the night air.

Similarly, more than two years later, I was at the kitchen table in the apartment here in Stratford, talking to a young Findley fan, when I suddenly felt overwhelmed by Tiff's absence. I tried to make it to my room to recover, and couldn't even make it to the door. I ended up on the floor, noisily and wetly gulping and gasping my grief.

And then I got back up to the table and continued talking about Tiff.

And what you need to know about the young Findley fan, I will tell you later. Now—on with the grief.

What follows is not a prescription for dealing with death and grief. It is how I deal with them—which has nothing to do with devising strategies or making conscious decisions.

It has to do with who I am and what I believe—and especially what I do not believe. And if I tell you that I do not
believe in God or the life hereafter, it does not mean that I
hold in any contempt those who believe other-wise. Nor do
I have any compulsion to force my beliefs on anyone else.

But I don't mind trying to articulate my beliefs.

For example, I spoke briefly to the small gathering of
friends at the crematorium—giving the version of life hereafter that would comfort me. I noted how the very substance
of Tiff's body would be changed by fire and permeate the
air and eventually be taken up to become part of other living
systems—plants, animals and people. I mentioned how many
lives his own life had touched—and possibly even changed
to some degree. And how, through his books, his life and
work would continue to affect others. Yes, Tiff was dead. He
was gone. But he had left a wondrous legacy.

Oddly enough, that was the first time I had ever actually tried to put my beliefs into words—even to myself.
Which is not to say that I had avoided thoughts of death.

I was approaching seventy-one when Tiff died, and had
already noticed that my built-in, gnawing fear of life's
ending had begun to fade. Certainly, I had no desire to live
long enough to be the victim of any of the physical or
mental infirmities that had visited my family and other loved
ones. Nor did I want to see Tiff suffer any such problems.
Otherwise, though, I felt more passive than panicked about
death, seeing it as a necessary ending rather than a mysteri-
ous rebirth. And I found evidence, after his death, that Tiff
had felt something the same. What follows is a journal entry

I found when putting together a selection of Tiff's personal writings, *Journeyman, Travels of a Writer*, published a year after I returned to Canada: *April 1968. I am afraid of death. But in saying so, I think I am saying, at heart, that I am afraid of pain— and I am afraid of "stopping." Nothing else frightens me in death but whatever is inherent in those two facets of it. I have absolutely no fear of the so-called unknown, basically because I have no formal concept about what people can possibly be talking about when they talk of "heaven"—or "the hereafter" or "what-have-you?" All that is merely comfort and consolation and so meaningless to the dead— although the living may draw some brief solace from it. What I fear is what I know—not what I do not know.*

One of Tiff's last public appearances was an interview by Eleanor Wachtel done before a Calgary audience in late 2001 and later broadcast by CBC Radio. Her final question was: "So, Tiff—what's next?" And his reply was just one word.

"Death."

Eleanor's response was to laugh and say something like, "Oh, surely not . . . ," to which Tiff said, "You bet!" But then he added: "Still . . ." and he began to sing a song from the musical *Annie*: "The sun will come *up* tomorrow. Bet your bottom dollar that tomorrow—there'll be sun!" Followed by thunderous applause and that gorgeous, husky Findley laugh.

That moment is one of my favourite memories.

Perhaps what you need to know now is something about what shaped my beliefs.

I grew up in Regina, through most of the Depression years. For many all around me, it was a time of bitterness, hardship—and survival. I was fortunate. Whatever losses my family suffered, our lives were relatively free of deprivation, in spite of the fact that my parents separated when I was eight. My father's epilepsy, particularly during those hard times, had put more stress on the marriage than it could bear. My mother and I ended up living with her parents—until her remarriage when I was fourteen. And so my grandparents came to play an important role in my upbringing.

The generation gap proved beneficial. Although I had to take on more responsibilities than many of my contemporaries, I was also able to achieve more freedoms. And I was blessed with a love of books—which meant that school was a breeze.

Church was not.

I never managed to take it seriously.

My grandmother professed to be a devout Anglican, but never attended services. She insisted, however, that I did—along with my grandfather, who had been brought up a Methodist. He was completely unaffected by the Anglican services, and used to hold his hymnal in such a way that when he dozed off, the sound of its falling would wake him up.

In the meantime, as I went through puberty—and partly as a result of the fact that nobody in the family ate breakfast—I was prone to fainting spells. This happened most frequently in church, usually during that part of the Lenten service that involved seven pages of kneeling. I can remember at least three occasions of keeling over and apparently getting wedged between what I was kneeling on and the pew in front of me. Let's face it—I was a somewhat chubby chap, and so it would take four strong men to rescue me. I would regain consciousness with the church ceiling swaying high above me, as the four strong men, one at each corner, carried me up the aisle and out into the fresh air.

Eventually, I was excused from Sunday services—to the intense relief, I suspect, of the local Anglican clergy.

And, to be honest, to my own relief. I had never managed to find believable most of what religion was trying to teach me. I quite liked the Golden Rule, but that seemed to me to be merely good sense rather than an example of divine inspiration.

My final brush with established religion was both ludicrous and disastrous.

In those days, Reginans who wished to attend the University of Saskatchewan in Saskatoon could take their first year's courses in Regina College. Shortly after classes began, the dean called a few of us locals into his office for "a little talk." He told us how he had noticed that the entire membership of the Student Christian Movement, that year, was made up of students from surrounding communities.

"Now, I don't want these young people to think that you Regina lot are snubbing them. I think it would be an excellent idea if a few of you turned up at some of their meetings . . ."

Obligingly, a couple of friends joined me in attending the next SCM get-together. We were warmly received. Too warmly.

They elected me president.

Of the Student Christian Movement.

I felt that to decline the honour would defeat the whole purpose of being there. So, I accepted. Little did I know then just what the honour would entail.

I was vaguely aware that the college had once been a Methodist institution. I may even have noticed, peripherally, that once or twice a week a few students gathered together for a chapel service.

What I soon discovered was that, on one of the semi-weekly gatherings, the service was led by . . . the president of the Student Christian Movement. Who was expected to deliver, weekly, a brief, uplifting sermonette.

Thus began my career in hypocrisy.

All my friends would crowd into the room to giggle at my dishonest shenanigans. I tried to make the best of it, but did not discover that "best" until the day I decided that if I was forced into this inappropriate situation, I might as well go all the way.

"All the way," in my terms, was to make the most of the theatricality of liturgical events. And so, I upped the intensity of my remarks until I was reaching for the ridiculous heights of a revivalist.

And the climax of my performance came with the exhortation that if you did this, that and the other: "IT WILL FILL YOUR SOUL WITH HOPE!!!"

That was when disaster struck—in the form of my weakness for unintentional spoonerisms.

What my riveted audience heard was: "IT WILL FILL YOUR HOLE WITH SOAP!!!"

Well.

Out of the shocked silence came a burst of raucous mirth. Some of my friends, screaming with laughter, ran from the room.

I stood in disarray until I finally managed to say: "I'm sorry—I can't do this . . ."

And simply left.

I wrote a letter to the SCM executive that was both explanatory and apologetic. They responded sympathetically, and even offered to send me as a delegate to the national convention of the movement. And I even went—but that's another story.

Suffice it to say that the whole experience was educational—especially about what good people can be found among those who do not share my own beliefs.

My negative reactions to religious ideas were strengthened by my choosing, initially, to be a biologist. I went as far as a master's degree in the subject, with a scholarship to Yale for the Ph.D. To the horror and puzzlement of my family and some of my friends, I took a sudden departure from that pathway into the future as soon as I had seen my first professional theatre. I relinquished the Yale commitment and headed for Ontario, where for five years I worked quite happily as an actor and eventually a producer. I have to consider it a good move, because it was in the theatre that I met Tiff. And when he decided to leave the theatre for writing, I joined him, heading into the documentary world of radio and television, with an initial speciality in scientific programming.

There were ongoing brushes with organized religion, especially after Tiff and I moved to rural Ontario, where evangelism can be frequently encountered. Too frequently. With both of us doing a lot of our work at home—with many deadlines to meet and a lot of concentration to be achieved, we were not best pleased to have people coming to the door wanting to convert us to their particular brand of worship.

Tiff was usually in his upstairs sanctuary. I worked just off the kitchen, and so I was the one who usually answered the doorbell. I tried to be scrupulously polite, quietly expressing my satisfaction with my own beliefs and my unwillingness to spend time listening to someone else's beliefs. With fewer deadlines, I might have found the time to argue—especially with Jehovah's Witnesses—that I found Divine Creation much less impressive than the existence of a world whose nature was such that life could come into being and evolution could produce astounding variety without the ongoing intervention of anything but natural processes.

As it turned out, I discovered by accident how to handle these unwanted interruptions. On one especially busy afternoon, with the lunch dishes in the dishwasher but still unwashed, with the telephone and fax constantly requiring time and attention I couldn't spare, the doorbell rang. From my desk, I could see the front door. Pale faces and pamphlets. I sighed. On the way to the door, I automatically turned on the dishwasher in an attempt to catch up. I opened the door and suddenly remembered.

"Christ!" I exclaimed. "I forgot the mouse!"

And hurried back into the kitchen.

You see, one of the many mice who ran inside of our walls had found a way to get into the dishwasher—even when it was closed. And so we always had to check the machine's interior before turning it on.

And there it was—startled with jets of water. I grabbed a tea towel, took hold of the poor little beast and called out, "I'll be right with you. I'm just drying the mouse!"

And of course, by the time I'd shooed the creature away and made it back to the door—there was nobody there.

I guess you also need to know that more than once I re-enacted this event, sans mouse, as new Christian soldiers were dispatched to recruit in our direction.

Now, back to basics.

So here I am, confessing that it doesn't seem arrogant to feel that I don't need to take on what—to me—are beliefs that at best are artificial, and at worst, terrifying and dangerous. Look at the world today, and the religious extremism that currently threatens so many. "My God is better than your God!" "My way of worshipping our God is better than your way!" "If you don't follow my beliefs I will kill you!"

Good grief!

That was my grandmother's favourite expression.

So now you need to know what all this has to do with how I coped with Tiff's death.

I simply followed my instincts. I acted according to who I am. And I still do. I will never cease to be achingly aware of his absence, and there will always be a measure of grieving in my life. In my life. That's important. I'm still alive. And Tiff does live on, for me—but only in my memory. I love to relive some of our times together. I love imagining how he would react to what has happened since he died.

And I love the fact, that as I sit at the computer, I am surrounded by images of Tiff. There are exactly a dozen photographs of him in my room—five of them showing us both (including a shot of the only time we ever appeared onstage together—when, in that 1962 season of repertory, I took over the role of one of our actors who had to leave the company because of ill health.)

I can't help wondering how Tiff would have wanted me to behave after his death—if such a thought had ever occurred to him. You see, we had an agreement. He agreed to die first. Seriously. Given how our lives were structured—what aspects I looked after and what aspects he looked after—it would have been unmitigated disaster for him if I had died first and left him alone.

And so that's one of the ways in which I can view his death as "right." The other way, of course, is that I'm happy he was spared a life that continued on past the point at which he was capable of doing the thing he loved most—writing. A Tiff with diminished mental or physical abilities is unthinkable.

And I feel the same about my own life. I am alive and I enjoy being alive—but I am also ready for death, because I know that life doesn't last forever.

The last thing you need to know is about the young Findley fan I mentioned in my confession about crying.

His name is Trevor Greene. He is from northern British Columbia, and he is currently in his early twenties.

He is extraordinarily lively, bright and well-read. He is good company and he is kind. Ultimately, I believe he will undertake something to do with writing or publishing, because he has such a great love of books. And whatever he does, I think it will have an entrepreneurial aspect to it. He is an energetic organizer of thoughts and actions. And he has dedicated himself to seeing me all the way to death.

I will leave you with something you don't really need to know, but might simply enjoy. It's something that happened before Trevor entered my life, and perhaps it sums up both what it is to survive the years and how difficult it can be to keep up with changing ideas, technologies and generations.

There came a time, a year or so after Tiff's death, when I met another young man. A very pleasant and good-looking young man. He, too, was interested in my life with Tiff, and asked me if I had any photographs of where we had lived in rural Ontario—as well as the little writing retreat in the south of France. As it happened, I did have photographs. Tiff and I had put together a couple of small albums to take on book tours, because so many people asked us about our two homes.

And so I hauled out the albums and sat beside the young man on the living-room sofa as I began leafing through the photographs. To be honest, I have to tell you that a moment arrived in which we were no longer looking at photographs. And to be brutally, almost embarrassingly honest, I also have to tell you that another moment arrived when it seemed appropriate—perhaps even obligatory—for me to reach down and indulge in a bit of fondling.

Suddenly, my fingers detected a kind of delicious little shudder running beneath the clothing I was touching.

"Heavens!" I said. "How on earth did you do that????"

His hesitant reply left me speechless.

"Actually," he said, "what you've been hanging on to is the cellphone in my pocket, and I just got a call . . ."

Good grief, indeed.

THE CONTRIBUTORS

BRIAN BRETT is the author of ten books of poetry, fiction and memoir. Active in promoting Canadian literature and culture, he is a retired Chair of the Writers Union of Canada. *Uproar's Your Only Memoir* was published in 2004, and in the fall of 2009, his new memoir/natural history, *Trauma Farm*, was released. He lives with his family on Salt Spring Island.

CATHERINE BUSH is the author of three novels. *Claire's Head* was chosen as a Best Book of the Year by *The Globe and Mail*. *The Rules of Engagement* was chosen as a *New York Times* Notable Book and a Best Book of the Year by the *L.A. Times* and *The Globe and Mail*. Bush has a degree in Comparative Literature from Yale University, has held a variety of Writer-in-Residence positions and has taught Creative Writing at universities including Concordia, the University of Florida, the University of Guelph and the University of British Columbia. Her non-fiction has appeared in *The Globe and Mail* and *The New York Times Magazine*. She is at work on a new novel.

In addition to the 2003 Commonwealth Writers Prize, **AUSTIN CLARKE** is the winner of the 2002 Giller Prize and the 2003 Trillium Prize for *The Polished Hoe*. Clarke is the author of six short-story collections and ten novels. His latest novel is *More*. He was born in Barbados and immigrated to Canada to attend the University of Toronto. He became a leader of the civil rights movement. Clarke has been a visiting professor at Yale, Brandeis, Williams, Wellesley, Duke and the universities of Texas and Indiana, and has served in prominent cultural and political positions in his native Barbados.

GEORGE ELLIOTT CLARKE, O.C., O.N.S. is a poet and scholar, and the E.J. Pratt Professor of Canadian Literature at the University of Toronto. He received the Governor General's Award for Poetry in 2001 and the Trudeau Fellows Prize, 2005–2008.

Poet **STEPHEN COLLIS** is the author of *Mine*, two parts of the ongoing "Barricades Project"—*Anarchive* and *The Commons*—and two books of criticism: *Through Words of Others: Susan Howe and Anarcho-Scholasticism* and *Phyllis Webb and the Common Good*. A long-standing member of the Kootenay School of Writing, he teaches poetry, poetics and American literature at Simon Fraser University.

FRANK DAVEY is a past editor of *Tish* and the Coach House Press, founder and editor of *Open Letter*, the Canadian journal of writing and theory, and trainer and handler of nationally ranked Great Dane show dogs. He is the author of twenty-two books of poetry, including *The Abbotsford Guide to India* and *Back to the War,* and twelve books of literary criticism and cultural theory, including *Post-National Arguments: The Politics of the Anglophone-Canadian Novel Since 1967, Canadian Literary Power, Karla's Web: A Cultural Examination of the Mahaffy-French Murders* and *Mr & Mrs G. G.*

ENDRE FARKAS is a poet and playwright who has published ten books of poetry and two plays. His work has been translated into French, Spanish, Italian, Turkish, Hungarian and Slovenian. He has read and performed his work across Canada and in the United States, Europe and Latin America. His most recent book is *Quotidian Fever: New and Selected Poems 1974–2007.* He is currently working on a play about the poet A.M. Klein.

BRIAN FAWCETT lives in Toronto and is trying to write a book about the Epic of Enkidu. His most recent non-fiction book is *Virtual Clearcut: Or, The Way Things Are in My Hometown.*

JILL FRAYNE is the author of a travel memoir, *Starting Out in the Afternoon.* She lives at the top of Algonquin Park.

JOAN GIVNER was professor of English at the University of Regina. She is the author of two biographies, an autobiography, two novels and several collections of short stories. Most recently she has written the Ellen Fremedon series of young adult novels.

HIROMI GOTO was born in Japan and immigrated with her farming family to Canada in 1969. She no longer picks mushrooms long into the night, but she can be found searching for matsutake in the mountains in the autumn. Her latest novel is *Half World*.

MARNI JACKSON has written for *The Globe and Mail*, *The London Times*, *Rolling Stone*, *Outside*, *Explore* and *The Walrus*. She is the author of *The Mother Zone* and *Pain: The Science and Culture of Why We Hurt*. Her new non-fiction book is about coming of age (or not) in your twenties.

Based in Cape Breton, **LINDA MCNUTT** writes novels and teaches literary theory and Shakespeare. She recently completed a follow-up to her first novel, *Summer Point*. Her current project is a novel about new beginnings and is set in Calgary circa 1912.

ERÍN MOURE is a Montreal poet and translator. Her most recent book is *O Cadoiro*.

PAUL QUARRINGTON is a writer and musician. He has won many awards for his fiction, including the Stephen Leacock Medal for Humour, Canada Reads and the Governor General's Award. His most recent novel is *The Ravine*. He sings and plays in the band Porkbelly Futures.

STEPHEN REID, author of *Jack Rabbit Parole*, is on day parole and living in the Victoria area. He divides his time between there and his home on Haida Gwaii. He continues to write and live with the poet Susan Musgrave.

RENEE RODIN was born in Montreal and moved in 1968 to Vancouver, where she raised her three children. She ran R2B2 Books, along with its weekly reading series, from 1986–1994. Her books of poetry are *Bread and Salt* and *Ready for Freddy*. A collection is forthcoming in 2010 with Talon.

ANNE STONE, a Vancouver-based teacher and novelist, is senior editor at *Matrix Magazine*. She is the author of three novels: *Jacks: a gothic gospel*, *Hush* and, most recently, *Delible*. *Delible*, chosen as a *Globe and Mail* Best Book, tells the story of Melora Sprague, a fifteen-year-old girl whose sister is missing.

WILLIAM WHITEHEAD, was born in 1931, grew up in Regina, worked initially as a biologist, then as an actor and ultimately, for twenty years, as an award-winning writer of documentaries for radio, film and television. In 1982, he began devoting himself full-time to the editing and managing of the work of Timothy Findley, until their forty-year partnership was ended by Findley's death in 2002.

CONTRIBUTORS' CREDITS

PERMISSIONS

All photos courtesy of the authors unless otherwise noted.

Excerpt from "A Book of Hours," as in *The Martyrology Book Six Books* by bpNichol, (Toronto: Coach House Press, 1987). Used with permission of Eleanor Nichol. [vii]

Excerpt from "Local Heroes" by Thomas Lynch. National Public Radio, 2005. Used with permission of the author. [8]

"They are there like breath . . . ." Private letter from Rudy Wiebe. Used by permission of the author. [15]

"A/Cross Sections" in *New Manitoba Writing,* ed. Katherine Bitney and Andris Taskans, Manitoba Writers Guild, 2007, 145. Used with permission of the author. [61]

Of Woman Born: Motherhood as Experience and Institution by Adrienne Rich, copyright 1976, 1986 by W.W. Norton Company, Inc. p 237. [174]

"I am writing just because I can" by Jaszon Camlot appears in *The Debaucher* (Toronto: Insomniac Press, 2008)—it originally appeared as part of the "Adios Sonnets: # 38" in *Matrix* 76 (2007): 27. Used with permission of the author. [311]

JEAN BAIRD has been an English professor, magazine publisher, consultant for non-profit organizations and creative director of Canada Book Week for the Writers' Trust of Canada. **GEORGE BOWERING** is a poet, novelist, essayist, critic, historian and editor. In 2002 he was appointed Canada's first Parliamentary Poet Laureate. He is an Officer of the Order of Canada.